W9-ASX-602

Regional and Local Economic Analysis for Practitioners

Regional and Local Economic Analysis for Practitioners

fourth edition

Avrom Bendavid-Val

PRAEGER

Westport, Connecticut
London

Library of Congress Cataloging-in-Publication Data

Bendavid-Val, Avrom.
Regional and local economic analysis for practitioners / Avrom Bendavid-Val.—4th ed.
p. cm.
Includes bibliographical references and index.
ISBN 0-275-93520-5 (alk. paper) — ISBN 0-275-93751-8 (pbk.: alk. paper)
1. Regional economics. 2. Economic zoning. I. Title.
HT391.B38 1991
338.9—dc20 90-41092

British Library Cataloguing in Publication Data is available.

Copyright © 1991 by Avrom Bendavid-Val

All rights reserved. No portion of this book may be reproduced, by any process or technique, without the express written consent of the publisher.

Library of Congress Catalog Card Number: 90-41092
ISBN: 0-275-93520-5 (hb.)
0-275-93751-8 (pbk.)

First published in 1991

Praeger Publishers, 88 Post Road West, Westport, CT 06881
An imprint of Greenwood Publishing Group, Inc.

Printed in the United States of America

The paper used in this book complies with the Permanent Paper Standard issued by the National Information Standards Organization (Z39.48-1984).

10 9 8 7 6 5 4

For Leah,
who has never let June go by,
and for
Naftali, Ronnit, and Oren
whose generation their visions belie

Contents

Part IV: Methods of Project Identification and Evaluation

Part V: Approaches to Regional Development Planning

Tables and Figures

TABLES

FIGURES

Preface

This edition represents the third and most far-reaching revision of this book. The previous edition was published in the early 1980s. The preface of that edition, referring in turn to its predecessors, both published in the early 1970s, reads in part:

> The earlier editions were an attempt at simplified presentations of the more common and most widely useful descriptive methods of regional economic analysis. They were aimed at practitioners who needed to understand and use the analytical tools but who did not have a solid grounding in mathematics or economics. They stressed the pliability of the methods and encouraged practitioners to exercise creativity in molding them into forms suitable for application in the particular regions and working situations in which they found themselves. The style and format were designed to enable the books to serve both for purposes of independent or classroom study and as working references.
>
> Quite a body of experience with the original editions in a wide variety of learning and working environments has now accumulated. . . . To me, [this experience] has confirmed the two basic premises on which the earlier editions were written, namely: (1) that there is a need for literature in the field of regional development planning that collects, selects, organizes, and spreads existing knowledge effectively, a need no less worthy or urgent than the need for new knowledge; and (2) that the worldwide usefulness of such a book is enhanced by presenting the material in a manner that stresses basic principles and is fairly independent of place-specific circumstances such as the particular types of data available.

In this third edition, which incorporates and builds on the earlier ones, the basic style, format, and approach are preserved. This will disappoint those users of the earlier editions who claimed that they needed guidance in obtaining data, wanted more detailed discussions of the methods of analysis, or yearned for case studies of applications. Those things are important, but this book, meant to be a broad introduction, is not the place for them. Other literature, a portion of which is listed in the Bibliography, should be consulted by readers who want to know more.

But working experience with the earlier editions has also confirmed the need for some changes. Those books were written with a certain regional planning frame of reference in mind. In the intervening ten years there has been an increasing interest in regional development planning and an associated proliferation of courses and programs in the subject. . . . There has been a growing awareness that the tools and concepts of regional analysis and development planning have applications in a wide variety of situations, including rural, local, district, county, multicounty, provincial, and state planning. All you really need is an open economy and some concern with the spatial distribution of economic activity. Virtually any subnational area will do.

For the most part, those paragraphs apply to the present edition as well. Again, though the term ''region'' is used throughout, the material presented in this book is directly applicable to a wide range of subnational areas. Again, it is my purpose, without altering the basic style, format, and approach of the book, to improve the presentations of methods of regional analysis covered in earlier editions and to add new material reflecting developments in the intervening years. This time, however, developments in the intervening years have been much more dramatic and extensive.

Some say that during the 1980s regional development finally came into its own. Certainly that decade saw a much expanded interest in decentralization, and one result of this was that regions and local areas came to be regarded more than before as important arenas for development planning and management activity. This has led to more experience with regional analysis and with regional development planning frameworks that use the analysis.

For example, in the United States, the national government withdrew from many of its previous roles in support of welfare and local development at subnational levels. State and local governments, as well as nongovernmental organizations, responded in many cases by taking more active roles in planning for economic stability and growth in their areas. In Western Europe the Economic Community, even while expanding and preparing for broader integration in 1992, increased its efforts to promote economic development planning in lagging regions and support projects intended to strengthen regional economies. To say that there was also a growing interest in decentralization in Eastern Europe would be an understatement; but in that case, by the end of the 1980s, the decentralization movement had only just begun the process of organizing for more independent economic planning by subnational regions.

In developing countries, central governments, often at the urging and with the support of foreign assistance agencies, initiated decentralization programs on a widespread basis. Provincial, district, and municipal governments were offered more authority to determine development investments, and efforts were made to improve their capabilities for development planning and management. These programs produced a great deal of experimentation with subnational planning in areas that were poor in planning resources, such as economic data, equipment and financial resources for analysis, technicians trained in analytical methods, institutional mechanisms for using analytical output in a planning process, and, most important, planning experience.

Another manifestation of the decentralization movement was increased reliance on markets to provide signals of demand and economic rewards, and increased reliance on the private sector for production and marketing. In many countries the spectrum of legal private enterprise was broadened, government supports were reduced, the role of government in resource allocation was diminished, marketing infrastructure was improved, government organizations that had legally monopolized the buying and selling of certain goods were dismantled (or steps were taken in that direction), and other measures were adopted to encourage private sector activity.

Administrative decentralization meant that subnational levels of government needed more revenue to support the broader array of responsibilities they were offered or given. Economic decentralization meant that the potential of the private sector as a source of that revenue was greatly expanded. Together, administrative and economic decentralization created a need for subnational development planning to direct the use of public resources so as to encourage private economic activity that would broaden local revenue bases.

And so new approaches, new concepts, and new analytical tools emerged from the planning experiences. These have not so much displaced what went before as expanded the tested choices available for regional analysis and development planning. They have also resulted in a more refined articulation of different types of regional analysis, resulted in a clearer understanding of the objectives of regional analysis in the development planning process, and expanded knowledge about how analysis and effective planning work together. All this has influenced the content and organization of this book.

Part I sets the stage with three chapters that introduce important aspects of the overall economic and development context within which methods of regional analysis are used. The first chapter contains basic introductory material about regions as economies within national economies, and notes some implications of this status for regional development planning and aggregate analysis. The second chapter dwells on what goes on inside a region, and reflects a heightened awareness of the importance of intraregional analysis for development planning.

The third chapter of Part I concentrates on specific development interventions, or projects. For the most part, notions of comprehensive planning have now given way to an emphasis on project identification through the regional planning process. This chapter explains why. It also discusses what has been learned about the nature of viable regional development projects that affects the focus of analysis for regional development planning.

The three chapters of Part I establish a pattern of concerns: the region as a whole and in relation to the larger environment, the internal operations of the region, and project interventions in the regional economy. This pattern reflects the three essential aspects of the regional development process: the region as a whole deriving income and employment from its export sales to the rest of the country and the world; the expansion, or multiplication of that income and employment through trade within the region; and the specific policies, institutions, infrastructure, and technologies that influence the levels of export sales and multiplication of the associated income and employment. Parts II, III, and IV also conform to this pattern by presenting, in turn, methods of aggregate regional analysis, intraregional analysis, and project identification and evaluation.

As in past editions, what is provided in Parts II, III, and IV is an introduction to common descriptive methods of analysis for use in regional planning: the emphasis is on description, not prediction or prescription. Descriptive methods employ factual information about the past and present to help understand how the economy of a region works, how it is performing, and where there are opportunities for intervening in ways that will enable it to perform better. These methods do not provide ''answers'' to questions about the future or ''solutions'' to planning problems the way projection, optimization, and simulation techniques, which are based on much more than factual information, are meant to do. Descriptive methods provide the basic insights essential for effective regional planning, whether the planning approach used is rudimentary or sophisticated.

Part V contains three chapters dealing with approaches to regional development planning. Inclusion of this material reflects an important lesson of the experience of the past decade, namely, that analytical tools appropriate in a given situation can be determined only in association with the planning process appropriate for that situation. Parts II, III, and IV represent menus of analytical methods; Part V is meant to provide help for selecting the methods most useful in a given situation. It does this by discussing basic planning logic and how that logic has been and can be adapted to different circumstances, and then by suggesting a general framework around which a specific regional planning process can be designed. The nature of a particular adaptation will play a major role in determining the methods of regional analysis that can be used effectively.

Also as in past editions, the text is not interrupted by reference to endnotes, footnotes, or bibliographic citations. Money values are given in terms of abstract *monetary units* indicated as Mu. Years involved in comparisons over time are indicated as *19XX* (the earlier year) and *19YY* (the later year). The Bibliography at the end of the book is organized in five sections corresponding to the five parts of the text. Each section stands as a complete bibliography for the corresponding part of the book, since if an entry is relevant to more than one part it appears in more than one corresponding section of the bibliography. An index is also provided.

It is more than likely that for the forseeable future the movement toward increased administrative and economic decentralization will continue. True decentralization means a distribution of decision-making authority between higher and lower levels that most empowers communities and individuals to exercise control over their destinies without compromising the general public interest. Decentralization is thus closely associated with political and economic democracy.

The more decision-making authority resides at lower levels, the more numerous and complex are the decisions to be made, and the more important it is that decisions be made within an analysis and planning framework that seeks to optimize the use of available resources. It is hoped that this edition, in reflecting some of the experience of decentralization in the past decade, will contribute to more widespread and productive efforts at decentralization in years to come.

Acknowledgments

While only I am accountable for the views expressed and for any errors, a book like this obviously benefits from the direct and indirect contributions of many people. Of course, all those who contributed in one way or another to previous editions have indirectly contributed to this one as well. But in addition, the years since the last edition have brought me into close working relationships with many people and organizations from which the present edition has benefitted considerably. Principal among them are:

Susan Escherich and Frederick Krimgold, of the Center for Development Policy; Dr. Herbert Stoevener, Head of the Department of Agricultural Economics; Dr. Mary Hill Rojas, Acting Director, and the staff of the Office of International Development; and other colleagues at Virginia Polytechnic Institute and State University;

Maria Grazia Quieti, of the Policy Analysis Division Training Service, and her colleagues at the United Nations Food and Agriculture Organization;

my colleagues at the U.N. Centre for Human Settlements (Habitat) and the U.N. Environmental Programme (UNEP) in Nairobi;

Dr. Raphael Bar-El, and my many friends and colleagues at the Development Study Centre;

Dr. Gerald J. Karaska and other associates of the Settlement and Resource Systems Analysis (SARSA) project too numerous to name, representing Clark University, the Institute for Development Anthropology, Virginia Polytechnic Institute and State University, and other institutions;

Dr. Eric Chetwynd and other associates in the Office of Rural and Institutional Development, U.S. Agency for International Development (USAID);

the staffs of USAID Missions and Regional Housing and Urban Development offices in Thailand, The Philippines, elsewhere in Asia, and throughout Africa;

local government officials, students, and the people of regions and countries in which I have worked and taught, and the central government officials who supported these efforts, throughout the world;

Judy Baker, who provided research support during preparation of the manuscript; and

James R. Dunton, Senior Editor, Business and Economics, Praeger Publishers, who encouraged me to prepare this revised and expanded edition, and who provided important guidance for the project.

I

The Economic and Development Context

1

Regional Development in the National Context

FROM NATIONAL TO REGIONAL ECONOMICS

For the most part, methods of aggregate regional analysis are based on theories and analytical tools developed for national economies. This is because national and regional economies can be viewed as being made up of the same fundamental components and the same sorts of relationships among those components. In practice, many of the important forces at work tend to be rather different, in relative order of magnitude if not in their essential natures, at the national and regional levels. Making good use of the methods of regional economic analysis requires an appreciation of essential differences in the ways national and regional economies operate.

We know, for example, that economic trade between nations tends to come about when, because of absolute or comparative advantages, the trading countries both gain from the exchange. A country may have production advantages that result from natural resource endowments, unique human or institutional resources, strategic locational features, or other special economic resources. The greater the national advantage in some type of production for which there is outside demand, the more profitable will be specialization and trade, and generally, the greater will be the volume of trade.

These notions can serve as a foundation for understanding interregional trade as well as international trade. Yet we know that in most cases external trade plays a much greater role in the economy of a region than in the economy of a nation. Why is this? What are the barriers to trade among nations that do not exist, or are not as serious, at the regional level?

For one thing, distances between national trading partners, and therefore the transportation costs of trade, are generally greater among countries than among regions trading within the same country. Also, defense and political considerations that are not factors at the regional level sometimes encourage countries to maintain production capabilities in certain commodities that might be purchased more cheaply in the international marketplace.

And then, national full-employment policies, cultural differences, xenophobia, balance of payments and exchange rate problems, administrative red tape, and other trade-inhibiting factors found at the national level are generally absent or much less intense at the level of trade between subnational regions. Moreover, a nation has the legal tools—tariffs, quotas, and other institutional devices not available to regions—to enforce a restriction of trade when that is determined to be in its best interests.

With fewer natural and institutional barriers, regions tend to specialize and trade to a much greater degree than nations. But not only goods flow more freely across interregional borders than across international borders; factors of production that are not fixed in place by nature—capital, labor, ideas, and techniques—also flow more freely. All this gives the regional economy a greater quality of general openness than is usually found at the level of the national economy. The economic implications of the general openness that characterizes a regional or local economy are vast. Again, they can begin to be understood by starting with what is known about the economies of nations.

Take, for example, what is known about the way national income is determined. In the traditional commodity market model of the economy national income, roughly the same as gross national product (GNP), arises from—and is the sum of—four types of spending: domestic consumption spending, private domestic investment spending, domestic government spending, and net exports (exports minus imports). An increase of a certain amount in one of these types of spending immediately causes income and product to increase by the same amount—in fact, since spending equals product equals income, by definition they all increase the same amount. But ultimately, owing to the process of *income multiplication*, the initial increase in spending results in income (and product) increases that are much larger.

The initial increase in income is multiplied into more income because it is spent by whoever earned it. This *respending* generates additional income for someone else. The additional income is also spent, and this generates still more income that is again spent, and so on, round after round, generating more and more income.

But only a portion of the income in each round is spent in a way that generates more income; the rest is used for taxes, savings, purchases of imports, remittances abroad, and so on. These types of outlays do not create additional current domestic income, and are considered *leakages* from the income generating stream. Since a portion *leaks out* in each round of spending, the amount of income that is generated in each round becomes smaller and smaller until at last

Figure 1.1
Illustration of Income Multiplication

Round	Amount Spent	Amount That Leaks Out (40%)	Income Generated
			Export sales: Mu 100
First	MU 100	Mu 40	60
Second	60	24	36
Third	36	14	22
Fourth	22	9	13
Fifth	13	5	8
Sixth	8	3	5
Seventh	5	2	3
⋮	⋮	⋮	⋮
Total	Mu 250	Mu 100	Mu 250

Mu = Monetary Units

it disappears altogether. Figure 1.1 shows a numerical example of the income multiplication process.

Imagine that something caused export sales to rise, generating Mu 100 of "new" income (shown in the first row of Figure 1.1). Imagine also that people tend to spend 60 percent of their income buying goods and services from each other, thereby generating more income, while the remaining 40 percent goes to outlays that represent leakages from the stream that generates current domestic income. Thus, in the first round of spending, Mu 60 of additional income is generated. When that income is disposed of in the second round of spending, 40 percent leaks out again, so only Mu 36 of further income is generated. On it goes, with less income generated in each round, and therefore less available to be spent in the next round.

Finally in the Figure 1.1 illustration, when the full Mu 100 has leaked out and there is nothing left to be respent, a total of Mu 250 of income will have been generated—the original Mu 100 plus another Mu 150 resulting from the rounds of respending. The *multiplier* in this case is calculated as 2.5. That is, any initial increase in income will multiply to a total increase of 2.5 times the initial increase. The multiplier is arithmetically determined as 1 divided by the leakage fraction. In Figure 1.1, the leakage fraction was 40 percent, and 1 divided by 0.4 is 2.5.

The smaller the leakage fraction, the larger the multiplier. Conversely, the more spending leaks out into taxes, imports, savings, and the like, the smaller will be the multiplier and the income generated. That is one reason most national governments concern themselves very much with ways to expand export sales and reduce imports. Income multiplication is at the very heart of both national and regional economic growth processes.

When we examine the factors that determine changes in levels of spending and the factors that determine the value of the multiplier, however, we find significant differences between the economies of nations and the economies of regions. In most countries, domestic consumption is determined largely by how much people have to spend and how willing they are to spend it on domestic goods; in regions an additional factor of major consequence is the willingness to spend in the region and on products made in the region. In most countries, private domestic investment is determined largely by the availability of capital and the relative attractiveness of investing it; in most regions an additional factor of major consequence is the relative attractiveness of investing in that particular subnational area.

Government spending nationally is determined by authorities internal to the system; government spending in a region may be determined largely by authorities outside the region. Exports from the country can be encouraged and imports to the country can be discouraged through a variety of devices available to the national government; municipal, provincial, or regional governments generally do not have such devices available to them. Furthermore, many of the leakages from the income-generating stream, such as taxes and savings, are not actually *lost* to the national economy. Taxes or savings that leak out this year may return as government spending or investment the next. That is far less likely to be the case in a region.

Indeed, the conventional national income determination model derives from a view of the economy as an almost abstract and more or less closed system in which income is determined largely by what goes on internally, and the interest rate, government spending, investment, saving, the multiplier, and so on, happen in a spaceless place. It is clear that, by contrast, income in a particular region is determined no less, and often much more, by what goes on outside regional borders than by what goes on within them.

A high rate of interest nationally may be reflected in a flight of capital from the region. A relatively high national multiplier may arise from factors that cause the multiplier of a particular region to be low. A region faces political and resource allocation problems quite different from those of the nation, because it competes with other regions within (as well as outside) the national territory. The region can lose income and resources to the rest of the world or gain income and resources from the rest of the world to a relative degree generally unknown to sovereign countries.

IMPLICATIONS FOR REGIONAL DEVELOPMENT PLANNING

This understanding of the differences between national and regional economies draws our attention to three major implications for regional development planning practitioners. The first is that realistic regional planning requires an understanding of the relationship of the region to the national environment of which it is part, the principal linkages through which the two interact, and the ultimate consequences these interactions could and do have on the region.

The second is that what appears to be good for the nation may not necessarily be good for the region, and what is good for the region may not necessarily be perceived as good for the nation. As an illustration, suppose that a plant for processing agricultural produce were established in a rural region that had formerly sent its produce to a distant city for processing. The new plant might provide off-farm employment for regional labor and increase the regional multiplier by eliminating the need to "import" the processed product produced in the plant. It might thereby have a beneficial effect on the level of regional income. However, transfer of the processing to the hinterland may result in displacement of higher-paid urban workers and, through a reverse multiplier effect, ultimately reduce the GNP. Moreover, the displaced urban workers who have been removed from the tax base may now constitute, together with their families, a greater drain on the national public services budget.

This is not to say that the region must be viewed as necessarily at odds with the nation. It is only to say that in regional development planning, national realities must be taken into account. This is particularly true if support for implementing a regional plan is needed from higher levels of government.

The third implication for regional development planning is that the institutional tools available for regional development—the administrative and policy-making bodies and authorities—are generally quite different at the regional level from those available at the national level; and in any event, the degree of policy control is vastly different at the two levels. For example, at the national level a reallocation of resources for development can be brought about by printing money and using it for development investment. This causes inflation and a reduction of the demands on resources for consumer goods production.

It is easy to see that, for better or for worse, such a policy could not be pursued at the regional level. Moreover, policies that perhaps could be pursued at the regional level, such as tax incentives or fee reductions for certain types of activities, tend to be relatively less effective regionally than at the national level because of competitive policies of other regions and the ability of resources to move freely across the region's open borders.

These implications all carry a single message: regions are unique entities; they are lesser and open parts of a larger whole, both economically and administratively. Much of the effective planning latitude available at the national level is unavailable at the regional level. Effective regional planning requires keeping very clear the distinction between what should be done and what can be done, making the best use of development resources that really can be accessed, and taking advantage of the superior information available at the regional level because of the closeness of planners to the object of their planning.

IMPLICATIONS FOR AGGREGATE REGIONAL ANALYSIS

Before selecting and adapting methods of analysis, a framework of important questions that the analysis will help address should be formulated. The questions that are most important will vary from region to region in accordance with the overall nature of the region, the national context, major development concerns, the programmatic and legal context of the regional planning effort, the type of planning process being used, and many other factors. But for all regions there are important questions that can be answered quantitatively and others that can only be answered in non-quantitative terms. Also, for all regions there are important questions about the fundamental characteristics of the region and important questions about how it interacts with other regions, the rest of the country, and as appropriate, with the rest of the world.

This suggests a structure for an aggregate analysis framework that includes quantitative and non-quantitative questions about the region, and quantitative and non-quantitative questions about the region's interactions. Figure 1.2 illustrates the matrix structure for a framework of aggregate analytical questions that reflects this and indicates the sorts of topics on which the questions should focus.

Our primary subjects in this book are quantitative, and particularly economic, descriptive methods of regional analysis and the regional planning frameworks in which they can be used. So it will have to suffice for present purposes to stress that quantitative analysis serves the planning process most effectively as part of a larger analytical framework that encompasses non-quantitative information equally essential to regional development decision making.

In fact, very broadly speaking, the relationship between the topics of quantified and non-quantified analysis is this: quantified analysis deals mostly with indicators of regional economic performance; non-quantified analysis deals mostly with the factors behind that performance. This comes through clearly in Figure 1.2. The art of regional analysis ultimately involves determining the causal relationships between the indicators of performance and the factors behind that performance. The art of regional development planning ultimately involves identifying practicable interventions in the latter that will result in desirable types of changes in the former.

A good way to begin the economic analysis of a region is to write a broad description of the regional economy in terms of its openness, spatial relations, and overall pattern of development as reflected in its principal economic activities, its structure, and the lives of the people who live there. This description should be based on experience and readily available information rather than on field research. It provides a coherent point of departure for deciding on the most important specific questions for the analytical framework. These questions, in turn, provide a basis for selecting the appropriate methods of regional economic analysis and for adapting them to the needs of the situation at hand.

There is not likely to be a simple one-to-one relationship between important analytical questions in any situation and particular methods of analysis presented

Figure 1.2
A Framework for Aggregate Regional Analysis Questions

	Quantitative	Non-Quantitative
The Region	Questions about levels, sources, and distribution of income and employment, sectoral and industrial composition of the region's economy, quality and availability of factors of production, interindustry linkages, and related matters; questions about patterns of change in these things; and questions about how the region compares with other regions and the country.	Questions about the institutions, public policy tools, and other administrative and organizational factors and resources in the region that have been significant in determining the direction of the region's economy; questions about patterns of change in these things; and questions about the potential problems and opportunities they represent with respect to further regional development.
The Region's Interactions Across Its Borders	Questions about the character and intensity of flows to and from suppliers and purchasers across the borders of the region, including final and intermediate markets, sources and destinations of income transfers, and flows of factors of production; questions about the consequences of these economic flows; and questions about patterns of change in the flows and in their consequences.	Questions about national policies and their implementation, major public and private institutions and their operations, infrastructure, and markets through which the region interacts with other regions and the country; questions about the general nature and consequences of the interactions; and questions about the potential problems and opportunities the interactions represent with respect to further regional development.

in this book. Some methods of aggregate regional analysis address questions about both the economic composition of the region and its interactions with areas beyond it borders. Some methods address the same question, but from different perspectives. Some were designed to focus on one kind of question, but can with some modification be used to focus on another. In fact, as will be seen, some methods originally developed for intraregional analysis can be adapted to aggregate regional analysis, and the other way around. Finally, most methods of quantitative regional analysis are oriented to a dominant question and one or more lesser questions as well.

The presentations of aggregate methods of analysis in Part II are designed to provide a good sense of the types of questions each method can be used to address and how each can be modified to serve different purposes and situations.

Figure 1.3
Methods of Aggregate Regional Analysis in Part II: Dominant Analytical Questions

Method of Aggregate Regional Analysis	Dominant Analytical Question
Basic statistical compendium	What is the overall economic profile of the region in terms of a wide range of characteristics reflecting its current status?
Income measures	What are the levels of different types of income in the region?
Income and product accounts	What are the values of different types of production and total production in the region, and how is this reflected in different types of regional income?
Balance of payments statements	What are the values of different types of flows, total flows, and net flows across the borders of the region?
Production linkage investigations	What are the forward and backward production linkages across the borders of the region?
Commodity flow studies	What volumes of selected goods flow between origins and destinations across the borders of the region?
Friction analysis	What are the major factors inhibiting interaction between important concentrations of economic activity in the region and other areas?
Mix-and-share analysis	What is the relationship between the changing relative composition of production and total employment in the region?
Location quotient and related indicators	What is the degree of comparative specialization of the region in selected activities or characteristics as associated with related activities or characteristics?
Economic base analysis	What is the relationship between outside demand for the products of the region and regional economic expansion based on general multiplier relationships?
Input-output analysis	What are the regional interindustry linkages and their multiplier effects as related to outside demand for the region's products?

By way of a broad introductory summary, though, Figure 1.3 shows the dominant analytical questions to which each of the methods of aggregate regional analysis in Part II is oriented. Most of the questions are expressed in current terms, but should be understood as referring to changes over time as well.

2

Inside the Region

INCOME AND EMPLOYMENT MULTIPLICATION DYNAMICS

Just as the regional economy must be understood in aggregate terms both as an entity in its own right and as an element of the national economic complex, so also it should be understood as composed of interconnected subregional places. Interactions among these places can be of a nature that contributes more or less to, or that even detracts from, regional welfare and development.

To illustrate, suppose that to create employment in a poor region incentives were provided that induced an investor to establish a bicycle assembly factory there. For purposes of efficiency, the factory is sited in the largest urban center in the region, the place in the region that is best connected to the rest of the country. This secondary city also appears to be where many of the region's unemployed people are concentrated. All the bicycle parts are brought in from outside the region, and the profits ultimately accrue to the factory owner, who lives in the country's capital city. So of all the factory's outlays, only a portion, say 40 percent, is spent in the region, mostly on wages of factory workers; the rest, 60 percent, leaks out of the regional income multiplication stream to pay for ''imported'' parts and as a profit ''transfer'' to the investor.

Now imagine that in addition to the secondary city there are several smaller towns, each a market town serving an agricultural area of the region. And instead of a bicycle factory, regional planners induced the investor to establish a cold-storage facility for agricultural produce that would produce an equally profitable return on the investment. Only 15 percent of the facility's outlays goes for wages and other local operating costs; 75 percent pays for farm produce to be stored and later sold both to local wholesalers and to those from the capital city; 10 percent is transferred out of the region as profits to the owner.

Although the cold storage facility employs fewer people than the bicycle factory, the 75 percent of outlays that are for farm produce is spent among the smaller market towns, most of it ultimately going to farmers in the region. The farmers tend to spend a higher proportion of their income locally than do workers in the main regional city. The cold storage capability expands the effective market for regional farm produce, so farm incomes in the region rise. The cold storage capability also means that people in the region can substitute off-season purchases of local produce for products that were previously imported to the region.

The cold storage facility may at first appear of lesser benefit than the bicycle factory to the city in which it is located, since from the perspective of that city it employs fewer people and has expenditure leakages of 85 percent. But from the regional perspective, the leakage is only 10 percent, and the increased incomes and higher regional spending multipliers of the farmers, together with the larger regional multiplier resulting from import substitution, ultimately mean higher incomes and employment throughout the region. In the end, more employment may even be created in the major town through intraregional multiplier effects.

Measures that result in the generation of more "new" income and employment in the region (through regional export sales) by definition result in regional economic growth. Measures that result in a larger regional multiplier improve the regional growth dynamic. Measures that result in both, such as the cold storage facility (if they are financially viable in their own right) accelerate economic growth in the near term and help lay a foundation for continuing expansion over the long run. But, as the illustration was meant to suggest, the income and employment multiplication process takes place between farms and towns and between towns and towns of a region, as well as within towns. Hence, intraregional interactions are at least as important to the regional development process as interactions between the region and other areas.

That is why methods of aggregate regional analysis are not enough for development planning purposes. Aggregate methods may break down the regional economy in terms of components of production, expenditure, income, or employment, and even the interactions among components; but they do not incorporate the element of space—where in the region different things happen and between which places different types of exchanges take place—explicitly. True, there is often a relationship between types of economic activities and locations within the territory of a region: certain types of crops tend to be grown in certain areas, larger manufacturing activities tend to be concentrated in the larger towns, and so on. But this relationship is far from absolute or well defined with respect to either activities or places, and in any case does not help to understand intraregional interactions sufficiently.

Intraregional exchanges are the vehicle of regional income and employment multiplication. The volume and diversity of these exchanges in the region as a whole and among certain specific areas and groups in the region are heavily influenced by the unique characteristics of different locations and the lines of communication between them. The characteristics of different locations, the channels of communication between them, and the natures of the interactions among them are the subject of intraregional analysis. Intraregional analysis adds the depth of "where" and "why" understanding to the "what" emphasis of aggregate regional analysis.

URBAN PLACES IN REGIONAL GROWTH

Urban places represent specific locations within regions that play a central role in regional economic development. This was hinted at earlier, where income multiplication was said to take place between farms and towns, towns and towns, and within towns of a region. Towns play a central role even in the development of predominantly agricultural regions in developing countries. Most farm produce is marketed in or through towns, and most farm inputs and farm household consumer goods originate in towns or are marketed through them. This is usually true even when the final transaction takes place in a periodic market or at the farm gate rather than in an urban place.

Since most of the population in rural regions of developing countries lives on farms, and most of the household income in these areas is spent on food, what about farm-to-farm sales? Studies have shown that even these most often take place in towns. In fact, it is now widely confirmed that in developing countries, farm households commonly earn a significant proportion of their cash income, often between one-third and two-thirds, from nonfarm activities. Most of this nonfarm income, including both self-employment and wage labor pursuits, is derived from town-based enterprises that serve a predominantly rural clientele. Thus, even in regions where much of the income multiplication takes place through farm household–to–farm household exchanges of goods and services, urban places are critical to facilitating the income multiplication process.

We have so far spoken of the income multiplication process as one that generates income through current buying and selling. The amount of current buying and selling depends on the level of effective demand—that is, the amount of money available to be spent. The amount of money available to be spent is, as we have seen, heavily influenced by the amount of money earned by generating income from regional exports and by multiplying income within the region. But the amount of money that can be earned through regional exports and the amount of this that is spent *in the region* is heavily influenced by the local supply of goods and services for marketing the region's products to the outside world and the local supply of goods and services for sale to people who live in the region. In other words, there must be income to create effective demand, and there must be a supply of goods and services in the region on which the income can be spent so that it can be multiplied. Urban places play an important role on the supply side of the regional economic growth equation, too.

For example, if farm households earn a significant proportion of their cash income from town-based activities, including self-employment activities, how do these activities become established? Many—in some places most—of the enterprises in rural towns are established by farm households using earnings from farming. Farmers in developing as well as industrialized countries tend to be seasoned businesspeople who know that a balance must be struck between short-term profits, medium-term returns, and long-term security. They know that farm households are the largest market segment in rural areas, and they know well what that market segment demands and the best locations for serving the demand. They will often invest in town enterprises, even when investments on the farm would yield productivity gains, both to diversify their "investment portfolios" and to obtain higher medium-term returns. They thereby help create a diversified supply of goods and services that increases the local multiplier.

Incidentally, it has been found that often these same farm households, after securing a larger and steadier flow of income, then invest more heavily in raising farm productivity. Hence, their investment in the supply of town-based goods and services ultimately serves to increase the supply of agricultural produce, and thereby to expand the flow of export earnings into the region.

This is not to suggest that farmers are the only ones who invest in towns. Indeed, given a conducive business environment, towns are the logical enterprise locations for most entrepreneurs who want to tap a regional market. Towns offer economies of agglomeration—the cost-lowering benefits of having other businesses nearby—that make them favored locations for businesses that supply goods and services to people in the surrounding area. And they offer opportunities for economies of scale because they are locations in which large numbers of buyers congregate. Many studies have shown that regional income multiplication from farm earnings is higher from consumer expenditures than from other types of expenditures. Urban places offer a venue for supplying a wide variety of consumer goods and services to a dispersed rural population in a way that is beneficial to both sellers and buyers.

Consumer goods and services do not necessarily originate in the town where they are sold, though small craft or manufacturing enterprises are frequently found in even the smallest urban centers. A good portion of the consumer goods sold in towns, as we have seen, is food that is produced on farms in the area. Many other items come from other urban places in the region, from cities elsewhere, and even from abroad. They frequently arrive at regional market towns through a distribution chain that involves other towns. Similarly, farm produce that is exported from the region frequently flows through marketing chains that involve grading, storing, bulking, and perhaps processing at a sequence of urban centers.

Hence, towns serve as a mechanism to facilitate the supply of goods flowing out of the region that provide export earnings, and also to facilitate the supply of goods flowing into and within the region that are the basis of income-multiplying intraregional trade. Moreover, in most regions the efficiency and regional income-multiplying benefits of this trade are related to the way a regional system of urban centers, including the transportation links among them, functions.

Regional towns also play a critical role in the supply of goods and services that are essential for growth in agricultural productivity and output. Some of these goods and services are provided commercially, and so their provision also multiplies regional income. Some of them are government services that, while having minimal income-multiplication effects, are vital to expanding the basic production that fuels income multiplication. Urban centers provide the same economies of agglomeration and scale to suppliers and purchasers of farm inputs that they do to sellers and buyers of consumer goods and services. Farm inputs include products such as seeds, fertilizers, veterinary chemicals, pesticides, equipment, repair services, and so on. But they also include equally important, if less tangible, items that can be supplied effectively only in or through towns: banking services, extension information, laboratory services, legal services, market information, technological information, medical and education services, government administration services, cooperative facilities, and the like.

As regions develop, their towns expand, urban economic bases become more diversified, and many towns become less dependent on their agricultural hinterlands. Also as regions develop, the relative proportions of employment, value added, and income derived directly from farming eventually begin to decrease in favor of urban activities, even when agriculture remains the foundation of the regional economy. As the proportions continue to shift, the roles of regional towns as centers of economic growth begin to depend on their absolute and comparative advantages with respect to much larger market areas than their agricultural hinterlands. Frequently, as regions become more urbanized, the number of distinct economically active urban places decreases as efficiency in serving larger markets requires larger urban concentrations and the regional population becomes more mobile. In time, many regions come to be defined by their urban complexes.

IMPLICATIONS FOR REGIONAL DEVELOPMENT PLANNING

The implications for regional development planning are vast. They make the art of regional planning one that is distinctly apart from the art of generally spaceless, often target-oriented, aggregate planning that conventionally takes place at the national level, whether for the country as a whole or for specific national sectors. And they set it distinctly apart from the more spatially and economically confined, often specifically problem-focussed and physically oriented planning that tends to characterize planning for individual urban areas.

First, the aim of regional development planning is not simply to expand regional income; regional income can be expanded in a hundred ways without development planning, as was the case in the example of the bicycle factory.

The effort and expense of regional development planning is warranted when the purpose is to accelerate the development process by improving the growth dynamics of the regional economy. This means improving the comparative advantages of the region in its export products and improving the opportunities for intraregional trade through which income is multiplied within the region. If successful, the measures that accomplish this will lead to a steadily expanding and diversifying regional economy with the flexibility to respond to changing market conditions and withstand setbacks in individual sectors.

Second, a major aspect of regional development involves improving the conditions that facilitate intraregional trade, and thereby an expanding regional income (and employment) multiplier. Particularly in developing countries, the measures that facilitate intraregional trade often will also facilitate higher levels of regional exports. Facilitating trade means that while the requirements for specific sectors of economic activity must be taken into account, the focus is on places and areas and the trade that does and could take place among them. Economic sectors are convenient ways of defining types of economic activity that are the current agents of regional development, not the objects of regional development.

Facilitating intraregional trade entails planning that accounts for location, demand, and supply. Measures that raise income are not enough; measures that increase supply are not enough; and measures that do not address the specific potentials for trade expansion in specific places within the region are likely to be cost-ineffective at best, and to represent completely wasted development resources at worst. But people seeking economic opportunity are ultimately the best judges of the natures of those potentials; so regional planners, in accounting for location, demand, and supply, need to walk a thin line between enabling people in various parts of the region to seize opportunity better and defining the opportunity for them.

Accounting for location, demand, and supply means exercising sensitivity to the fact that, excluding metropolitan regions, a regional economy is a fabric of intimate connections among rural areas and urban places. The potentials for economic expansion vary among the region's agricultural areas and towns, and usually vary among particular towns and their surrounding areas in some association. Yet measures causing change in one part of a region may, through trade linkages, have ramifications in another part of the region that ultimately affect net regional consequences in ways unforseen in the absence of a true regional perspective. A true regional perspective views the settlement system and the agricultural areas of a region as a multifaceted economic organism operating over the entire territory of the region.

Finally, the regional economy is a living, dynamic, responding organism. The regional planner needs not only to understand this, but to help improve the sustainability of its growth forces and its adaptability to changing circumstances in the national, and indeed the world, environment. Setting employment or income or output targets, or defining roles for specific urban places, may be among many useful exercises employed during a planning effort, but they are hardly legitimate regional development objectives.

Planning meant to achieve specific quantified economic measures representing a desired status in the region at a target date (sometimes called *blueprint planning*) involves heroic assumptions. It requires assuming that markets, competition from other regions, the roles and comparative advantages of regional towns or agricultural zones, the weather, and a myriad of other significant factors beyond planning control can be predicted or assigned, or assuming by default that they will remain unchanged. Responsible planning involves concentrating on factors within planning control. What is within the control of regional development planning is really quite limited. But it is enough to improve the regional environment in ways that enable the forces currently working to expand economic well-being to work better, and to enable new forces to emerge that increase opportunities for broad-based economic adaptation and expansion.

IMPLICATIONS FOR INTRAREGIONAL ANALYSIS

What was said in the last section of Chapter 1 about a framework of quantitative and non-quantitative analytical questions for aggregate regional analysis applies to intraregional analysis also. While specific intraregional analysis needs and priorities will naturally vary considerably among different regions, the basic types of analytical questions are the same for all. For all regions there will be important analytical questions about the economic characteristics, functions, and performance of places within the region and the interactions among them; and for all regions there will be questions about the factors in the overall environment in different areas of the region that influence the character and performance of intraregional economic systems.

The first category is a counterpart to the set of quantitative questions in Chapter 1, and the second category is a counterpart to the set of non-quantitative questions in the same chapter. Again, the art of regional analysis ultimately involves determining the causal relationships between the indicators of performance and the factors behind that performance. And again, the art of regional development planning involves identifying practicable interventions in the overall environment that will result in desirable types of changes in the performance, in this case, of intraregional economic systems. Figure 2.1 summarizes the sorts of topics that would be covered in a framework of questions for intraregional analysis.

The four broad types of questions under ''Economic characteristics of places and the interactions among them'' in Figure 2.1 coincide roughly with the four chapters covering methods of intraregional analysis in Part III of this book. By way of an introductory summary, Figure 2.2 shows the dominant analytical questions to which each of the methods of intraregional analysis in Part III is oriented. The questions are expressed in current terms, but should be understood as referring to changes over time as well. Some of the methods of intraregional analysis are adaptations of aggregate methods of analysis, some are by their

Figure 2.1
A Framework for Intraregional Analysis Questions

Economics characteristics of places and the interactions among them	Questions about: a) absolute and comparative economic characteristics and activities of subareas and urban settlements of the region; b) major trade channels operating within the region, and flows of major goods or categories of goods in intraregional trade; c) regional income and employment multiplication dynamics within the region in terms of sectors, locations, demand, and supply; d) the system of urban settlements, and relationships between rural and urban areas.
The overall environment in regional subareas	Question about: a) social structure and cultural characteristics that influence economic behavior; b) availability, use, and management of natural resources; c) attributes of the physical infrastructure that facilitates intraregional exchange; d) technologies and production processes utilized by farmers, transporters, and town-based enterprises; e) institutional capital as reflected in local governments, marketing institutions, trade organizations, financial institutions, and voluntary organizations and their operations; f) the local policy environment as reflected in the policies of local institutions with a bearing on production and trade.

fundamental natures suitable for aggregate and interregional as well as intraregional application, and some have been designed explicitly for intraregional analysis.

Figure 2.2
Methods of Intraregional Analysis in Part III: Dominant Analytical Questions

Method of Intraregional Regional Analysis	Dominant Analytical Question
Basic statistical compendium	What are the overall economic profiles of the region's subareas and towns, and how do they compare with each other in terms of important characteristics
Income measures	What are the levels of different types of income in different parts of the region?
Social accounts	What is the relationship between income levels in different parts of the region and the different prevailing production patterns, and in turn, the values of flows across the region's borders?
Economy composition analysis	What are the relative levels of concentration or specialization in selected characteristics or activities among different parts of the region, and what are the associated consequences?
Natural resource assessments	What are the natural resources endowments of different parts of the region, and what are the associated problems and potentials?
Linkage investigations	What are the major types of linkages and their magnitudes among central places in the region?
Flow studies	What volumes of selected goods flow between major points of origin and destination in the region?
Friction analysis	What are the major factors inhibiting interaction among central places in the region?
Extended commodity trade systems analysis	What are the intraregional marketing chains of important commodities, particularly rural commodities produced for sale outside the region?
Economic base and accrual analysis	What is the relationship between outside demand for the products of different areas in the region and economic expansion of those areas and of the region as a whole, based on simple multiplier relationships?
Input-output analysis	What are the interindustry linkages and their multiplier effects among different parts of the region as related to outside demand for the region's products?
Rural-urban exchange analysis	What are the comparative rural-urban income multiplication effects associated with different agricultural commodities in different parts of the region?
Access studies	What is the degree of access of the population of different parts of the region to functions provided by the region's central places, and what does this suggest about effective demand for those functions?
Functional analysis	What are the functions provided by the region's settlement system, what sorts of hierarchical networks prevail within it, and what does this suggest about effective supply of those functions?
Market center studies	What are the major trade functions of the region's market centers, and how are they linked through trade to other regional market centers and the rural areas of the region?

3

Project Interventions for Regional Development

THE NATURE OF REGIONAL DEVELOPMENT PLANNING

Regional development planning is not planning *of* a region; it is planning *for* a region. It is an effort organized to establish overall regional economic development objectives, collect and analyze information, and generate and evaluate project proposals within a strategic framework for regional development.

Regional development planning leads to projects that most often involve public sector actions or actions of a public sector nature undertaken by nongovernmental organizations. Worldwide experience has shown that efficient economic development involves recognizing the appropriate roles of the public and private sectors, and enhancing their capabilities to carry out their respective roles effectively. While there are always legitimate roles for both sectors, they vary from country to country and change over time within countries.

Broadly speaking, however, it is the role of the private sector to create value by producing tradable goods and services and engaging in their exchange. And it is the role of the public sector to facilitate and promote the creation of value by the private sector, and to ensure that it is done in a way that serves the interest of the broad population in both the short and long runs. It is also up to the public sector to create value directly by performing certain functions, for example transportation or police services, when these functions are essential but the private sector does not have the capacity to perform them or cannot do so in a way that is both financially viable and responsive to social values.

Regional development planning can be thought of as planning for the improved use of public resources available to the region so as to improve private sector capacity to create value responsibly with private resources. The private sector plans, usually very carefully, for the use of its resources. It is generally sensitive to the need for public sector support for its plans, and often actively seeks that support. Efficient economic development requires equally careful planning for the use of public resources; and the private sector—farmers, small entrepreneurs, voluntary organizations, cooperatives, and operators of larger businesses alike—must have a part in the planning process.

Project interventions in the regional economy that emerge from regional development planning are generally aimed at improving and expanding the economic options available to the people of the region. To be successful in this with lasting effect, proposed projects need to meet tests of technical feasibility, economic viability, environmental sustainability, and social acceptability. Evaluating proposed projects for these qualities and their responsiveness to the economic needs of the population requires knowledge that is possessed and judgments that can be made only by those who live in the region and will live with the projects. People who live in the region must therefore be the primary participants in regional development planning.

Through regional development planning the region is considered as a whole, as an economic entity with diverse interacting elements. Local project proposals for public action are identified on the basis of an analysis of the regional economy, or at least are comparatively and collectively evaluated against region-wide economic conditions and opportunities. In this way regional development planning is different from other types of planning for regions, such as planning for a single social or economic sector within a defined region, or planning for individual villages in a region as isolated entities, or planning to carry out several foreordained projects within the territory of a particular region.

The planning process produces a regional development plan. The heart of this plan is a limited set of proposed projects identified, justified, and evaluated within a framework of current strategic regional economic priorities and relationships. The purpose of the plan is to lay out project interventions in the regional economy that, based on the best information available, are most likely to lead to important improvements in the way the economy operates and in the ability of the region's population to prosper through that economy.

Whether regional development planning is undertaken in a relatively decentralized national environment or one that is newly struggling with decentralization efforts, there are several reasons why it is important to focus the planning process on identifying and assessing a limited set of specific projects of a public sector nature. First, it is with respect to identifying specific priority projects that can be publicly implemented and managed with good effect (as against, say, comprehensive planning or planning that encompasses establishing an array of economic enterprises) that the development planning need is almost always most pressing. Second, that is the type of public planning that can be undertaken most competently at the regional level, where trained technical personnel, socioeconomic data, financial resources, and most important, public planning experience are often least available.

Third, project identification and evaluation represents a decision-making level at which planning can most readily produce proposals attuned to regional realities, and therefore is most likely to be followed by implementation and achievement of objectives. This is essential for the progress of an administrative decentralization process as well as a regional economic development process. For people ultimately judge the credibility of a decentralization process by the degree to which decentralized planning results in implementation of projects that expand their opportunities and respond to their needs. The history of regional planning in developing countries suggests that when the emphasis is on producing comprehensive plans, little implementation takes place; and when the emphasis is on identifying and establishing economic enterprises through public planning, little economic development takes place.

Finally, encouraging planning that is focussed sharply on identifying a limited set of project interventions in the regional economy is the easiest way for a central government to promote true decentralization. This sort of regional planning does not require an intricate and administratively cumbersome national system of oversight, clearances, technical assistance, and coordination for planning or implementation. It thus allows decentralization to proceed not by burdening central government with massive new responsibilities, control functions, and bureaucratic structures, but by enabling central government to shed some of these burdens and to clarify and simplify the purposes of others.

REGIONAL DEVELOPMENT PROJECT INTERVENTIONS

In the previous chapter the point was made that the most essential elements in regional economic development are expanding returns from regional export activities coupled with expanding intraregional income and employment multiplication. In this light, improving and expanding the economic options available to the people of the region implies, above all, project interventions that lead to improved efficiency in the operations of regional producer and consumer markets, including production for those markets. This, in turn, means an emphasis on project interventions that reduce the costs of buying and selling in regional markets in which people participate, and that reduce barriers to entry, such as outright restrictions or lack of access to resources or technologies, into markets in which people could be participating.

Regional project interventions of this sort generally fall into three broad categories:

1. Infrastructure and other physical capital;
2. The array of public and private institutions and institutional operations; and
3. Public sector policies.

Regional development planning is done for the purpose of identifying and evaluating priority practicable project interventions in these categories, including their natures, scales, and specific locations.

Improving the efficiency of important regional market systems may require more than one type of project intervention for maximum effectiveness. For example, improving marketplace facilities in a regional market town may be of little benefit to local farmers, consumers, and traders if marketplace fees are so high as to make doing business there too costly for many. Policy changes, possibly including new sources of local authority revenue, may need to accompany physical marketplace improvements in order to achieve the full potential of development benefits. It is for reasons like this that projects must be evaluated in relation to each other and considered in terms of strategic packages.

Moreover, accelerating regional development most efficiently and effectively, especially in developing countries, usually requires improvements in infrastructure, institutions, and policies at the national level as well as at the regional level. For example, if farm prices fixed by central government policy discourage commercial farming, improving a farm-to-market road may be of minimal benefit. This means that in the course of determining current regional project priorities, the national environment of infrastructure, institutions, and policies needs to be realistically taken into account. It also means that an important type of regional development project may be to exert pressure on central government agencies for improvements that can only be undertaken at the national level.

An emphasis on project interventions that improve regional market efficiency does not mean that other types of measures, such as those aimed at directly improving productivity, are not also important to regional development. But if markets do not function efficiently to convert improved productivity into increased income that is then multiplied among the farms and towns of the region, new production methods and technologies may have little lasting effect on development. This is another reason why regional development projects, whether directly related to market efficiency or not, must be evaluated in relation to each other and considered in terms of strategic packages.

PROJECT IDENTIFICATION AND EVALUATION

Part IV of this book concerns methods of project identification and evaluation. Again, it is best to begin the process of project identification and evaluation with a framework of analytical questions. The fundamental types of questions, applicable to all regions, are shown in Figure 3.1.

The chapters of Part IV are meant to help determine the specific project identification and evaluation questions applicable to the development planning situation in a particular region, and to devise the analytical tools for addressing those questions. Chapter 15 deals with project identification and Chapter 16 deals with project evaluation. The sections of each of these chapters correspond to the analytical questions shown in Figure 3.1 under each heading.

Figure 3.1
A Framework for Regional Development Planning Project Identification and Evaluation Questions

Project identification	Questions about: a) the indicators through which aggregate and intraregional analysis suggest that project interventions could accelerate regional economic development; b) the elements in the larger environment that are major factors in causing those indicators to be what they are, and that can be favorably influenced through project interventions; c) preliminary evaluation of numerous possible project interventions in light of their relative practicability and roughly estimated incidence and magnitude of their consequences.
Project evaluation	Questions about: a) the likely positive and negative consequences of proposed projects; b) the relationship of each project to regional development goals, objectives, and strategies; c) comparative and combined assessment of project intervention proposals.

Together, Chapters 15 and 16 reflect a process that begins with indicators of potentially beneficial projects, then moves to development of a large list of specific possible projects based on those indicators, and then proceeds through a sequence of activities for refining the list into a limited set of priority and practicable proposed project interventions in the regional economy. Chapter 17 of Part IV discusses benefit-cost analysis, a specific approach to evaluation of project proposals that is in widespread use and deserving of separate treatment.

Armed with menus of methods for aggregate regional analysis, intraregional analysis, and project identification and evaluation, how does one design a regional development planning process so that the appropriate methods of analysis can be selected, adapted, and combined for a particular regional planning situation? Part V of this book offers ideas that speak to that question.

Part V does not offer a menu of regional development planning processes the way Parts II, III, and IV offer menus of methods of analysis. The three chapters of Part V discuss first an idealized planning model, then options for launching and selecting a routine overall approach to planning, and finally a general framework on which a specific regional planning process can be designed. On the basis of material in Part V, regional planners can consider approaches to regional planning that would be most suited to the contexts of their work. It will then remain for them to determine the breadth and nature of planning focus, points and mechanism of public participation, administrative framework, detailed procedures, time frame, and analytical methods through which the approach is elaborated into an explicit planning process that leads to effective project interventions in the regional economy.

II

Methods of Aggregate Regional Analysis

4

The Basic Statistical Compendium

Usually quite early in a regional development planning endeavor, attention turns to the task of collecting data for regional analysis. It is a task that can be costly in terms of time, labor, and funds. In order to ensure that data collection is done efficiently, it is a good idea first to work out a preliminary framework of methods of analysis for which the data are needed. The last sections of Chapters 1 and 2, dealing respectively with methods of aggregate regional and intraregional analysis, provide some help for devising such a framework.

Devising a framework of analytical methods, however, requires basic knowledge about the region sufficient for determining the types of analytical tools that are likely to yield the most valuable development planning information and for which the needed data can be obtained. Some preparatory work will often be necessary to develop this basic knowledge. The preparatory work can begin with the sort of broad regional description mentioned in the last section of Chapter 1, but can also go beyond that to the preparation of a regional statistical compendium. A statistical compendium is a document made up of statistical tables, often accompanied by diagrams, charts, maps, and explanatory text, and covering a wide range of subjects important to a preliminary understanding of the region's unique nature.

FUNCTIONS OF THE COMPENDIUM

A regional *profile* in the form of a statistical compendium has the potential to fulfill many functions. It can serve to help present the region's case to agencies of the central government and other potential sources of development support outside the region. For local leadership, the compendium can serve as a handbook of information on characteristics of the region and as an introduction to a broad array of regional problems and potentials. For all levels of government, the statistical compendium serves as a sort of regional calling card, announcing that regional development planning work is in progress and that more can be expected from this enterprise in the near future.

For the planning staff, the completed compendium provides a basis for selecting subject areas for further intensive study and for devising a regional analysis framework. It enables a first rough overall analysis of the region sufficient for setting initial planning priorities. Moreover, the compendium constitutes a sourcebook for data that will later be used in some of the formal methods of regional economic analysis.

The task of designing and putting together the statistical compendium has usefulness in its own right. It is often the first of the actual major planning (rather than administrative) tasks that requires the coordinated participation of the entire planning staff and that has an immediate tangible objective. As such, the effort helps crystallize working relationships and areas of specialization among development workers. Beyond this, the compendium effort provides a framework for a first systematic review of the entire regional complex by the planning team; brings about contacts with concerned bodies in the region; and, for future reference, familiarizes the analysts with sources, types, and characteristics of available regional data.

COMPONENTS OF COMPENDIUM TABLES

Usually, the maps, charts, diagrams, and text of a regional compendium are based on the statistical tables that make up the heart of the document. The statistical tables have four essential structural components, as illustrated in Figure 4.1.

1. *Overall analytical rubrics*: the broad categories of information covered by the compendium and reflected in the sections or divisions into which the document is organized;
2. *Table subjects*: the specific types of information covered within each analytical rubric and reflected in the table titles;
3. *Column headings*: representing the specific data selected to describe the subject with which each table deals; and
4. *Row headings*: representing the list of geographic areas for which the data indicated in each column heading are provided.

Compendium tables do not have to follow the format of the Figure 4.1 illustration, but whatever the format, table components remain essentially the same. When the tables are being designed, decisions must be made about these components. The decisions should not be made casually; ultimately, they determine

Figure 4.1
A Compendium Table and Its Components

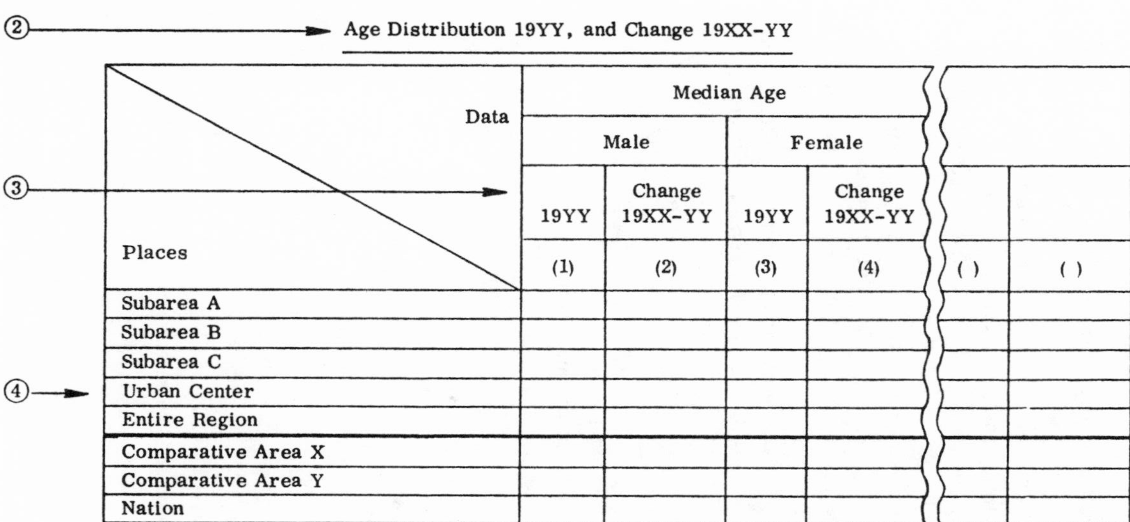

Places \ Data	Median Age					
	Male		Female			
	19YY	Change 19XX–YY	19YY	Change 19XX–YY		
	(1)	(2)	(3)	(4)	( )	( )
Subarea A						
Subarea B						
Subarea C						
Urban Center						
Entire Region						
Comparative Area X						
Comparative Area Y						
Nation						

the quality and quantity of information about the region that will be communicated by statistical data in the compendium.

ANALYTICAL RUBRICS AND TABLE SUBJECTS

The overall analytical rubrics, or information categories, into which the statistical tables are organized encourages compendium readers to think about the region with a certain analytical orientation. Chapter 18 points out that the set of analytical rubrics can be used as an organizing framework throughout the planning process, promoting clarity and consistency as the process progresses from one step to the next. Thus, while the analytical rubrics may be revised as the planning process matures, their initial selection is sufficiently basic to the planning frame of reference to warrant a good deal of careful thought. The only fixed rule is that taken together they must in some sense reflect the relevant whole of the region.

For example, one government agency in the United States charged with a special concern for the welfare of the poor in its development activities published guidelines for local statistical compendiums that called for compendium divisions in accordance with the following analytical rubrics:

—Profile of the poor

—General demographic characteristics

—Geographic characteristics

—Economic characteristics

—Social characteristics

At the same time, another U.S. government agency charged with a special concern for unemployment and community development used the following set of analytical rubrics to organize the statistical compendiums for areas it assisted:

—Characteristics of the unemployed

—Community facilities

—General population characteristics

—Economic structure and activities

—Physical resources

One approach often used is the regional resources or assets approach, in which all the features of the region are seen as greater or lesser resources that can serve to advance economic development. The set of specific analytical rubrics devised would reflect the dominant exploitable features of the particular area. In a region heavily dependent on extractive industry, the analytical rubrics might be:

—Human resources

—Institutional resources

—Energy resources

—Mineral resources

—Timber resources

Imagination can be used to consider how the analytical rubrics might appear under this approach in regions with economies dominated by tourism, manufacturing, or agriculture.

Another approach often used is known as the HINCO view of the region or local area: Tables are organized under analytical rubrics highlighting the human, institutional, natural, capital, and other components of the regional complex. Figure 4.2 shows the subjects of tables that might appear in each division of a compendium organized along HINCO lines.

Many regional planners prefer analytical rubrics that cause the compendium to highlight aspects of the area that relate more directly to key issues as they perceive them. Thus, they have often promoted organizing tables under compendium sections such as social aspects, physical aspects, institutional aspects, and economic aspects, with the last category further subdivided into regional export-related activities, regional import-related activities, and regional activities that serve regional markets. A variation on this approach involves subdividing economic aspects into extractive, manufacturing, commerce, agriculture, and perhaps tourism subcomponents.

Figure 4.3 is an illustration of a compendium model based on a population-location-activities approach. This approach is oriented to highlight what goes on within a region and how this is related to the region's location. The locational characteristics have both a physical dimension and a relative spatial dimension. Figure 4.3 suggests the analytical rubrics and the table subjects that could be included under each. It also provides a brief summary of the contributions that data within each division of the compendium might make toward a comprehensive regional description.

Neither Figure 4.2 nor Figure 4.3 are suggested as checklists of requirements for basic regional statistical compendiums. Certainly first efforts to produce such compendiums should aim at much more limited documents than are implied by the illustrations. The illustrations can be used to help think about those data that really are important, as well as available, in the case of a particular region. As planning efforts continue over the years, there will be time enough to modify, elaborate, and expand the compendium.

Some overlap and repetition of information will be noticed in Figures 4.2 and 4.3. The purpose of the set of overall analytical rubrics is to focus attention on major discrete components of the regional socioeconomic system in order better to observe and understand the functioning of the whole. But the whole really is a system, and its components are linked and interdependent. As a result, there

Figure 4.2
A Compendium Model Organized on the HINCO Approach

Analytical Rubric	Table Subjects
1. Human aspects	Population size and demographic characteristics Education Work experience, skills Income and wages Expenditure patterns Employment, unemployment, labor force participation Health Population subsets (for example, minorities, rural, urban) Housing Productivity Commutation Labor-market areas
2. Institutional aspects	Regional and local governments Public revenue and expenditure patterns Social and municipal services Labor-to-capital ratios Business barriers Business institutions Institutional coordination Institutional participation Trade and labor organizations Cooperatives Economic activity mix characteristics Land ownership patterns
3. Natural aspects	Land use patterns Mineral resources Soil types Water resources Topographic features Recreation assets Scenic assets Locational characteristics Historic sites Other heritage-related features Environmentally sensitive zones Hazard-prone zones
4. Capital aspects	Infrastructure Land use potentials Transportation and communication Public investment Private investment Savings rates External capital sources Housing stock Unutilized/underutilized structures Firm size Concentration ratios Gross product Capital-to-output ratios Public-capital construction
5. Other aspects	Development plans and planning at higher and lower levels Trade areas Special relationships with other areas Special information on major economic activities, problems, or potentials Results of surveys designed to obtain the views of the leadership or the general public on development problems, potentials, or desired directions Energy resources

Figure 4.3
A Compendium Model Organized on the Population-Location-Activities Approach

Analytical Rubric	Table Subjects	Insights Provided
1. Population and social characteristics	Population size, age distribution, family characteristics, vital statistics, growth components, and so on Education Work experience Income and wealth Personal income and expenditure patterns (sources and uses) Employment and unemployment, labor force participation, worker-to-total population ratio, and so on Health, living conditions, and so on Welfare Government Subsets, for example, farmers, minorities, rural populations, urban population, and so on	Status, problems, and potentials of human resources; social organizations; local culture; and so on
2. Location characteristics	Physical resources Other natural geographic, locational, climatic features, and so on Social capital, infrastructure, and rates and sources of investment in these Governments Inter- and intraregional orientations and spatial relationships Transportation and communications mixes and links	Spatial and physical qualities of the location, both natural and man-made, including general inter- and intraregional lines of communication, commerce, and central-place hierarchy patterns

Figure 4.3 (Continued)

3. Economic activities characteristics	Firm size Concentration ratios Value added Gross regional product Productivity Sales Farm characteristics Detailed characteristics of major economic activities Investment and capital accumulation Capital-to-output ratios Industry mix characteristics	Levels and types of economic activities, industrial linkages, producer or consumer goods orientations, local and export consumption orientations, investment, credit, and other aspects of the region's structure of economic activities
4. Population-location relationships characteristics	Population extent, density, and frequency measures, such as population per square mile, location and extent of population centers, distribution of settlements by population size, distribution of population by settlements and settlement size, and so on Travel patterns Commutation External travel Migration Land ownership patterns	The manner in which the characteristics of the population and of the location result in and result from interactions between then
5. Population-activity relationships characteristics	Employment by industry Income and wages by industry Unemployment by industry experience Labor-to-capital ratios Labor productivity by industry	How efficiently human resources are being utilized in economic activity, and the benefit to the population from engaging in the activities and utilizing the technologies prevailing in the region
6. Location-activity relationships characteristics	Location of commerce and industry Intra- and interregional flows and linkages Trade areas Labor market areas Special relationships with other regions	The characteristics, problems and potentials of economic activity as related to and determined by spatial and physical features of the regional location

is bound to be overlap among subjects handled under different analytical rubrics. A relaxed attitude should be taken about this. Related information that common sense suggests ought to be seen together should not be separated just for the sake of adhering strictly to the subject matter confines of different analytical rubrics. This may lead here and there to data appearing under more than one analytical rubric, which would simply reflect their relevance to more than one major component of the regional complex.

CONSIDERATIONS REGARDING COLUMN HEADINGS

The column headings of a table reflect the selection of measures and indicators thought most informative with regard to the subject of the table. This is not a trivial point. It means that column headings do not merely describe the data that were available and have been included in the compendium, and table titles do not merely describe the general subject tying the data in the table together. It means that the decision process goes in the other direction: table titles reflect decisions about the subjects best suited for informing the compendium reader, and column headings reflect decisions about the most important statistical measures regarding that subject—all, of course, in light of the data available.

Column headings may call for absolute measures, such as regional income, or for data derived from these measures, such as percentage increases in regional income. Derived data usually involve a comparison of absolute measures over time, among different places, among different population groups, or among different types of economic activities. Often they deal with a combination of these things, such as comparative changes over a certain period among selected economic activities in different places. Such comparisons are usually accomplished by means of percentages or indexes, both of which are the products of ratio computations. Ratio computations—dividing one number by another—are the simplest of all methods of analysis. As the following chapters show, they are often the point of departure for more elaborate methods, such as input-output analysis.

Table 4.1 shows unemployment for a province and for the nation in 19XX and 19YY (say, the beginning and end of a five-year period), in columns (1) and (2). A first ratio computation converts these numbers into unemployment *rates*, or percentages of the total labor force (figures for the total labor force are not shown), as shown in columns (3) and (4). This increases the available information by revealing the proportion of individuals not able to find work from among those able and willing to work. It is readily apparent from columns (3) and (4) that while the rate of unemployment in the province showed improvement (decline) over the period 19XX–19YY, it compared rather unfavorably with the nation in both years.

How unfavorably? And was the position of the province improving or deteriorating relative to the nation over the period? Column (5) shows the percentages by which the two unemployment rates changed over the period, the result of

Table 4.1
Illustration of Comparisons over Time and among Places

	Number of Unemployed People		Unemployment Rates				
			Rates		Percentage Change	National Indexes	
	19XX (1)	19YY (2)	19XX (3)	19YY (4)	19XX-19YY (5)	19XX (6)	19YY (7)
Province	6,000	5,440	7.8	6.8	–12.8	173	179
Nation	850,000	760,000	4.5	3.8	–15.6	100	100

calculating a ratio of ratios in columns (3) and (4). It is apparent from the figures in column (5) that the amount of the decrease in the unemployment rate in the province lagged behind that of the country. The computation of a ratio over time has further increased the available information from the absolute measures.

If the provincial unemployment rate has declined more slowly than that of the nation as a whole, then despite the improvement in the provincial unemployment rate, its position relative to the nation must have been deteriorating over the period. Computing a ratio among places—in this case, the province and the nation—quantifies and thereby highlights and gives more substance to this fact, increasing the available information from the absolute measures still further.

Columns (6) and (7) show index numbers resulting from computing ratios of the figures for the province and the nation in columns (3) and (4), respectively. In column (3), for example, the 7.8 unemployment rate for the province was divided by the 4.5 unemployment rate for the nation, resulting in a ratio of 1.73 (or 1.73/1.00). By convention, the ratio is multiplied by 100, producing a whole number index for the province that uses the national unemployment rate as the base for comparison. Columns (6) and (7) show unemployment in the region relative to the nation at the end of the period to be six index points higher than at the beginning of the period. This suggests a growing polarization between the province and the rest of the country that could have extremely serious consequences for the province over the long run, especially if something were to cause the general decline in unemployment to be arrested.

CONSIDERATIONS REGARDING ROW HEADINGS

The geographic areas listed in the row headings (often referred to as the table stub) may include the region's principal towns and subareas and also reference areas outside the region selected for comparison. The reference areas provide a background against which to consider local data.

National figures are popular as standards of comparison because national figures reflect the larger environment of which the region is a part. But for many regions, particularly rural ones, national socioeconomic measures are often of questionable comparative value. For one thing, a major component in the calculation of national figures may be an urbanized population with tastes, needs, standards, and a way of life in general very different from those prevailing in rural areas. Moreover, a comparison with the national average, median, or the like, while in a sense a comparison with a national composite, is not a comparison with anything that really exists. People tend most frequently to view their region, its progress, and their own welfare as relative to other specific regions and their populations. In many cases, then, other reference areas are needed as standards of comparison in addition to or instead of the nation.

There is a wide variety of alternatives to national norms as standards of comparison. Other possible reference areas include other regions, medians or averages of all other regions, medians or averages of selected groups of other regions, and so on. In the search for standards of comparison to complement or replace the nation in the row headings of a particular table, the analyst may look for real or fictitious (composite) areas that are similar to the region under study in terms of population or social, economic, and cultural characteristics, or that have a functional similarity. The standard of comparison that will be most informative depends on the subject with which the table deals and the point that is to be made.

5

Income Measures, Income and Product Accounts

Regional income measures are important because they provide indications of personal and community economic welfare and, compared over time, of economic growth. Regional income and product accounts are more difficult to assemble, but can be designed to provide a great deal more. The accounts can be a powerful tool for description and analysis of a region's economic structure, and can be made to reflect an underlying social, geographic, sectoral, or other substructure as well.

Income-based analysis does, however, have certain limitations when used to indicate levels of welfare and regional economic health. These limitations arise from the fact that the analysis is usually based on money income derived largely from economic product, or goods and services being traded in the marketplace, while in fact, the benefits of goods and services not currently traded in the marketplace often figure very substantially in levels of individual, family, and community welfare in both industrialized and developing countries. For example, the current status of housing, health, recreational opportunities, nutrition, job satisfaction, the physical and natural environment, and many more welfare factors are not indicated in the slightest by current levels of individual or regional income.

Perhaps even more important from the regional development planning perspective is the fact that current levels of income (and product) say little about the underlying health of the economy or its prospects for the future. Today's income may reflect yesterday's investments and decisions more than anything else. Moreover, a high current money volume of product may have come about at the expense of efficiency or resources for tomorrow.

Figure 5.1
Conceptual Structure of Income Measures

Gross Regional Product (at market prices)	
less	capital consumption allowances of enterprises in the region
equals	**net regional product**
less	business (including government enterprises) payments other than those to or on behalf of local factors of production
plus	subsidies to enterprises in the region
equals	**regional income** (paid to local factors of production)
less	regional income not accruing to persons
plus	other income accruing to persons residing in the region
equals	**regional personal income**
less	personal taxes paid by residents of the region
equals	**regional personal disposable income**
less	personal consumption expenditures by residents of the region for subsistence
equals	**regional personal discretionary income**
which is used for:	regional personal savings and regional personal discretionary consumption

Nevertheless, income measures and income and product accounts, taken for what they are, provide useful indicators of levels of economic activity, economic returns, and the relationships between different types of economic activity and economic returns, especially when compared over time. As the foregoing implies, these analytical tools provide the most useful insights when employed in combination with other methods of analysis.

THE STRUCTURE OF BASIC INCOME MEASURES

The basic income measures employed by analysts at the regional level are, for the most part, based on counterpart measures commonly employed at the national level. Figure 5.1 shows the conceptual structure of the many related income measures that might be used in regional analysis.

Gross regional product, or GRP, is the total value, at market prices, of final goods and services produced in the region during the accounting year. The word *final* means that the goods and services are not purchased for further processing or resale within the region.

Gross regional product can be estimated in several ways. The first involves:

adding up

—personal consumption expenditures in the region;

—private investment in the region;

—local and central government expenditures in the region; and

—all sales of the region's products and services to buyers outside the region (regional exports);

and then subtracting

—the value of goods and services purchased outside the region and resold in the region or used as inputs to regional production (imports).

A variation on this approach is to add up total, not just regional, expenditures by regional people, firms, and governments, plus all expenditures by outsiders in the region; but then imports subtracted would have to include all purchases by regional residents, firms, or agencies outside the region, not only those used for resale or as inputs.

Another approach, one that is probably more practicable for many regions, is to sum the value, at market prices, of final goods and services produced in the region, minus the value of imported inputs, for each sector or industry category. The simplest approach, where record keeping permits, is to sum the value added by each sector or industry category. Because expenditure and product are, by economic definition, the same, all these approaches should yield the same GRP figure. In fact, they can be used as cross-checks for each other.

Figure 5.1 begins with GRP and then makes certain adjustments in it to arrive at regional income, or payments to the owners of regional *factors of production* (land, labor, capital) used to create the GRP. One of the adjustments is subtracting the cost of capital equipment consumed in the production process. This capital consumption contributes to the value of final production, but does not represent current income to anyone. Moreover, *allowances* must be made, (that is, money must be set aside) to replace the used-up capital if production levels are to be maintained. When capital consumption allowances are netted out of gross regional product, the resulting figure is net regional product, NRP.

NRP is adjusted further in two ways. First, other costs of production that do not represent payments for regional factors of production, such as certain taxes and profit payments to outside owners, are subtracted. Then business earnings indirectly associated with production, particularly subsidies, are added in. The resulting figure is regional income, which represents the actual earnings accruing to owners of the factors of production in the region in consequence of their production of gross regional product.

Regional personal income includes that part of regional income that people take home in the form of personal earnings from all sources before taxes. To arrive at regional personal income, regional income must be reduced by the amounts that do not accrue to people, such as social insurance contributions, corporate income taxes, retained corporate profits, and the like. And it must be increased by the amounts that accrue to people from sources other than regional product, such as investment income, gifts, and so on.

When personal taxes are deducted from regional personal income, the resulting figure is regional personal disposable income, the money people can spend. In many cases, however, people have payments due on commitments made previously. In the context of a poor region, commitments made previously may meaningfully include minimum subsistence expenditures, such as those for basic food and shelter. When these are deducted from the figure for disposable income, the resulting figure is considered regional personal discretionary income, the money people can spend or save as they please.

Regional per capita income is usually based on regional personal income or regional disposable income, and is simply income divided by population. Regional average household income is income divided by the number of households in the region, or, alternatively, regional per capita income multiplied by average household size. While per capita income and average household income have identical analytical value in a statistical sense, for interpretation purposes one or the other may be more informative in light of prevailing cultural practices.

Any of the income measures can be derived by building up or by breaking down. In the foregoing, the structure of income measures was explained as if one began with a building-up process involving estimation and then summation of the various expenditure or production components, leading to GRP, and then proceeding to a breaking-down process in order to arrive at various income measures. But the regional analyst could just as well begin with disposable income or personal income estimates and go the other way, if it were more suited to the situation. Furthermore, one does not need to go the whole way. One could, for example, use aggregate estimation techniques based on secondary data to arrive at GRP, and sample surveys to estimate personal disposable and discretionary income. The purpose of Figure 5.1 and the discussion around it is to show the relationships among different types of income measures, not to suggest a computation procedure that must necessarily be followed.

Two important income measures that cannot be explained through the scheme presented in Figure 5.1 are median household income and median household per capita income. The first is simply the midpoint in the array of all the family household incomes in the region, such that 50 percent of the households have an income that is greater and 50 percent have an income that is lesser. The second is computed by dividing the median household income by the region's average household size. These measures can be developed only through household surveys.

DEVISING REGIONAL INCOME AND PRODUCT ACCOUNTS

The discussion of income measures has already suggested an accounting system in which the components of regional expenditures, the components of re-

Figure 5.2
Income and Product Accounts for Region Z, 19YY
(in thousands of monetary units)

Regional Income and Other Charges against Gross Regional Product		Gross Regional Product	
Personal savings	0	Regional personal consumption expenditures	18,500
Personal consumption expenditures	18,500		
Subtotal Personal disposable income	18,500	Gross private regional investment	1,500
Personal taxes	0		
Subtotal Personal income	18,500	Government expenditures in the region	0
Transfer payments	0		
Undistributed profits	0		
Corporate income tax	0	Net exports	0
Subtotal Regional income	18,500	Exports 15,000 Imports (15,000)	
Indirect business taxes	0		
Subtotal Net regional product	18,500		
Capital consumption allowances	1,500		
Gross regional product	20,000	Gross regional product	20,000

gional product, and the components of regional income should, with some adjustments perhaps, tally to the same total for any accounting year. This is the basis of regional income and product accounts. Imagine the components of income shown in Figure 5.1 that add up to GRP in one column, and the components of GRP in terms of different types of expenditures in an adjoining column, and you have imagined the basic framework of regional income and product accounts.

The basic regional income and product accounts framework is illustrated in Figure 5.2. Using this framework as a point of departure, regional income and product accounts can be devised to cover all the economic activity of the region, or only a component of that activity, and to do so with greater or lesser precision and in greater or lesser detail. The accounts may be organized along any desired lines in accordance with analytical needs and data availability.

The first step, then, in devising a set of regional accounts is to consider carefully what are to be the analytical objectives of the accounts. In figuring out how to achieve these objectives through the design of the accounts, the analyst should consider questions such as the following: How can the accounts reflect and help throw light on elements of major analytical importance to regional development considerations? How can relevant ethnic, sociocultural, administrative, and other substructures be reflected in these accounts? How can relationships with the rest of the world be usefully but concisely examined? What meaningful balancing devices can be employed? What types of data are available?

To illustrate different ways of approaching regional income and product accounting, we begin with a simplified example. Imagine a region, Region Z, with the following analytically convenient characteristics:

1. All residents are members of farm households, and farm households earn all their income from farming.
2. There is an uninhabited marketplace in the region where all farmers sell their produce to merchants who come there to buy on traditional market days.
3. In this same marketplace residents of the region purchase their household and farmyard goods from dry goods merchants who also come there on traditional market days. There is no other expenditure outlet.
4. Both the produce merchants and the dry goods merchants live outside the region. The produce merchants take all the produce they purchase with them for resale outside the region. The dry goods merchants bring all their wares with them when they come to market, and they take what remains with them, along with their earnings, when they leave the region at the close of market days.
5. All transactions in the marketplace are for cash.
6. The government neither collects taxes nor spends money in the region.

Available data indicate that in 19YY:

7. The total value of farm production at local market prices was Mu 20 million (Mu = monetary units).
8. On average, farm families retained 25 percent of what they produced for their own use (including exchange with neighbors), and sold the remainder.
9. Of residents' purchases at the marketplace, 10 percent was for replacement of worn-out farm equipment.
10. There were no personal savings.

If we follow the general rules and format of conventional income and product accounting, a set of accounts for Region Z might be devised as shown in Figure 5.2, with expenditure components on the right and income components on the left, and with each adding up to GRP. The income side of the accounts is essentially the same as Figure 5.1, but it has been turned upside-down so that the components add up to GRP at the bottom. Because in Figure 5.1 GRP was broken down into income components while in Figure 5.2 income components have been built up to GRP, items that were subtracted at each step in Figure 5.1 have been added at each step in Figure 5.2.

Available data inform us that in 19YY farmers in Region Z consumed Mu 5 million of their produce and sold Mu 15 million in the marketplace. Their earnings of Mu 15 million were used to purchase goods in the marketplace, of which personal consumption expenditures accounted for Mu 13.5 million and expenditures for replacement of farm equipment accounted for Mu 1.5 million. Thus, Mu 13.5 million in marketplace personal consumption purchases plus Mu 5 million in produce consumed on the farm have been registered as total personal consumption expenditures of Mu 18.5 on the right side of the accounts in Figure 5.2. Farm equipment replacement purchases of Mu 1.5 million have been registered as gross private regional investment. Government expenditures were zero.

The Mu 15 million of cash expenditures in the marketplace, however, were entirely for imports. Because residents of the region produced no product and earned no income in connection with these sales, they are shown in the accounts as imports of Mu 15 million that have been subtracted from total GRP. Export sales of Mu 15 million have to be added to the accounts, since residents of the region did produce product and earn income in connection with them, and they are not reflected in the other expenditure categories. Import purchases exactly offset export sales, so net exports amounted to zero.

On the left side of the accounts in Figure 5.2, the estimate of capital consumption allowances is based on actual spending for replacement investment.

A set of regional income and product accounts based on a national accounting framework has the advantage of enabling a comparison with national accounts. In many cases, however, regional analysts are not likely to find this framework particularly useful. In the case of Region Z, for example, even the simplified national accounting-based framework in Figure 5.2 contains a considerable amount of detail that is analytically unimportant—in fact, irrelevant—for purposes of descriptive regional analysis. Excessive clutter can obscure essential information.

Beyond this, the income and product accounts, if not devised in a way that is suited to the region in question, can actually be misleading. For example, the accounting framework in Figure 5.2 provides no indication of the rather important fact that one-quarter of Region Z's farm production did not enter the commercial economy. Also, one might conclude from those accounts that capital consumption allowances were calculated on the basis of refined business practices: the way investment decision making really works—when a piece of equipment breaks, the farmer goes to the marketplace to buy a new part or a new implement—is not reflected in the accounts. In general, the accounts in Figure 5.2 convey no real feel for the economy of Region Z. In fact, the accounts give no indication that the region is exclusively agricultural.

Using the national accounting framework as a starting point, however, a set of accounts might be devised along the lines illustrated in Figure 5.3. Here, the

Figure 5.3
Income and Product Accounts for Region Z, 19YY, Modified Format (in thousands of monetary units)

Gross Regional Income		Gross Regional Product		
Personal cash savings	0	Personal consumption expenditures		
Cash income used for farm capital replacement purchases	1,500	Imputed value of produce consumed on the farm		5,000
		Cash purchases		13,500
Cash income available for purchases of household and farmyard consumption goods	13,500	Gross private regional investment		
		Replacement investment		1,500
		Growth investment		0
Subtotal Personal cash income	15,000			
Imputed income from sales of farm produce to self	5,000	Government expenditures		0
		Net exports		0
Income from nonfarm activities	0	Exports	15,000	
Income from all other sources	0	Imports	(15,000)	
Taxes	0			
Gross regional income	20,000	Gross regional product		20,000

explicit shortcomings of the previous set of accounts have been overcome. The structure and operation of the farm-based economy stand out relatively clearly. Even the zero entries have been thought out and contribute useful information about the region.

But the accounts are a highly flexible tool. The analyst may choose to minimize detail and emphasize a particular aspect of the economy to which attention should be drawn for development planning purposes. The illustration in Figure 5.4 represents an approach to accounting for Region Z that emphasizes sources of income and uses of product of the region's residents. In this format, uses of income are not dealt with, and product is computed directly by industry category (in this case, there is only one category), instead of through the summation of expenditure categories.

Or the analyst may prefer to use an accounting framework other than income and product in the strict sense. Sales, expenditures, product, and income are all equal, or can be made to be so, from an annual accounting perspective. In Figure 5.5 the data for Region Z have been organized according to expenditures of and purchases from (sales by) residents of the region. In this case, detail has again

Figure 5.4
Income and Product of Residents, by Source and Use, Region Z, 19YY
(in thousands of monetary units)

Residents' Income		Residents' Product		
Income from exports	15,000	Value of farm products		20,000
Imputed income from sale of farm produce to self	5,000	For export For local consumption	15,000 5,000	
Total residents' income	20,000	Total residents' product		20,000

Figure 5.5
Expenditures of and Purchases from Residents, by Origin, Region Z, 19YY
(in thousands of monetary units)

Residents' Expenditures		Purchases from Residents	
Imports	15,000	By rest of world	15,000
Local Goods	5,000	By local resident	5,000
Total expenditures of residents	20,000	Total purchases from residents	20,000

been suppressed, and the analyst has emphasized the relative roles of internal and outside markets.

All the illustrations so far have been based on the residence principle. That is, they are concerned with the region in terms of the resident population and not with the region as geographic territory. They do not, for example, convey a sense of the implications of the fact that the marketplace is physically within the region but economically outside it; Figures 5.2 through 5.5 would be unchanged if the marketplace were also physically outside the region.

If the accounts for Region Z were constructed on a geographic basis alone, GRP would be Mu 35 million: Mu 20 million in farm production and Mu 15 million in marketplace sales to farmers. This would obviously not be a very useful way of representing the economy of the region. Constructing the accounts in a way that enables comparison of the economy of the region as a geographic unit with the economy of the region as a population unit, however, could be very useful for development planning purposes. Figure 5.6 illustrates how this might be done for Region Z. The accounts in Figure 5.6 draw attention to total product created within the geographic territory of the region, and then to the portion that leaks out of the regional income multiplication stream and the reason it leaks out.

Figure 5.6
Regional Income and Product with Explicit Locational Adjustment, Region Z, 19YY
(In thousands of monetary units)

Regional Income			Regional Product		
Farm income		20,000	Value of farm products		20,000
From imputed value of produce consumed on the farm	5,000		For home consumption	5,000	
			For export	15,000	
From cash sales to exporting merchants	15,000		Gross sales by merchants		15,000
			Consumption goods	13,500	
			Capital goods	1,500	
			Subtotal:		35,000
			Minus: value of goods imported and earning taken abroad by nonresident merchants		(15,000)
Total income of region's residents		20,000	Total products of region's residents		20,000

AN EXPANDED EXAMPLE OF REGIONAL ACCOUNTING

Figure 5.7 illustrates a set of regional accounts that follows a format quite different from any of the previous illustrations. In this case, the accounts are concerned only with personal income, and particularly with personal income derived from current production in the region. The data are shown for two years that obviously bound a period of considerable growth for Region Q. The figures are presented in *constant* monetary units, meaning that they have been adjusted by inflation factors so that they are expressed in terms of monetary units of constant value over the period, and figures for the two years are therefore comparable.

Data on earnings have been collected at the paying business establishments rather than at the earning households. They are shown first by type of earning, or payment, and then by sector (farm/nonfarm), subsector (government/private nonfarm), and industry category making the payments. Despite its very different appearance, the type-of-payment/source-of-payment system of accounting shown in Figure 5.7 represents a double-entry framework similar to conventional income and product accounts.

In order to convert earnings paid by establishments in the region into earnings of the region's residents, a net residence adjustment is included. The negative residence adjustment figures result from the fact that earnings of residents commuting to work in the region exceed those of regional residents commuting to

Figure 5.7
Income Accounts for Region Q, 19XX and 19YY
(in thousands of constant monetary units)

	19XX	19YY
Earnings by type of payment		
Wages and salaries	650	1,750
Other labor income	15	50
Proprietors' income	110	200
Total earnings by type of payment	775	2,000
Earnings by industry category		
Farm	425	575
Nonfarm	350	1,425
Government	35	250
Central	30	175
Civilian	30	100
Military	0	75
Local	5	75
Private nonfarm	315	1,175
Manufacturing	110	635
Mining	5	5
Construction	40	100
Communication and transportation	35	80
Trade	70	175
Finance and related services	20	45
Other services and utilities	30	125
Other	5	10
Total earnings by Region Q establishments	775	2,000
Residence adjustment	(10)	(295)
Total earnings of Region Q residents	765	1,705
Property income	75	260
Transfer payments	20	75
Less personal contributions to social insurance	(5)	(50)
Total personal income of Region Q residents	855	1,990
Population (thousands)	57.5	80.5
Per capita income (monetary units)	15.0	25.0
Index: national per capita income = 100	60.0	85.0

work outside the region. Were the data available, it would be useful to have the residence adjustment disaggregated by inflows and outflows, by type of payment, and by industry category.

Next, other types of income are added to total earnings of residents, and other adjustments are made in order to arrive at the total personal income of the region's residents. As a useful addendum to the accounts, per capita personal income is computed and indexed on national per capita income for the two years (absolute figures not shown).

The accounts shown in Figure 5.7 enable the regional analyst to answer or suggest possible answers to a wide variety of questions of major importance to development planning, such as the following: What changes have taken place in the economic structure of the region over the period? What might have caused the basic structural changes? What have been the changing relative roles of the various types of income and the various sources of earnings? What change has taken place over the period in earnings of residents as a proportion of total earnings generated in the region? What change has taken place over the period in the relationship of per capita income to total earnings? How has the region fared in per capita income terms relative to the nation? To answer these questions with as much precision as possible, the analyst might compute (a) the percentage change for each entry over the period; (b) the percent of total earnings paid by each category of Region Q business establishments in each of the two years; and (c) the change in these latter percentages over the period. The reader may care to try this exercise.

Figure 5.7 is one of an endless variety of ''correct'' regional income accounting methods. In some regions, for example, a breakdown of income by cultural groups might be more meaningful than earnings by type of payment. In many cases, it may be useful to construct several different types of complementary accounts and take advantage of the unique benefits that each offers. Other variants are discussed in Chapter 11, in connection with intraregional analysis. Further discussion on the use of aggregate income and product accounting for regional development analysis will be found in Chapter 10, and a discussion of regional income determination that combines income and product accounting and economic base multiplier concepts will be found in Chapter 8.

6

Balance of Payments Statements, Linkages and Flows

There is a multitude of interregional linkages—physical, social, technological, political, institutional, and economic—through which regions interact with each other. These interactions, in turn, generate impulses that work their way through the regional economy by means of an equally complex intraregional linkage system. This chapter begins by introducing a tool for analyzing the payments inflow/outflow consequences of the region's economic interactions with the rest of the world. This tool, the regional balance of payments statement, in effect enables estimation of the current net payments flow resulting from the prevailing system of interregional linkages.

The following sections of the chapter introduce methods for examining the natures of those linkages and also potential linkages, the flows that give them economic import, and factors inhibiting economic flows between the region and other areas. These methods aim at highlighting economically beneficial interactions, both actual and potential, between the region and the rest of the world.

BALANCE OF PAYMENTS STATEMENTS

Balance of payments statements are valuable as complements to other studies, such as income and product accounts and flow studies, but also have substantial analytical value in their own right. Regional balance of payments statements provide, at a glance, a large quantity of information about two key elements of the essential regional growth dynamic, returns to exports and import leakages from the regional income multiplication stream. Prepared at regular intervals, balance of payments statements also enable analysis of changing regional terms of trade with the rest of the world, and provide useful insights into export/import-related regional growth trends and prospects.

The objective of the balance of payments statement is to record the money value of inflows to and outflows from the region. The statement may deal with one or more selected types of flows, such as services or commodities, or it may record all flows. The precise structure of the balance of payments statement, the level of detail, the way in which the double-entry balance is brought about, and the way in which various substructures of the region are highlighted are matters for consideration on a case by case basis, in light of analysis objectives, data availability, and research resources available. Figure 5.5, in the previous chapter, can be viewed as a simple form of a regional balance of payments statement.

Since a balance of payments statement reflects the financial consequences of interregional transactions, it might seem that the regional analyst would want to tally all such transactions in the accounting year to arrive at the balance of payments statement figures. Developing the figures this way would involve an inflow-outflow double-entry accounting system based on the *goods flow* principle. According to this principle, each movement of a commodity, service, debt paper (ownership of a financial obligation), or cash is recorded in accordance with whether it physically moves into or out of the region. As Figure 6.1 illustrates, each interregional exchange would have both an inflow and an outflow component.

Let us turn to the fourth example in Figure 6.1. If the region exported Mu 500 of grain, this would be recorded as an outflow from the region, according to the goods flow principle. And if, in exchange, the region received Mu 100 in cash, a sewing machine, and an IOU for Mu 200, these would be recorded as inflows to the region and would balance the outflow.

In practice, it is not possible to record each exchange between the region and the rest of the world; nor is it necessary. Because earnings from exports in general are viewed as paying for imports in general, what really concerns the analyst is the net or balance of payments rather than each individual payment and the specific exchange that accounts for it. The traditional balance of payments statement uses the *payments equivalent* principle rather than the goods flow principle. Under this principle, net payments figures are arrived at through a system that records flows in accordance only with the movements of the payments to which they typically give rise. Under the payments equivalent principle, an export of Mu 500 worth of grain would be recorded only as a payment inflow of Mu 500.

A common format used in regional balance of payments statements is based on that used at the national level. This format contains four major headings, or types of accounts:

1. *Current account*: The current account shows the money value of goods, services, and transfers of gifts flowing into and out of the region during the accounting year. The term *current* refers to the fact that flows of goods, services,

Figure 6.1
Illustrations of the Goods Flow Accounting Principle

Example: Export of Mu 500 of grain in exchange for cash

Inflows		Outflows	
Cash (sales receipts)	Mu 500	Grain	Mu 500

Example: Export of Mu 500 of grain in barter exchange for sewing machine (based on market price of grain)

Inflows		Outflows	
Sewing machine	Mu 500	Grain	Mu 500

Example: Export of Mu 500 of grain in exchange for promissory note

Inflows		Outflows	
Short-term credit abroad	Mu 500	Grain	Mu 500

Example: Export of Mu 500 of grain in exchange for Mu 100 cash, a sewing machine, and a promissory note of Mu 200

Inflows		Outflows	
Cash (sales receipts)	Mu 100		
Sewing machine	Mu 200		
Short-term credit abroad	Mu 200	Grain	Mu 500

and transfers registered in this account are considered complete in the current year for accounting purposes.

2. *Capital account*: The capital account shows long-term and short-term debt and equity purchased or sold during the accounting year. Capital movements may arise from a current account transaction or a current cash movement, or from either of these in past or future years.

3. *Cash movements*: These refer to bank demand deposits and currency (and, traditionally, gold) that move into or out of the region as a result of current account or capital account transactions. This represents the ''bottom line'' of net payments flows in the accounting year, and at the regional level is usually computed as a residual.

4. *Errors and omissions*: Records on inflows and outflows are never complete,

even at the national level. Thus, after careful independent computation of the current account, the capital account, and cash movements, any imbalance that remains is attributed to errors and omissions. If cash movements are computed as the residual net of current and capital accounts, there will be no errors and omissions, as these will have been implicitly incorporated into cash movements. However, if there is a basis for independent estimation of errors and omissions, cash movements would be computed as a residual of the current account, capital account, and errors and omissions.

Figure 6.2 provides a schematic representation of a regional balance of payments statement in a modified version of the national format. Along the left are listed the item entries in the current and capital accounts. Column (1), Exports and Payments Inflows, records the money value of current and capital movements that result in "new" money flowing into the region. Column (2), Imports and Payments Outflows, records the money value of current and capital movements that result in payments by the region to the rest of the world. The third column provides the net balance for each of the four accounts, and, where desirable, for individual items. Thus, the inflow and outflow represented by each interregional exchange are not recorded as such in the balance of payments statement. Instead, all movements resulting in payments inflows are recorded only in Column (1) and all movements resulting in payments outflows are recorded only in Column (2).

In some regions the capital account, or certain items in it, may be impracticable or irrelevant. In such cases, a revision of accounting procedures will be necessary. One possibility is to record values for those capital account items that are relevant and obtainable, and replace cash movements with a residual account entitled "Cash and Debt Residual." In the extreme case, data could be recorded for current account only and everything else computed as a residual.

Data from Figure 6.1 will help illustrate how the balance of payments statement format of Figure 6.2 would work. Figure 6.3 shows how the entries would appear. In the current account, the export of grain amounting to Mu 500 would be entered in Column (1), as if a money inflow had already taken place as a result of the export. The import of a sewing machine of Mu 200 value would also be entered in the current account, but in Column (2), as if there had been a money outflow in payment. Thus, the net balance on current account would be +Mu 300.

In the capital account, opposite the item "Short-term loans," Mu 200 would appear in Column (2) as if there had been a money outflow in order to purchase (import) the debt. Thus, the net balance on capital account would be −Mu 200. When the net balances on current account and capital account are added together, there remains Mu 100 of the +Mu 300 imbalance on current account that is not covered by the net balance on capital account. Therefore, +Mu 100 must have been the net cash movement and would be entered as such in Column (3).

In computing the accounts, many items may cause some confusion at first. In general, it can be determined whether a particular value belongs in Column

Figure 6.2
Schematic Representation of a Balance of Payments Statement

Item	Exports and Payments Inflows (1)	Imports and Payments Outflow (2)	Net (1) – (2)
Current Account			
Commodities			
Commodity 1	Money value of goods exported	Money value of goods imported	
:			
:			
:			
Commodity n			
Services			
Tourism	Foreign tourist expenditures in region	Residents' spending abroad	
Transportation, financial and other	Receipts from foreigners by local firms	Payment by residents to foreign firms	
Interest, dividends, other earnings, and transfers and gifts	Receipts from abroad by residents	Payments abroad by residents	
Totals on current account	Total (+)	Total (–)	Net balance (+ or –)
Current Account			
Long term	Long term commitments of residents to foreigners through foreign investment in the region, sales of equity and bonds abroad, and so on	Long–term commitments of foreigners to residents through residents' investment abroad, residents' purchases of equity and bonds abroad, and so on	
Short term	Short–term borrowing abroad	Short–term loans to foreigners	
Other			
Totals on capital account	Total (+)	Total (–)	Net balance (+ or –)
Cash Movement: Net movements of currency and demand deposits			(+ or –)
Errors and Omissions			(+ or –)

Note: "Foreign" and "abroad" refer to the rest of the world, including other regions of the country.

Figure 6.3
Illustrative Entries for a Balance of Payments Statement
(in monetary units)

Item	Exports and Payments Inflows (1)	Imports and Payments Outflows (2)	Net (1) - (2)
Current account			
Grain	500	0	
Sewing machines	0	200	
Totals on current account	+500	-200	+300
Capital account			
Short-term loans	0	200	
Totals on capital account	0	-200	-200
Cash movement (residual imbalance)			+100
Error and omissions			0

(1) or Column (2) by carefully considering whether the effect is equivalent to a payment inflow or a payment outflow. For example, the excess of taxes paid to the central government over central government expenditures in the region would be entered in Column (2) because it is a net money outflow. Recorded individually, rather than net, taxes paid out are a payment outflow, and government expenditures are a payment inflow to the region.

The point must be emphasized that the balance of payments statement may be designed along lines deemed most suitable by the regional analyst in each particular case, as long as the basic accounting principles adopted are sound and are adhered to consistently. Indeed, the net exports entry in conventional income and product accounts can be viewed as a primitive and partial form of balance of payments accounting. The analyst can start with this and expand in stages to a full-fledged regional balance of payments statement.

Further discussion on the use of aggregate balance of payments statements in a regional planning context will be found in Chapter 10.

PRODUCTION LINKAGE INVESTIGATIONS

Linkage investigations are undertaken to identify major economic linkages, particularly production linkages, between the region and other areas that exist or could potentially be established. Knowledge of existing linkages is important for a basic general understanding of how the region's economy operates. For regional development planning, interregional linkage investigations serve the primary purpose of identifying major avenues through which the region gains returns from exports and loses income multiplication potential because of imports. This knowledge is especially important for considering how beneficial economic flows can be expanded and nonbeneficial flows can be reduced between the region and other areas.

There are two principal kinds of interregional production linkages:

—forward production linkages, involving further processing toward a finished product; and

—backward production linkages, involving a supply of inputs to the production process.

Related interregional linkages that may also warrant investigation are:

—distribution linkages, which capitalize on the region's location in the interregional transportation network; and

—consumer trade and public service linkages, through which the region is connected with larger consumer market and public service trade areas that extend beyond the borders of the region.

There is no single general tool to apply in the investigation of linkages or linkage potentials. In fact, many of the methods of analysis discussed in other chapters of this book can provide clues to existing, potentially expanded, and potential new linkages. If the sole aim, however, is to examine existing and potential linkages, there are several specific methods that can be used.

One of these is the production linkage survey. This is simply a survey of firms in selected industry categories in the region and in certain other regions, especially neighboring ones. A carefully selected sample of firms in the central or other major metropolitan area might also be included in the survey. The information sought from firms in the survey falls into two major categories: information related to outputs of the production process (forward production linkages) and information related to inputs to the production process (backward production linkages).

For any type of economic activity or production process being investigated, the analyst would want, at a minimum, to develop answers to the following questions through the survey.

Regarding Outputs

—What are the specific outputs?

—What are they used for?

—How are they marketed?

—What are their prices and what are the major factors determining prices?

—In what quantities, to where, and how are they delivered?

—If they are intermediate goods, why are they not processed further in the region?

—What substitutes compete in the same markets?

Regarding Inputs

—What are the principal inputs?

—What are they used for?

—How are suppliers identified?

—What are their prices and what are the major factors determining prices?

—In what quantities, from where, and how are they delivered?

—Why are they not produced in the region?

—What substitutes are technologically acceptable?

A less direct technique for exploring production linkages involves an investigation of national input-output relationships. If a national input-output table is available, the forward and backward linkages of industries on a national basis can be studied for their relevance to the potential expansion of the economic base of the region. In the absence of national input-output tables, linkages of industries actually or potentially represented in the region can be determined by interviewing representatives of selected industries at the national level and by reviewing industry trade journals. In some cases more valuable linkage information will be obtained at the national level, because at this level a broader perspective on industry input-output technologies may prevail.

The location quotient constitutes what is perhaps the simplest of all devices for providing at least a first indication of areas where more detailed linkage investigations are warranted. The location quotient technique involves a comparison of the extent to which selected economic activities are found at the regional and national levels in relation to other activities to which they are linked. For example, the throughput capacity of canning facilities per 100 hectares of vegetables and fruits grown by commercial farmers might be calculated and compared at the regional and national levels. If there is a great disparity between the regional and national ratios, this might suggest that a linkage investigation is warranted.

A number of cautions need to be borne in mind when using the location quotient for insights into linkages and linkage potentials. In the first place, the analyst must know something about the production process before meaningful ratios can be computed. Assistance from persons familiar with various production processes may be required to identify appropriate ratios for linkage investigation. Also, because the region is part of the nation, and therefore influences national ratios, reference areas other than the entire nation may be more appropriate in some cases.

Finally, it does not necessarily follow that what is found in the nation or other reference area should or could be found in the region as well. For this reason, the location quotient should be viewed only as a quick and easy way of helping to identify possible sectors, industries, or production processes for true linkage investigations. A full discussion of the location quotient appears in Chapter 7, which deals with methods for analyzing the composition of the regional economy.

Though the foregoing has concentrated on production linkages, much of what has been said clearly applies as well to distribution linkages and to consumer trade and public service linkage investigations. Further detail concerning specific linkage studies related to these types of activities, especially transportation, trade, and public service linkages, has been reserved for Part III of this book, especially chapters 11, 12, and 14. This material has been reserved for Part III, which deals with intraregional analysis, because in-depth investigations of these types of linkages are most frequently necessary—and most frequently undertaken—as part of an effort to document the internal structure and operations of the regional economy.

Nevertheless, the basic methods discussed in Part III are applicable also to interregional analysis. The reader consulting this book specifically for guidance in designing interregional linkage investigations should review related sections of chapters 7, 11, 12, and 14 at this time as well. However, balance of payments statements, economic base studies, and input-output studies also provide insights into existing, potentially expanded, and potential new interregional linkages.

COMMODITY FLOW STUDIES

Commodity flow studies identify by origin and destination commodities and their quantities that flow to and from the region. Usually, origins and destinations are given in terms of regions or cities, but other major breaking, bulking, processing, or trading points may be used also. Information of this sort can highlight important and less important interregional linkages and provide a commodity-specific picture of the region's role in national trade patterns. Analysis of data from flow studies can provide a basis for assessing the relative distance frictions of commodities exported by the region and clues to commodity and market combinations with the greatest potential. Conducted at several short and long time intervals, flow studies provide insights into seasonality and secular shifts in important supply sources and export markets of the region, and give valuable clues to likely future developments.

Commodity flow studies are also commonly used to provide data for other analysis techniques. They are often important elements, for example, in commodity trade systems analysis (discussed in Chapter 12), rural-urban exchange analysis (discussed in Chapter 13), and balance of payments statement estimates.

General commodity flow studies invariably base annual estimates on sample surveys. Complete counts may be possible only when the period of time or number of commodities covered by the study is very limited. Surveys can be conducted by direct counting techniques at the borders of the region or at origin and destination points in the region. Where a tradition of record keeping prevails, the survey can be conducted by indirect techniques.

However conducted, the objective of the survey is to gather information that enables the construction of tables and maps showing the origins and destinations of at least major flows of specific commodities, by quantities. Figure 6.4 illustrates the conceptual framework for presenting commodity flow information. It represents data that in practice would be contained in a series of related statistical tables and maps designed to provide the type of detail most important for analytical purposes in the study region. Greater or lesser detail may be provided by individual commodity; by commodity flows exceeding a certain weight, count, or money volume; by points of origin and destination; by flows exceeding or less than a specified distance; by mode of delivery; by a final or intermediate goods distinction; and so on.

Figure 6.4 indicates that quantity information is presented in terms of money value. This means that weight, volume, or unit count information has been converted to money value equivalents using market prices. Such conversions can be problematic, because prices vary during the year and among different buyers and sellers; moreover, prices sometimes are quoted free of transportation costs (FOB, ''free on board'') and at other times as including transportation costs (CIF ''cost, insurance, and freight''). Still, if reasonably meaningful conversion to monetary value is possible, it is worth the effort to prepare commodity flow tables in both physical and monetary terms. While much of the information indicated in Figure 6.4 can be presented in weight, volume, or unit count terms, additivity and comparability among commodities, routes, and modes of transport are possible only when quantities are expressed in monetary terms.

Thus, data from a general commodity flow study might be presented first in a table listing major commodities flowing out of the region and into the region. For each, the annual flow in terms of weight, volume, unit count, and/or money value would be shown. This summary table could be followed by others dealing in detail with commodity flows by mode of transportation; by quantities traveling over a certain range (for example, 50 kilometers or more); by destinations and origins of special interest, such as neighboring regions or a metropolitan area; by the three largest points of origin or destination; by commodities having annual flow volumes over a certain weight or money value; or by other criteria that may be of special interest or concern.

FRICTION ANALYSIS

Friction analysis aims at determining key factors inhibiting beneficial economic flows—or, viewed from a positive angle, opportunities to facilitate greater beneficial interaction—between the region and other areas. The starting point for analysis of factors inhibiting specific types of flows usually is what is commonly called a *gravity study*. Gravity studies are based on the proposition that the intensity of potential interaction between two places varies directly with their

Figure 6.4
Conceptual Framework for Presenting Commodity Flows Data

Commodity Flows to and From Region Z, by Mode, 19YY[a] (thousands of monetary units, FOB value)						
Commodities, Origin Region Z	Region X	Region Y	Big City A	Big City B	Total	Other Countries[b]
Cart: Commodity 1 : : : : Commodity n						
Truck: Commodity 1 : : : : Commodity n						
Train: Commodity 1 : : : : Commodity n						
Boat: Commodity 1 : : : : Commodity n						
Totals: Commodity 1 : : : : Commodity n						
All Commodities						
Commodities, Destination Region Z [Use same format as above]						

[a]Estimates for 19YY based on surveys conducted Tuesday of first full week of each month.

[b]No overseas port in Region Z. Shipments to or from other countries also counted in region or city through which shipped.

combined mass and inversely with the distance between them: hence, the term *gravity*.

Imagine a country in which the friction of distance is zero—or put simply, where it costs nothing in time, money, or anything else to travel. It would not be unreasonable to suppose that under such circumstances the amount of travel from Place A to any other place would be directly related to the size, or mass, of that other place. If we take population as the measure of mass, and Place B as the other place, then the proportion of all the trips from Place A that terminate in Place B would be the same as Place B's proportion of the population of the country (excluding the population of Place A). The proportion of all the trips from Place A that terminate in any other place would be calculated the same way.

If we conduct a survey and determine the actual proportion of all the trips taken from Place A that terminate in Place B in, say, the course of a year, that proportion is likely to be rather different from the proportion calculated on the basis of mass alone. The difference between the actual proportion and the mass-based hypothetical proportion is taken as a measure of distance friction (which we brushed aside by imagination at the outset) between the two places. The comparison of the two proportions could be expressed as a friction ratio:

$$\text{Effects of distance friction from A to B} = \frac{\text{Actual proportion of trips from A that terminate at B}}{\text{Hypothetical proportion of trips from A that terminate at B}}$$

A ratio of 1/20 would mean that the actual proportion of trips from A that terminate at B is only 1/20 of what would be expected on the basis of mass alone. Thus, a smaller ratio indicates greater distance friction.

Starting with this relatively simple idea, a structure of friction analysis can be erected that is as simple or as complex as the analyst desires. The approach can be used to assess one type of interaction within one industry from the region to one other place, or it can be used to construct a generalized friction map showing relative intensity of distance friction between the region, or major points in the region, and major destinations throughout the country. The measure of mass need not be population: gross product, retail sales, employment, per capita income, units of market space, or any other measure appropriate to the analysis can be used.

In fact, a number of friction ratios can be calculated using different measures of mass as a means of trying to ascertain those that seem to matter most or that seem to be closely related, or for purposes of averaging and generalizing. Similarly, interaction need not be measured in terms of trips. It could be measured in terms of volume of a specific commodity that flows from the region to outside destinations, or it could be measured in terms of any other interaction of analytical interest. Or, a number of friction ratios could be calculated using alternate interaction measures.

Of course, the ultimate purpose of calculating friction ratios is to identify important sources of distance friction operating on routes of interaction that bring, or could bring, significant benefits to the regional economy. These sources of friction would then be analyzed through special studies, and ways of reducing them would be explored. Calculating several types of friction ratios using a variety of measures of mass will begin to reveal patterns suggesting important sources of distance friction. In addition, means can be devised for attempting to identify the relative significance of different types of ''distance'' that cause flow-inhibiting friction.

Distance can be expressed in terms of kilometers along transport routes, money or time cost of travel, red tape, or other relevant measures. By comparing the friction ratios between the major city of the region and two outside places equidistant from it in kilometers, for example, one could account for the difference in the friction ratios entirely in terms of other kinds of distance. By doing this with several sets of places, one could derive a relationship between kilometers of distance and other kinds of distance that could be applied to all friction ratios. One could use the same technique to isolate the effects of other kinds of distance.

Gravity studies—that is, calculation of friction ratios—have limitations for purposes of regional analysis. One important limitation arises from the fact the ratio can only be calculated between points, and this means that individual places—usually towns—within the region must serve to represent the region as a whole or major parts of it. The component of friction represented by distance from true points of origin to these representative places cannot be accounted for in the ratio. Also, the effects of mass are probably not entirely linear. That is, the significance of mass when two places are close together will be different from its significance when two places are very far apart. This means that the notion of potential interaction based on mass alone is truly hypothetical in the fullest sense of the word.

Nevertheless, friction ratios have considerable usefulness. Full analysis of a major component of distance friction can involve a serious commitment of planning resources. Friction ratios are tools for helping identify the factors on which such analysis should focus that are inexpensive, easy, and quick to apply in many different ways that can cross-check each other. They must, however, be viewed in perspective as preliminary indicative devices.

7

Economy Composition Analysis

What is the composition of the regional economy? How does its composition compare with that of the country or of other regions? How is it changing? Which changes should be fostered, and which discouraged? Mix-and-share analysis, location quotients, and related techniques provide means of understanding the regional economy in terms of the influences of the different activities of which it is composed, they help evaluate those activities in relation to each other and similar activities elsewhere, and they help identify opportunities for altering the composition of the regional economy in ways that will improve its performance.

MIX-AND-SHARE ANALYSIS

The change in regional employment relative to the change in national employment over a period can be viewed as the net of three effects. The first effect is the impact on the region of the change in total employment nationally over the period, the *national growth effect*. The second effect stems from the *industry mix* in the region—that is, the distribution of regional employment among faster- and slower-growing types of economic activities relative to the distribution prevailing nationally. The third effect is a consequence of changing *regional shares* of total national employment in each industry category. The notions of industry mix and regional shares are compared with the help of a diagram in Figure 7.1.

The formula $R = N + M + S$ (where R is the total change in regional employment and N, M, and S are the individual components of the change reflecting the national growth, industry mix, and regional shares effects respec-

Figure 7.1
Diagrammatic Representation of Mix-and-Share Concepts

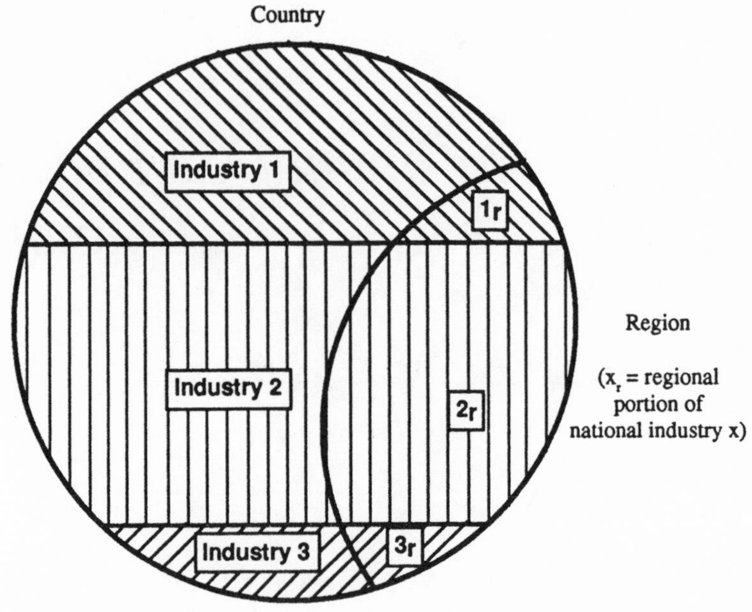

Industry Mix

$$\frac{1_r}{1_r + 2_r + 3_r}, \frac{2_r}{1_r + 2_r + 3_r}, \frac{3_r}{1_r + 2_r + 3_r}$$

relative to

$$\frac{1}{1+2+3}, \frac{2}{1+2+3}, \frac{3}{1+2+3}$$

Regional Shares

$$\frac{1_r}{1}, \frac{2_r}{2}, \frac{3_r}{3}$$

at the start of the period, relative to

$$\frac{1_r}{1}, \frac{2_r}{2}, \frac{3_r}{3}$$

at the end of the period

tively) is the basis for mix-and-share analysis. Mix-and-share analysis provides a descriptive explanation of the change in regional employment over a period by isolating the individual components of change representing each of the three effects.

Suppose changes in employment in a nation and in one of its regions, Region Z, over the period 19XX–19YY are represented by the data in Table 7.1. Total

Table 7.1
Changes in National and Regional Employment, Region Z, 19XX–19YY (absolute numbers in thousands)

Industry	Employment		Employment Change, 19XX-YY	
	19XX (1)	19YY (2)	Absolute (3)	Percent (4)
Nation				
Agriculture	10,000	10,000	000	00
Manufacturing	5,000	10,000	+5,000	+100
Services	6,000	9,000	+3,000	+50
Government	3,000	7,000	+4,000	+133
Total nation	24,000	36,000	+12,000	+50
Region Z				
Agriculture	150	120	-30	-20
Manufacturing	50	80	+30	+60
Services	50	95	+45	+90
Government	10	20	+10	+100
Total Region Z	260	315	+55	+21

Table 7.2
National Growth Effect, Region Z, 19XX–19YY (all figures in thousands)

Industry	Employment 19XX (1)	N = (1) x National Growth Rate of 50% (2)	R = Actual Growth (3)	R – N = M + S = Net Relative Change to Be Accounted for (4)
Agriculture	150	+75	-30	-105
Manufacturing	50	+25	+30	+5
Services	50	+25	+45	+20
Government	10	+5	+10	+5
Total Region Z	260	+130	-55	-75

employment in the nation grew by 50 percent over the period, while total employment in Region Z grew by only 21 percent, less than half the national rate. How can the difference be explained?

By how much would regional employment have grown had each of its industries—agriculture, manufacturing, services, and government—and, therefore, the regional total, grown at the same rate as employment nationally? Table 7.2 shows the individual industry and total computations for N, the national growth effect. Column (2) shows that when regional employment in each industry in the base year is multiplied by the national rate of growth (which is the same as the average rate of growth among industries nationally) over the period, it is

Table 7.3
Industry Mix Effect, Region Z, 19XX–19YY
(absolute numbers in thousands)

Industry	Distribution of Total 19XX Employment (in percent)		Deviation: Industry Growth Rate Minus National Growth Rate (in percent)	Employment 19XX	M = (3) x 4
	Nation (1)	Region (2)	(3)	(4)	(5)
Agriculture	42	58	-50	150	-75
Manufacturing	21	19	+50	50	+25
Services	25	19	0	50	0
Government	12	4	+83	10	+8
Total	100	100	0	260	-42

found that 130,000 new jobs in Region Z can be attributed to a regional reflection of growth in national employment.

But actual growth in Region Z amounted to only 55,000 new jobs over the period. Something obviously transpired in the regional economy to offset the national growth effect by 75,000 jobs. If R = N + M + S, then M + S = R − N. Thus, the net relative change of minus 75,000 jobs by which the region grew more slowly than the nation can be accounted for by the industry mix and regional share effects.

What was the industry mix effect? To what extent is the regional deviation from the national growth rate attributable to the fact that the composition of the regional economy included a higher proportion than nationally of employment in industry categories with growth rates below the national average? Table 7.3 supplies the answer. The numbers in Column (3) represent the individual industry deviations from the national growth rate. The deviations were computed by subtracting the national average growth rate (in this case, 50 percent) from individual national industry growth rates shown in the upper half of Column (4) of Table 7.1.

These deviations are then multiplied by regional employment in the respective industries in the base year, 19XX. In this way, regional employment in each industry category in the base year is weighted by individual national industry deviations from the national average growth rate. The results of these computations, shown in Column (5) of Table 7.3, represent the regional industry mix effect.

Table 7.3 shows that the industry mix effect was negative in the case of Region Z. Columns (1) and (2) confirm that in the base year the industry category with a rate of growth below the national average, agriculture, represented a higher proportion of total employment in the region than in the nation. The other industry

Table 7.4
Employment and Components of Employment Change, Region Z, 19XX–19YY (in thousands)

Industry	19XX (1)	19YY (2)	R Change 19XX-YY (3)	Components of Employment Change: N National Growth Effect (4)	M Industry-Mix Effect (5)	S Regional Shares Effect (6)
Agriculture	150	120	-30	+75	-75	-30
Manufacturing	50	80	+30	+25	+25	-20
Services	50	95	+45	+25	00	+20
Government	10	20	+10	+5	+8	-3
Total	260	315	+55	+130	-42	-33

categories, which grew at rates equal to or greater than the average, represented smaller proportions of total employment in the region than in the nation. The result was a negative industry mix effect that offset the national growth effect by 42,000 jobs.

The regional shares effect remains to be computed for Region Z. If R = N + M + S, the regional shares effect can be calculated residually as S = R − N − M, or 55 − 130 − (−42) = −33. In other words, the regional shares effect can be computed as that part of the net relative change (in this case, minus 75,000 jobs) that was not accounted for by the industry mix effect (in this case, minus 42,000 jobs). This residual can be computed for each industry category separately.

If each entry in the lower half of Column (1) of Table 7.1 (regional employment by industry category in the base year) is divided by its counterpart in the upper half (national employment by industry category in the base year), and if the same is then done for Column (2) of Table 7.1 (same data for the end year), a comparison of the results will confirm the computations of the regional shares effect. It will be found that regional shares of agriculture, manufacturing, and government declined in Region Z between 19XX and 19YY. Only in the case of the services industry category did the regional proportion of total national employment increase.

Summary mix-and-share data can be presented in a single table. Table 7.4, which presents the data for Region Z in terms of absolute numbers only, shows how such a table might appear. Columns (3) through (6) of Table 7.4 could have been presented in percentage terms as well as absolute numbers.

The analyst who compiled Table 7.4 and the previous tables might have provided an interpretive analysis of the agricultural sector in Region Z for the period 19XX-19YY as follows:

Had the national agricultural sector grown at the national growth rate, and had regional employment in agriculture reflected this same growth rate, the number of jobs in agriculture in Region Z would have grown by 75,000, from 150,000 in 19XX to 225,000 in 19YY. The gap between 225,000 and the actual employment of 120,000 in 19YY, a net relative change of minus 105,000 jobs over the period in Region Z, can be accounted for by two factors.

First, employment in the national agricultural sector grew by much less than national total employment, which grew by 50 percent. As a matter of fact, employment in agriculture did not grow at all in the nation over the period. Because it "grew more slowly" than the national average, agricultural employment decreased as a proportion of the national total. A larger proportion of the region's total employment was in agriculture in 19XX than was the case nationally. As a result, the relative decline experienced by this sector nationally affected the region more severely than the nation, and was responsible for a relative loss of 75,000 jobs in the region.

Second, during the period 19XX–19YY, the region's share of employment in agriculture nationally declined. This decline expressed itself as a relative decrease of 30,000 agricultural jobs in Region Z over the period.

Hence, the net impact of industry mix and regional share effects offset the national growth effect of plus 75,000 jobs by a net relative change of minus 150,000 jobs. The result was that the region experienced a decline of 30,000 in agricultural employment.

Interpretations along similar lines could be provided for each of the other industries and for total employment in the region.

Many variations are possible on the basic mix-and-share method illustrated in the Region Z example. The analysis can be performed for subareas and towns in the study region as well as for the region as a whole, as discussed in Chapter 11. If more appropriate, a reference area other than the nation, such as a "parent" region, state, or province of which the study region is a part, can be used for the analysis. The industry categories into which the regional economy is divided for purposes of the analysis may be as disaggregated as available data permit, even to the level of individual crops or products, and all categories covered need not be at the same level of disaggregation.

Mix-and-share analysis can be performed for several historical periods, and will always yield greater insights when performed for several shorter periods rather than for a single longer time span. Employment is most often used as the unit of measure because it is generally the most available in a form suitable for mix-and-share analysis, but value added, gross revenues, sales, or some other output or earnings measure could in principle be used just as well. When a money measure is used in addition to employment, the analysis may provide insights concerning relative productivity impacts.

Like all methods of analysis, mix-and-share analysis should be undertaken with a full awareness of its limitations. One limitation arises from its ability to focus on only a single variable at a time. For instance, in the Region Z illustration, the analysis concentrated on employment, while value added, investment, public spending, and other factors perhaps critically related to the composition of the regional economy were ignored. In fact, the use of employment as the unit of measure systematically understates the overall growth impact of industry cate-

Figure 7.2
Illustrative Location Quotient Computation: Agriculture in Region Z, 19XX (in thousands)

$$LQ = \frac{\frac{150}{260}}{\frac{10{,}000}{24{,}000}} = \frac{0.58}{0.42} = 1.38$$

where

	Employment in Agriculture	Total Employment (reference variable)
Region Z	150	260
Nation	10,000	24,000

gories undergoing the most rapid gains in labor productivity. Furthermore, the analysis does not account explicitly for unemployment, and it remains for the analyst to relate data on changes in unemployment to the findings of mix-and-share analysis. As in all analysis methods, the source and quality of data used, the choice of base and terminal years, and the level of industry aggregation all seriously influence the results.

As a descriptive tool, mix-and-share analysis does not explain why a particular industry mix prevailed in the base year, why different industry categories experienced different growth rates nationally, or why changes in regional shares of national sectors took place. Nor does it evaluate whether or not the changes that took place were desirable. A decline in the regional share of a sector that is experiencing a relative decline nationally produces a double negative impact in terms of net relative change, for example. But the negative employment impact may result from workers shifting from slower- to faster-growing activities, which may be very desirable from the standpoint of long-term regional growth. Hence, mix-and-share analysis has the potential to answer, but also to raise, many important questions about the composition of the regional economy. Some of the questions it raises will have to be addressed through additional studies undertaken in the course of the regional development planning process.

THE LOCATION QUOTIENT

In its most common form, the location quotient is a device for gauging the relative specialization of the region in selected industry categories, or sectors. A unit of measure that is often used is employment. Employment in a selected sector is related to a reference variable, usually total employment, at the regional and national levels. The relationships at the two levels are then compared.

Employment in a selected sector of economic activity is related to total employment by means of a simple ratio computation, and the ratios at the regional and national levels are compared by means of another ratio computation: the location quotient is a ratio of ratios. Following are two alternative formulas, arithmetic equivalents, for computing a location quotient.

$$LQ = \frac{\dfrac{X_r}{RV_r}}{\dfrac{X_n}{RV_n}} = \frac{X_r \text{ as a fraction of } RV_r}{X_n \text{ as a fraction of } RV_n}$$

or

$$LQ = \frac{\dfrac{X_r}{X_n}}{\dfrac{RV_r}{RV_n}} = \frac{X_r \text{ as a fraction of } X_n}{RV_r \text{ as a fraction of } RV_n}$$

where

X_r = employment in industry X in the region

X_n = employment in industry X in the nation

RV_r = reference variable value for the region

RV_n = reference variable value for the nation

If, for example, X, the *specialization variable*, is employment in agriculture, and the reference variable is total employment, then the location quotient can be computed in either of two ways: (a) agriculture's proportion of total employment in the region divided by agriculture's proportion of total employment in the nation, or (b) the region's proportion of national agricultural employment divided by the region's proportion of total national employment. An illustration of location quotient computation using the first method is given in Figure 7.2. The illustration uses data from Table 7.1 for 19XX.

The arithmetic nature of the location quotient leads to the following rules of location quotient evaluation:

$LQ > 1$: If the location quotient is greater than 1, the region is more specialized than the nation in the study sector.

$LQ < 1$: If the location quotient is less than 1, the region is less specialized than the nation in the study sector.

$LQ = 1$: If the location quotient is equal to 1, the region and the nation specialize to an equal degree in the study sector.

In many cases the nature of the location quotient can be anticipated. For example, if a broad aggregate like total employment is used as the reference variable, a regional export activity (one that exports to outside the region) would be expected to have a location quotient greater than 1; manufacturing in a rural region of an industrialized country would be expected to have a location quotient less than 1; and a local service activity would be expected to have a location quotient equal to 1. Deviations from the expected nature or major deviations from the expected order of magnitude of location quotients suggest areas where further study may be warranted.

A time series of location quotients can be computed for relative trend detection, location quotients can be computed for subareas and towns in the study region, and employment can be considered at any level of disaggregation, down to a specific crop or product, in accordance with analysis needs and data availability. In some cases, it may be appropriate to employ a reference area other than the nation, such as a parent region or province, a median or average of other regions, or the nation excluding the study region.

The specialization variable and the reference variable need not be in the same terms. When the specialization variable is employment, for example, population might be used as the reference variable if the industry under study is a service industry and the location quotient is to be used as an indicator of adequacy of service. If the service is oriented to households rather than individuals, number of households might be the appropriate reference variable.

When the analysis is oriented toward productivity considerations, revenues, value added, or unit output measures could serve as reference variables. When using the location quotient as a tool in linkage investigations, employment or output in a linked industry might be appropriate reference variables. By setting the location quotient equal to 1 and solving for the regional specialization variable, an estimate can be made of the change needed in the region so that it reflects reference area proportions.

Moreover, the location quotient technique can help highlight regional relative inefficiencies, can assist in focussing on potential import substitutes or products with export expansion potential, and can provide an indication of industries for which further detailed study is most warranted. The location quotient has been found useful within the framework of linkage investigations, friction analysis, economic base analysis, input-output analysis, mix-and-share analysis, and more. Because of its simplicity, the location quotient can be computed many times, relative to many reference variables, time periods, and reference areas, and with a minimum investment in analysis time, effort, and money.

But the analyst should be mindful of the fact that the location quotient is, at best, a rough descriptive indicator. Results of location quotient computations are heavily influenced by the level of disaggregation of the specialization variables selected, the choice of reference variables, the choice of reference area, the choice of years, and of course, the quality of available data. Furthermore, the caveats implicit in any comparison among areas apply as well to the location quotient. Differences among areas in tastes and needs, levels of income, family sizes, exploitable resources, labor practices, and, therefore, economic structure, require that statistical results of location quotient computations receive cautious analytical interpretation.

RELATED INDICATORS

The location quotient has been found so handy that a family of related indicators has emerged for exploring the relative relationship between specific kinds of linked variables in different areas. All these amount to little more than imaginative applications of the basic location quotient approach in response to particular analytical needs. Even mix-and-share analysis can be understood ultimately to be a sophisticated application of the location quotient approach.

The following are examples of three types of indicators often used in regional analysis that are related to the location quotient.

1. *Index of concentration*: indicates the degree to which selected activities or characteristics are dispersed or concentrated, and where the study region stands in comparison with other regions in terms of the relative degree of concentration.
2. *Distribution quotient*: relates concentration of an activity or resource in a region to the proportion of the country's territory in the region, and is most often computed for several regions for comparative purposes.
3. *Index of association*: indicates the degree of association between two activities or between an activity and a resource in the way they are distributed among regions, and where the study region stands in comparison with other regions in terms of the degree of association.

These and other location quotient-type indicators are discussed in Part III, Chapters 11 and 14, of this book. The presentations have been reserved for Part III, which deals with methods of intraregional analysis, because these indicators are most often used to assess differences among subareas of a region. Employing them for interregional analysis requires obtaining data for the nation as a whole and some or all of its other regions. If such data are available, these indicators will be found to be very useful ways of summarizing key elements in the composition of the aggregate regional economy relative to other regions.

8

Economic Base Analysis

Underpinning economic base analysis is economic base theory. The heart of economic base theory is the proposition that the economic growth of a region ultimately depends on outside demand for its products. More precisely, whether a region grows or declines and at what rate is determined by how it performs as an exporter to the rest of the world. Exports to the rest of the world may be in the form of goods and services, including labor, that flow out of the region to buyers, or in the form of purchases inside the region by buyers who normally reside elsewhere. In the parlance of economic base theory, export industries constitute the *economic base*, or *basic sector*, of the region.

Numerous supporting activities are necessary to service industries in the basic sector as well as basic sector workers and their families. Of course, the supporting activities also service themselves and the workers and families of workers engaged in them. The supporting activities, such as trade, personal services, production for local markets, and production of inputs (or ''intermediate goods'') for products in the basic sector, together comprise the *nonbasic sector*.

If demand for exports of the region increases, the basic sector expands. This, in turn, generates an expansion in the supporting activities of the nonbasic sector. This latter phenomenon is the one with which economic base analysis is principally concerned. Earlier chapters have dealt with methods of analysis for exploring the overall performance and composition of the regional economy, and for examining regional exports and potentials for expanding regional exports. Economic base analysis is the first of two methods of analysis to be presented that explicitly address aggregate regional employment or income multiplication consequences of regional export activity. In its simplest form, economic base analysis answers the question: "What is the overall gain in employment or income in the region associated with each gain in export sales?"

THE BASE MULTIPLIER

Economic base theory views all regional economic activity as either basic or nonbasic. Thus, basic employment plus nonbasic employment equals total employment for the region. The ratio of basic employment to nonbasic employment is called the economic base ratio, or just *base ratio*.

If, in a particular region, for every worker in the basic sector there are two workers in the nonbasic sector, the base ratio will be 1:2. If the base ratio is 1:2, every new job in the basic sector is assumed to lead to two new jobs in the supporting activities of the nonbasic sector. Similarly, for every decline of one job in the exporting activities of the basic sector, two jobs will go out of existence in the nonbasic sector.

If the base ratio is 1:2, *the economic base multiplier* (or just *base multiplier*) is 3. This means that when basic employment increases by one job, it multiplies to a total of three new jobs, including new employment in both basic and nonbasic sectors. Thus, multiplying any change in the basic sector by the base multiplier yields an estimate of the total change resulting from a change in the basic sector in response to a change in demand for its exports.

The base multiplier, then, is the sum of the two components of the base ratio, with the basic component set equal to 1. The two components of the base ratio are basic employment and nonbasic employment, which together equal total employment. Setting basic employment equal to one means dividing basic and nonbasic employment, or total employment, by basic employment. Hence, the formula for computing the base multiplier is:

$$\text{Base multiplier} = \frac{\text{Total employment}}{\text{Basic employment}}$$

And the formula for using the base multiplier to estimate total employment, given basic employment would be:

$$\text{Total employment} = \text{Basic employment} \times \text{Base multiplier}$$

And the formula for estimating the change in total regional employment given a change in basic employment would be:

$$\text{Change in total employment} = \text{Change in basic employment} \times \text{Base multiplier}$$

CONDUCTING AN ECONOMIC BASE STUDY

On the surface, the steps involved in an economic base study appear relatively simple. First, a unit of measure is chosen. Then, economic activities in the basic and nonbasic sectors are identified and employment or income for each sector is tabulated. Once this is done, the base ratio and base multiplier can be computed in the manner described.

The first problem that confronts the regional analyst who sets out to perform an economic base study is the selection of a unit of measure. Most often employment data are used because of their availability. Employment as a measure also has the advantage of facilitating ready conversion of the results of an economic base study into population or household terms by means of a conversion ratio such as average number of dependents per worker.

But using employment as the unit of measure poses some troublesome problems. One problem is presented by the need to convert part-time and seasonal employment into equivalent full-time annual employment. There is also the problem of commutation. Residents of the study region who work beyond its borders and residents of neighboring regions who daily commute to jobs in the region must be sorted out and accounted for appropriately. Furthermore, owing to technological, productivity, management, and related factors, employment may be a relatively insensitive measure of change, especially in the short run.

Gross sales or value added by enterprises in the region have also been used as units of measure for economic base studies. Output units of measure such as these can be among those most reliable and easily obtainable in countries with well-developed taxation and economic census reporting systems. Naturally, the value of an economic base study is enhanced when results based on using different units of measure are compared.

Income can also be used as the unit of measure for an economic base study. For certain purposes, such as linking findings to income and product accounts or balance of payments statements, or for gauging potential change in the region as a market, this unit of measure has special advantages. Generally, income also provides a more meaningful measure of changes in individual and community welfare than do employment or output measures. But these advantages are also disadvantages. Assessing income consequences of changes in returns from regional exports involves a somewhat more complex procedure, one that entails eliminating returns from exports that do not enter the regional income multiplication process. Using economic base analysis for income determination is discussed separately in the next section of this chapter.

After a unit of measure has been selected (for discussion purposes, employment will be used in the rest of this section), the analyst must consider a method for determining which activities are in the basic sector and which are in the nonbasic sector. A direct method, such as a survey of businesses, would yield the most precise information. Direct methods, however, require a high quantity and quality of participation in the survey, and can be costly. Consequently, one of a variety of indirect methods is often used instead.

The simplest indirect method is the assumptions approach, in which it is assumed that all activities in certain categories are basic. A common assumption for purposes of economic base analysis is that all manufacturing and agricultural production is for export and that all remaining economic activity is supporting activity. In the majority of cases, however, many industry categories will be found to have significant components in both the basic and nonbasic sectors; that is, the regional economy will have an overall complexity that precludes the use of highly simplifying assumptions.

A second indirect method aims at estimating the separate basic and nonbasic components of each sector or industry category. It is based on the notion that the excess of the proportion of employment in any type of economic activity for the region over the counterpart proportion for the nation represents regional specialization that is aimed at export markets and therefore is in the basic sector. The estimate is made by using the following formula, derived directly from the location quotient formula given in Chapter 7, when LQ = 1; that is, when regional and national proportions for industry X are the same.

$$X_r = \frac{\text{National employment in industry X}}{\text{Total national employment}} \times \frac{\text{Total regional employment}}{1}$$

Solving for X_r indicates the number of workers that would be employed in industry X in the region if employment in this industry as a proportion of total employment in the region was the same as employment in this industry as a proportion of total employment nationally. X_r is taken to be nonbasic employment in industry X, and the difference between X_r and actual regional employment in industry X is taken as basic employment.

Estimating total regional basic and nonbasic employment requires applying the formula to every industry represented in the region. For this purpose the regional economy could be divided into as few as 2 or as many as 500 industries. The sum of the positive differences between actual and X_r values is the total for the basic sector, and everything else is taken as nonbasic.

Some regional analysts have employed variations of the location quotient method of estimating basic and nonbasic totals that tie the basic portion of a regional industry to the regional share of national population or income. Under this approach, if regional population or income is 5 percent of the national total, for example, then all employment in a regional industry in excess of 5 percent of national employment in that industry is taken as connected with production for export from the region, and is therefore basic.

Methods based on the location quotient have their weaknesses. General caveats regarding the location quotient are summarized in Chapter 7. Particularly serious when used in economic base analysis is the failure of the location quotient to account for nonuniformity of demand, productivity, and interindustry linkages throughout the country. Furthermore, the location quotient method ignores the fact that a certain proportion of national output is for foreign consumption. If the appropriate national data are available, this latter problem can be overcome, of course, by eliminating national employment in export production from the national employment figures used.

The best approach in many cases will be a combination of assumptions and location quotient approaches. The output of certain specific regional industries can usually be taken as essentially basic, and others can reasonably be taken as essentially nonbasic. The location quotient approach can be applied to those that probably are significantly active in both sectors. Or, a combination of direct and indirect methods of sectoral determination may be appropriate: reasonable assumptions can be made about some industries, a location quotient approach can be applied to others, and a few key industries can be surveyed.

Another problem that the economic base analyst will have to deal with is the time lag problem. One can readily appreciate that the base multiplier does not work instantaneously, that there is a time lag between the response of the basic sector to a change in demand for its export products and a time lag in the response of the nonbasic sector to a change in the basic sector. The period of time required for the multiplier to work itself through is not known, and for most practical purposes cannot be ascertained.

A common approach to this problem is to ignore it, on the argument that over the long run, whatever time lag may exist is not of much consequence. Some analysts, especially when performing an economic base study for projection rather than descriptive purposes, have tried to offset the problem through the way in which they calculate the base multiplier. Earlier, the formula for the base multiplier was given as:

$$\text{Base multiplier} = \frac{\text{Total employment}}{\text{Basic employment}}$$

Some analysts prefer the following formula, which employs data covering a period of time, on the assumption that it implicitly accounts for time lag factors:

$$\text{Base multiplier} = \frac{\text{Change in total employment}}{\text{Change in basic employment}}$$

Another approach is to deal with the time lag problem by computing a historical time series of base multipliers in which the latter formula is used over a number of three- to five-year periods. With the time series as a point of departure, an estimate of the value of the base multiplier at some point in the future could be made. A historical time series of base multipliers would also have descriptive analytical value with respect to the past development of the region. It is a matter of concern to regional development planning whether the trend has been to an increasing or decreasing regional base multiplier.

If it is executed carefully and the results interpreted cautiously, an economic base study can be a highly utilitarian tool for exploring, evaluating, and making rough estimates of trends in employment, revenues, income, population, housing needs, community service needs, and other aspects of the regional complex that are important to analysts and development planners. For an economic base study to be relevant, it is necessary only that economic base theory seem a reasonable way of accounting for the major part of the economic growth of the region.

REGIONAL INCOME DETERMINATION

Economic base analysis can be relatively simple when used for the kind of rough impact and trend assessment referred to so far. Or, it can be refined into a sophisticated and detailed tool for income, employment, or sales estimation, and for guidance with respect to development policy relating to various types of economic activities in the region. Input-output analysis, discussed in Chapter 9, turns out to be a form of economic base analysis taken to the limits of its possibilities. Between simple economic base analysis and input-output analysis lies a range of variants related to notions taken from income determination theory.

In Chapter 1, a discussion that led eventually to the multiplier concept began with the basic categories of expenditures that add up to income or product for a nation or region: consumption spending, investment spending, government spending, and exports. These components of income or product were discussed again in Chapter 5 in connection with income measures and income and product accounts.

Regional income is determined by those portions of the four types of spending that actually result in local income, as distinguished from the portions that leak out of the income generating (multiplying) stream. Leakages include spending on import purchases (including purchases made outside the region), taxes, savings, and the like from which local residents and businesses do not derive current income. In terms of economic base theory, regional income is determined by earnings being generated in the basic sector and multiplied through purchases in the nonbasic sector.

For purposes of economic base analysis, the basic sector must be thought of as encompassing those types of spending that are exogenously determined—that are not directly dependent on the current level of regional income or economic activity. It therefore excludes regional consumption spending and includes exports, but also includes investment and government spending, or at least large portions of them. Current levels of investment and government spending are determined substantially by decisions made in the past, by expectations concerning the future, and by other considerations that are not related to current levels of local income or economic activity.

Income earned by firms and individuals in the region is spent directly on leakage purchases, such as imported inputs and consumer goods, and on purchases from the regional nonbasic sector. Spending in the regional nonbasic sector includes regional input and consumer expenditures. However, not even all expenditures in the region's nonbasic sector generate regional income. To some extent they cover the cost of imports purchased through local agents or shopkeepers, indirect taxes, and so on. In other words, there is further leakage from expenditures in the nonbasic sector.

A change in total regional income would be equal to the change in income of the region's basic sector times a multiplier. Basic sector income results from purchases of the region's exports, regional investment, and government spending in the region. The multiplier reflects the proportion of income that is spent in the region's nonbasic sector times the proportion of spending in the nonbasic sector that in turn generates income in the region.

It will be recalled that the base multiplier formula is:

$$\text{Base multiplier} = \frac{\text{Total income}}{\text{Basic income}}$$

Since total income equals basic income plus nonbasic income, it follows that basic income equals total income minus nonbasic income, and the multiplier formula could be written as:

$$\text{Base multiplier} = \frac{\text{Total income}}{(\text{Total income} - \text{Nonbasic income})}$$

If the right side of this equation were divided through by total income to set the value of total income equal to one, the result would be:

$$\text{Base multiplier} = \frac{1}{(1 - \text{Proportion of income from nonbasic sources})}$$

Since nonbasic income results from nonbasic sector spending times the fraction of that spending that generates regional income, and since nonbasic sector spending is itself a proportion of total regional income, the multiplier formula in terms of 1 could be further detailed as follows:

$$\text{Regional Base Multiplier} = \frac{1}{1 - (\text{Proportion of income spent in the regional nonbasic sector}) \times (\text{Proportion that generates regional income})}$$

To digress for a moment, the two proportions multiplied in the denominator of the last equation represent the fraction of income that generates further income in the region, or the fraction that does not leak out of the regional income multiplication stream. By definition, one minus this fraction represents the fraction of income that does leak out. So the equation is the equivalent of:

$$\text{Base multiplier} = \frac{1}{\text{Leakage fraction}}$$

The reader should not be surprised to find that this is the same formula arrived at in Chapter 1, through different means.

We know that according to the economic base analysis framework:

$$\text{Change in total regional income} = (\text{Change in income in the region's basic sector}) \times (\text{Regional base multiplier})$$

We have so far developed the formula for the "regional base multiplier" part of the equation; what would be the formula for the "change in income in the region's basic sector" part? Using the components of the conventional income determination model:

$$\begin{aligned}\text{Change in income in the region's basic sector} = {} & \text{Change in regional export sales} \\ & + \text{Change in regional investment} \\ & + \text{Change in government spending in the region}\end{aligned}$$

Thus, the full economic base income determination formula can be expressed as:

$$\text{Change in total regional income} = \left(\begin{array}{c}\text{Sum of changes in spending} \\ \text{on regional exports, investments} \\ \text{and government activities}\end{array}\right) \times \left(\frac{1}{\begin{array}{c}1 - (\text{Proportion of income} \\ \text{spent in the regional nonbasic} \\ \text{sector}) \times (\text{Proportion that} \\ \text{generates regional income})\end{array}}\right)$$

Suppose research based on sample surveys indicated that of each Mu 1.00 of gross regional income, only Mu 0.60 was spent on purchases in the region's nonbasic sector. And suppose it was also found that of every Mu 1.00 spent in the nonbasic sector, only Mu 0.50 became regional income, while the remaining Mu 0.50 paid for goods imported for sale in the region. The multiplier would be computed as follows:

$$\text{Regional base multiplier} = \frac{1}{1 - (.6)(.5)} = \frac{1}{1 - .3} = \frac{1}{.7} = 1.43$$

Now, values for changes in spending on regional exports, investments, or government activities can be estimated or hypothesized and multiplied by 1.43, yielding the change in total regional income. More to the point for regional development planning purposes, however, might be assessing ways the multiplier could be increased by actions that reduce different types of leakages, and for indicative purposes comparing the consequences of these different actions given current levels of basic spending. The special value in economic base analysis is that it focusses planning attention on the individual elements of the two essential components of regional economic growth, returns from regional exports and regional income multiplication.

9

Input-Output Analysis

In the previous chapter, economic base theory was described as viewing the regional economy in terms of two fundamental sectors: a basic, export, or exogenous demand sector, and a nonbasic sector where income and employment multiplication take place. The multiplication process depended on two kinds of nonbasic demand for the region's goods and services: the demand for intermediate, or input, goods and services by the region's businesses; and demand for final goods and services by the region's consumers.

Input-output analysis focusses primarily on the business spending component of the nonbasic sector. It tracks the intricate web of production linkages among different industries in the region, and reveals the extent to which the natures of these linkages ultimately lead to more or less regional income for each unit of final sales of regional goods and services. In effect, through input-output analysis, an income multiplier is developed for each regional industry, and the reasons why each multiplier has a particular value can be clearly seen. Input-output analysis can thus be a powerful tool for identifying types of regional economic activities and linkages among them that may offer the greatest opportunities for expanding income-multiplying exchange within the region.

Input-output analysis takes demand for final goods and services by regional consumers to be exogenously determined: in economic base terms, it places regional consumption spending (as well as exports, investment, and government spending) in the basic sector. As a result, the exogenous expenditure (or purchases) components in input-output analysis are essentially the same as the expenditure components of gross regional product. Indeed, input-output analysis can be thought of as documenting and exploring the precise systems of interindustry exchange through which different components of regional product eventually become different components of regional income. In fact, as will be shown in Chapter 10, input-output analysis can link up directly with income and product accounting.

AN INPUT-OUTPUT PRIMER

The *total product* of an economy, by income and product accounting procedures, is the combined value of all the final products produced, or final sales, during a year. The *total output* of an economy, by input-output accounting procedures, is the total value of all sales—not just final sales—that took place during a year. Total output is much greater than total product because it includes interindustry sales of intermediate products sold as inputs to production processes. Final sales are made in response to final demand, or demand for final products. Interindustry sales come about in the course of satisfying input requirements to the production processes that ultimately lead to final sales.

An interindustry sale represents a flow of goods or services, expressed in money terms, between *intermediate industries*, industries that purchase inputs for processing and further sale. While there may be a "seller" or "supplier" and a "purchaser" in the common commercial sense, an interindustry transaction may be considered to have taken place even if these are absent. A transfer of goods among factories under a single ownership is considered an interindustry sale, complete with a supplier and a purchaser, in input-output terms. The same principle applies to final sales; even a transfer to inventory is considered a final sale with reference to the current accounting year.

Input-output analysis divides the economy into two major components, suppliers and purchasers. There are two types of suppliers:

1. *Intermediate suppliers*, who purchase inputs for processing into the outputs they supply. They sell their products to other intermediate suppliers or to final purchasers.
2. *Primary suppliers*, who do not need to purchase inputs to make what they supply. What they sell (labor, for example) is considered primary inputs to other industries. Payments to suppliers of primary inputs do not generate further interindustry sales because these suppliers purchase no inputs; payments to them are *final payments*. Earnings of these suppliers essentially represent value added.

And there are two types of purchasers:

1. *Intermediate purchasers*, who buy the outputs of suppliers for use as inputs for further processing.
2. *Final purchasers*, who buy the outputs of suppliers in their final form and for final use. The level and composition of demand by final purchasers are taken to be determined exogenously. Production to satisfy the demands of final purchasers generates intermediate purchases of inputs.

Intermediate suppliers and purchasers are the same entities. Their sales and purchases are related to each other, since their purchases of inputs are a function of the demand for their outputs.

Primary suppliers and final purchasers may or may not be the same entities. But in cases where they are the same (households, for example, both supply labor, a primary input, and purchase final goods), their activities as primary suppliers and as final purchasers are taken as completely independent of each other.

Input-output analysis employs three tables. The *transactions table* contains basic data concerning total flows of goods and services among suppliers and purchasers during the study year. The flows are represented in money terms and are viewed as sales transactions between suppliers and purchasers.

The *direct requirements table* is derived from the transactions table, and shows the inputs required directly from different suppliers by each intermediate purchaser for each unit of output that purchaser produces.

The *total requirements table* is derived from the direct requirements table, and shows the total purchases of direct inputs and indirect inputs (inputs to the production of inputs) that are required throughout the economy per unit of output sold to final purchasers by each intermediate supplier.

Imagine an isolated island economy: there are no imports, no exports, no government, no investment, no savings, no inventory. Thus, everything is purchased, processed, sold, and consumed on the island in the current period. There is only one type of final purchaser, households; and there is only one type of primary supplier, also households. Households supply primary inputs such as labor, management, and ownership. There are only two intermediate industries, agriculture and a collection of crafts industries that we will call manufacturing. Table 9.1 is the transactions table compiled for the island economy based on reported sales during the most recent accounting year.

The first row of Table 9.1 shows that in the accounting year, agriculture sold a total of Mu 100,000 of produce. Sales to final purchasers for household consumption accounted for Mu 60,000 of the total, and sales to intermediate purchasers accounted for the remaining Mu 40,000 in sales. Of its sales to intermediate purchasers, agriculture sold Mu 30,000 worth of produce to manufacturing (industrial crops and inputs for processed foods), and Mu 10,000 to itself (farm inputs such as seed, feed, and fertilizer). The first column of Table 9.1 shows that in order to produce the Mu 100,000 of total output, agriculture had to purchase Mu 10,000 in products from itself, Mu 5,000 in manufactured inputs (implements, repair services), and Mu 85,000 in primary inputs (farm labor, self-employment earnings) from households. The manufacturing row and column show counterpart information for that intermediate industry.

The rows of the transaction table, then, show the distribution of each supplier's sales to intermediate and final purchasers. The columns show the distribution of each purchaser's purchases from intermediate and primary suppliers. Naturally, for any intermediate industry, total inputs will equal total outputs. For the econ-

Table 9.1
A Simple Input-Output Transactions Table
(in thousands of monetary units)

	Intermediate Purchasers		Final Purchasers (households)	Total Sales (outputs)
	Agriculture	Manufacturing		
Intermediate suppliers				
Agriculture	10	30	60	100
Manufacturing	5	10	35	50
Primary Suppliers				
Households	85	10	15	110
Total purchases (inputs)	100	50	110	260

omy as a whole, total outputs of primary suppliers (for which primary supplier sales of Mu 110,000 are shown in Table 9.1) will equal total final purchases (for which expenditures of Mu 110,000 are shown in Table 9.1). This corresponds to the equality between income and product in income and product accounting. And of course, as the number in the bottom righthand corner of the table shows, total (final plus intermediate) inputs into the system will equal total outputs of the system.

The transactions table provides a rather complete view of the interindustry flows of goods and services in the economy during the study year. It does not, however, constitute a generalized analytical tool. How can the basic transactions data be transformed into a generalized statement of direct input requirements per unit of output for each intermediate industry? The answer is, by dividing the figures for input purchases in each intermediate purchaser column by the number at the bottom of the column, total inputs for that industry.

Since total inputs for each industry equals total outputs for that industry, dividing each intermediate purchaser column through by the total will provide a distribution of direct input requirements per unit of output for each intermediate industry. Table 9.2 shows the results of this simple computation, arranged in the format of a direct requirements table. The final purchasers column has been dropped from Table 9.2, because purchases by final purchasers do not represent inputs for further processing. The direct requirements table is often called the *table of technical coefficients*, because it shows the technical production relationships between outputs and direct inputs for each industry.

Table 9.2
A Simple Input-Output Direct Requirements Table

Mu 1.00 of Output By / Requires Inputs From	Agriculture	Manufacturing
Agriculture	0.10	0.60
Manufacturing	0.05	0.20
Households	0.85	0.20
Total direct inputs	1.00	1.00

The direct requirements table provides the coefficients needed to calculate direct inputs required for any level of demand for the output of any intermediate industry. Suppose, for example, demand for agricultural products is expected to amount to Mu 50,000 next year. Multiplying that figure through the agriculture column in Table 9.2 shows, based on what took place in the study year, what satisfying that demand would require by way of direct inputs to agriculture: Mu 5,000 in agricultural products, Mu 2,500 in manufactured products, and Mu 42,500 in primary inputs from households.

In effect, every artisan, factory manager, shopkeeper, and farmer has a one-column direct requirements table for the business or farm, in mind if not on paper. It is used to adjust orders for supplies in accordance with the output planned for delivery. From the perspective of the firm, all sales are final and all inputs are primary.

From the perspective of the regional economy, however, direct input requirements are only part of the story. Direct inputs (other than final inputs) must also be produced, and their production will require additional inputs, indirect inputs to final production. But then, where do the indirect inputs come from? Producing them will require even more indirect inputs. There emerges a pattern of successive rounds, with the outputs of each round creating demand for inputs supplied by the round that is one step further removed from final product. The reader with a long memory will find this somewhat reminiscent of the multiplier discussion in Chapter 1, and there is indeed a relationship that, if not already obvious, will become more so as we move along.

Direct inputs can be thought of as the first round of input supplies. The first set of indirect inputs, those required to produce the direct inputs, can be thought of as the second round of input supplies. The next set of indirect inputs, those required to produce the second round, are the third round of input supplies, and so on. Calculation of total input requirements from the direct requirements table by the *iterative method* refers to computing all the rounds and summing the results.

To illustrate, let us imagine that our island is suddenly discovered by a party of explorers. They inform us that, as they have already sent back word of their

Table 9.3
Total Requirements Computations from Direct Requirements Table (in thousands of monetary units)

	Sales to Final Pur-chasers	Sales as Direct Inputs			Second Round		
		To Agr.	To Mfg.	Total	To Agr.	To Mfg.	Total
By agriculture	200	(.1)(200) = 20	(.6)(100) = 60	80	(.1)(80) = 8.00	(.6)(30) = 8.00	26.00
By manufacturing	100	(.05)(200) = 10	(.2)(100) = 20	30	(.05)(80) = 4.00	(.2)(30) = 6.00	10.00
By households	--	(.85)(200) = 170	(.2)(100) = 20	190	(.85)(80) = 68.00	(.2)(30) = 6.00	74.00
Totals, indirect rounds							110.00
By all suppliers	300			300			

discovery, we can expect a substantial influx of population during the coming year. Incredibly, the explorers have brought with them estimates of the increase in final demand that will result from the influx of population. When these are added to existing levels of final demand, it is calculated that sales of agricultural products to final purchasers will amount to Mu 200,000, and that Mu 100,000 of manufactured products will be purchased by final consumers, provided of course, that these supplies are available.

The leaders of the island society, a congenial lot, are somewhat worried because they want to plan to accommodate the needs of the newcomers properly, and to do this they must know what the full impact of the higher level of final purchases will be on each supplying industry. In their wisdom, they immediately perceive that what is called for is an input-output total requirements computation.

Table 9.3 shows how total requirements might be computed from the direct requirements coefficients in Table 9.2. Multiplying agricultural final sales of Mu 200,000 through the agriculture column of Table 9.2 shows that direct inputs of Mu 20,000 are required from agriculture; Mu 10,000 are required from manufacturing; and Mu 170,000 are required from the primary suppliers, households. This computation is shown in the second column of Table 9.3.

Note that the first parentheses of each pair in the column contains the corresponding coefficient from the direct requirements table. The second parentheses

Table 9.3 (continued)

Sales as Indirect Inputs							Total Sales
Third Round			Fourth Round				
To Agr.	To Mfg.	Total	To Agr.	To Mfg.	Total	Total	
(.1)(26) = 2.60	(.6)(10) = 6.00	8.60	(.1)(8.6) = 0.86	(.6)(3.3) = 1.98	2.84	37.44+	317+
(.05)(26) = 1.30	(.2)(10) = 2.00	3.30	(.05)(8.6) = 0.43	(.2)(3.3) = 0.66	1.09	14.39+	144+
(.85)(26) = 22.10	(.2)(10) = 2.00	24.10	(.85)(8.6) = 7.31	(.2)(3.3) = 0.66	7.97	106.07+	296+
		36.00			11.90		
						157.00+	757+

of each pair contains sales for that industry shown in the sales column preceding it. In a similar fashion, the direct input requirements to enable manufacturing to satisfy the anticipated Mu 100,000 of final sales can be computed, as shown in the third column of Table 9.3. Total direct requirements for satisfying the expected final demand for both agriculture and manufacturing products are shown in the fourth column of Table 9.3.

Total direct requirements supplied by agriculture and manufacturing are, in turn, multiplied through their respective columns in the direct requirements table (Table 9.2) in order to arrive at second round inputs (the first set of indirect inputs) required. These computations are shown in the three columns under the heading "Second Round" in Table 9.3. These three columns show the same kinds of calculations shown in the three columns for direct inputs.

The totals for the second round are, in turn, multiplied through the direct requirements table in order to arrive at third round inputs required. In principle, this procedure can continue endlessly, but Table 9.3 does not go beyond four iterations. After four rounds, the numbers are relatively small in this example, and the error resulting from stopping after four rounds will be relatively minor. A plus sign has been added to the totals for indirect inputs in recognition of the fact that these totals represent slight underestimates.

The row at the bottom of Table 9.3 shows that in order to satisfy the anticipated

Table 9.4
Total Requirements Computations: Agricultural Sales of Mu 1.00 to Final Purchasers

	Sales to Final Pur-chasers	Sales as Direct Inputs			Second Round		
		To Agr.	To Mfg.	Total	To Agr.	To Mfg.	Total
By agriculture	1.00	(.1)(100) = 0.10	--	0.10	(.1)(.10) = 0.01	(.6)(.05) = 0.03	0.04
By manufacturing	--	(.05)(100) = 0.05	--	0.05	(.05)(.10) = 0.01	(.2)(.05) = 0.01	0.02
By households	--	(.85)(100) = 0.85	--	0.85	(.85)(.10) = 0.09	(.2)(.05) = 0.01	0.10
By all suppliers	1.00			1.00			

Mu 300,000 combined final sales of agricultural and manufacturing products, total sales of direct inputs of Mu 300,000 and of indirect inputs amounting to over Mu 157,000 will be required throughout the economy. The rightmost column of Table 9.3, total sales for each industry, shows that total (final plus intermediate) sales of agricultural products alone will amount to over Mu 317,000; total sales of manufacturing products will exceed Mu 144,000; and sales of primary inputs by households will total over Mu 296,000. This is the information that the island leadership needs in order to plan for the necessary expansion.

A word is in order concerning the role of primary suppliers (households) in the computations in Table 9.3. Because no inputs are required by primary suppliers, payments for primary inputs in any round are final payments that do not reappear as multiplication factors in the next round of computations. It will be noted that the figure representing combined total sales in each round is smaller than combined total sales in the preceding round by the amount of sales by households in the preceding round, which can be thought of as a leakage from the interindustry stream. In this example the leakage is not undesirable, as it represents income to regional households.

It was mentioned earlier that ultimately, total sales by primary suppliers must equal total final sales, just as income equals product in income and product accounts. In Table 9.3, combined final sales amounted to Mu 300,000, but through the iterative process, sales of primary inputs by households came to only Mu 296,000+. This is accounted for by the fact that only four iterations were worked through. The more rounds computed, the closer the total primary inputs figure will come to total final sales. The limit of the iterative process

Table 9.4 (continued)

Sales as Indirect Inputs							
Third Round			Fourth Round				
To Agr.	To Mfg.	Total	To Agr.	To Mfg.	Total	Total	Total Sales
(.1)(.04) = 0.00	(.6)(.02) = 0.01	0.01	(.1)(.01) = 0.00	(.6)(.00) = 0.00	0.00	0.05	1.15
(.05)(.04) = 0.00	(.2)(.02 = 0.00	0.00	(.05)(.01) = 0.00	(.2)(.00) = 0.00	0.00	0.02	0.07
(.85)(.04) = 0.03	(.2)(.02) = 0.00	0.03	(.85)(.01) = 0.01	(.2)(.00) = 0.00	0.01	(0.14) 0.15	(0.99) 1.00
						0.22	2.22

would be reached and actual total sales for all industries attained when total sales by primary suppliers equaled total final sales. The gap between these two figures after a number of iterations provides an indication of the distance from actual totals.

In most regions, intermediate industries, for purposes of input-output analysis, are likely to include at a minimum three principal categories of crops, three principal categories of crafts and manufacturing, three principal types of service sector activities, and something else, such as forestry, fishing, or mining activities. Commonly, regional input-output studies deal with between 10 and 50 industry categories. It is easy to see that running through the iterations in order to compute total requirements can be a rather cumbersome procedure. This cumbersomeness can rise to prohibitive dimensions when total requirements computations are needed for a large number of alternative levels and compositions of estimated final sales.

Before this observation is brushed aside by readers equipped with computers, two points need to be made. First, for purposes of descriptive analysis, a generalized statement of structural interdependence in the economy is needed. A set of total requirements coefficients arranged in a table would constitute such a statement, in the same way that the table of direct requirements coefficients constitutes a generalized statement of direct technical relationships among suppliers and purchasers. Second, in any case it would be useful to have a set of total requirements coefficients, just as there are direct requirements coefficients, that would enable ''solving'' readily and quickly for any estimated or hypothesized level of final sales, with or without computers.

A total requirements table can be computed from the direct requirements table

Table 9.5
Total Requirements Computations: Manufacturing Sales of Mu 1.00 to Final Purchasers

	Sales to Final Pur- chasers	Sales as Direct Inputs			Second Round		
		To Agr.	To Mfg.	Total	To Agr.	To Mfg.	Total
By agriculture	--	--	(.6)(1.00) = 0.60	0.60	(.1)(.60) = 0.06	(.6)(.20) = 0.12	0.18
By manufacturing	1.00	--	(.2)(1.00) = 0.20	0.20	(.05)(.60) = 0.03	(.2)(.20) = 0.04	0.07
By households	--	--	(.2)(1.00) = 0.20	0.20	(.85)(.60) = 0.51	(.2)(.20) = 0.04	0.55
By all suppliers	1.00			1.00			

by applying the iterative method for Mu 1.00 in sales to final purchasers by each intermediate industry in turn. This has been done for agriculture in Table 9.4 and for manufacturing in Table 9.5, again based on the direct requirements coefficients in Table 9.2. The figures in the rightmost column in each case show the total requirements from all components of the economy to supply Mu 1.00 of that industry's product to final purchasers. These two columns have been transferred to Table 9.6, the total requirements table for the island economy.

In Tables 9.4 and 9.5 it will be noticed that two sets of numbers are given for total sales of primary inputs by households. In parentheses are those that derive from the four rounds of computation. But it is known that ultimately, total sales by primary suppliers will equal final purchases. Since in our example there is only one primary supplier and one primary purchaser, households, its total sales must equal its total purchases. This allows us to set total primary input sales by households equal to final purchases, namely, 1.00, and then to calculate total indirect primary input sales residually as the difference between final purchases (1.00) and direct primary inputs (0.85 for agriculture, and 0.20 for manufacturing). This is shown by the two numbers, 0.15 and 0.80, not in parentheses in the rightmost columns.

The point was made earlier that the gap between computed total primary inputs and final purchases provides an indication of the magnitude of the error arising from limiting the computations to only a few rounds. In this case the gap would be the amount by which computed total primary inputs is less than 1.00 (.01 for agriculture and .04 for manufacturing).

The total requirements table shows, for each intermediate industry, total sales arising from each unit of output delivered to final purchasers. In Table 9.6, for

Table 9.5 (continued)

Sales as Indirect Inputs							Total Sales
Third Round			Fourth Round				
To Agr.	To Mfg.	Total	To Agr.	To Mfg.	Total	Total	
(.1)(.18) = 0.02	(.6)(.07) = 0.04	0.06	(.1)(.60) = 0.01	(.6)(.02) = 0.01	0.02	0.26	0.86
(.05)(.18) = 0.01	(.2)(.07) = 0.01	0.02	(.05)(.06) = 0.00	(.2)(.02) = 0.00	0.00	0.09	1.29
(.85)(.18) = 0.15	(.2)(.07) = 0.01	0.16	(.85)(.06) = 0.05	(.2)(.02) = 0.00	0.05	(0.76) 0.80	(0.96) 1.00
						1.15	3.15

example, it can be seen that for every Mu 1.00 of output delivered to final purchasers by agriculture, total sales by agriculture to final purchasers, to itself, and to other intermediate industries (in this case, there is only one other) will be slightly more than Mu 1.15; total sales by manufacturing to all intermediate industries will be slightly more than Mu 0.07. If primary sales by households are added in, total sales by all suppliers in the economy to all purchasers will be slightly more than Mu 2.22 per Mu 1.00 of output delivered to final purchasers by agriculture. Of the Mu 2.22 total, Mu 1.00 represents agriculture's sales to final purchasers, Mu 1.00 represents sales by primary suppliers, and Mu 0.22 represents interindustry transactions. The manufacturing column of Table 9.6 can be explained in a similar fashion.

The reader may be struck by the similarity between the total requirements coefficient and the economic base multiplier discussed in Chapter 8. If the total requirements coefficient for agriculture is 2.22, then for every Mu 1.00 of exogenous demand that is satisfied by agriculture, a total of Mu 2.22 in sales will have been generated. The economic base ratio can be thought of as 1.00:1.22 for agriculture. The interindustry base ratio can be thought of as 1.00:0.22, because for every Mu 1.00 of final sales, Mu 0.22 of intermediate sales are generated. A multiplier of 2.22 may seem somewhat high, but we have been illustrating with a closed island economy free of leakages.

Now, let us return once again to the final demand estimate for the island economy. Armed with the total requirements table, it would be unnecessary to compute total input requirements by the iterative method as was done in Table 9.3. In effect, this has been done in advance through the computation of total

Table 9.6
A Simple Input-Output Total Requirements Table

Requires Total Sales By \ Every Unit of Delivery to Final Demand By	Agriculture	Manufacturing
Agriculture	1.15+	0.86+
Manufacturing	0.07+	1.29+
Households	1.00	1.00
Total requirements from all suppliers	2.22+	3.15+

Table 9.7
Illustrative Total Requirements Computations Using the Total Requirements Table
(in thousands of monetary units)

Requires Total Sales by \ Final Delivery By	Agriculture	Manufacturing	Total
Agriculture	(200)(1.15) = 230	(100)(0.86) = 86	316
Manufacturing	(200)(0.07) = 14	(100)(1.29) = 129	143
Households	(200)(1.00) = 200	(100)(1.00) = 100	300
Total	(200)(2.22) = 444	(100)(3.15) = 315	759

requirements coefficients. All that need be done now is to multiply the coefficients in each column of the total requirements table by the corresponding final purchases estimate.

Table 9.7 shows these computations for the example of the island economy. The column for agriculture in Table 9.7 shows total sales by each supplier required to satisfy the anticipated Mu 200,000 of delivery to final purchasers by agriculture. The manufacturing column provides the same information for the anticipated Mu 100,000 of delivery to final purchasers by manufacturing. The total column corresponds to the total sales column of Table 9.3, and shows total sales by each supplier for the combined Mu 300,000 of delivery to final purchasers.

The total for each column can easily be disaggregated into its final purchases, primary supplies, and interindustry sales components. Of the approximately Mu 444,000 of total sales by agriculture, for example, we know that Mu 200,000 represents anticipated agricultural sales to final purchasers; Mu 200,000 represents primary input sales by households; and the remainder, Mu 44,000, represents interindustry sales. Of the approximate Mu 759,000 of total output for the economy, we know that Mu 300,000 represents total anticipated sales to

Figure 9.1
Regional Transactions Table Format

			Purchasing Industries and Sectors													Output Summary		
			Regional Intermediate Purchasers						Final Purchasers									
									Local			Export						
			Industry 1	Industry 2	. . .	Industry i	. . .	Industry n	Households	Investment	Government	Households	Business	Central government	Net inventory change	Total regional intermediate industries	Total final sales	Total sales (outputs)
Supplying Industries and Sectors	Regional Intermediate Suppliers	Industry 1	X_{11}	X_{12}	. . .	X_{1i}	. . .	X_{1n}										
		Industry 2	X_{21}	X_{22}	. . .	X_{2i}	. . .	X_{2n}										
		⋮	⋮	⋮	⋮	⋮	⋮	⋮										
		Industry i	X_{i1}	X_{i2}	. . .	X_{ii}	. . .	X_{in}										
		⋮	⋮	⋮	⋮	⋮	⋮	⋮										
		Industry n	X_{n1}	X_{n2}	. . .	X_{ni}	. . .	X_{nn}										
	Primary Suppliers (final payments) — Local	Households																
		Gross business savings																
		Government																
	Primary Suppliers (final payments) — Imports	Labor																
		Transfers to parent companies																
		Central government																
		Goods																
		Others																
Input Summary		Total regional intermediate industries																
		Total final payments																
		Total purchases (inputs)																

final purchasers; Mu 300,000 represents total sales by primary suppliers (income, or value added); and the remainder, Mu 159,000, represents interindustry sales.

THE REGIONAL TRANSACTIONS TABLE

Figure 9.1 provides a sample format for a regional input-output transactions table. Though the general principles are the same, it is considerably more complex than the illustration presented in Table 9.1. Figure 9.1 not only reflects the economic openness of a realistic regional situation, it reflects as well the need for regional development planners to distinguish among principal sources of final purchases and the principal sources of primary supplies both within and outside the region. The reader is urged to take a moment to examine Figure 9.1 and compare it with the structure of Table 9.1.

Input and output summaries have been added to the transactions table at the right and bottom, bringing together intermediate, final, and grand totals for inputs and outputs. Inside the double line, the data matrix can be divided into four quadrants. The upper right is the final purchases quadrant; this shows sales of commodities produced in the region by each regional intermediate supplier to each major category of final purchaser. The upper left quadrant is the interindustry quadrant, the heart of the input-output table, which shows interindustry sales by regional intermediate suppliers (listed at the left) to regional intermediate purchasers (listed at the top). The lower left is the final payments (primary inputs) quadrant, which shows sales by primary suppliers (for which they receive final payments) to regional intermediate industries. The lower right is the primary suppliers–final purchasers quadrant, which records sales by primary suppliers directly to final purchasers. Cells in this quadrant representing sales by entities outside the region (imports) directly to other entities outside the region (exports) will have zero values if regional agents have not been involved in these types of transactions. The data for the transactions table represent total sales that have involved any element of the regional economy during the study year.

For purposes of regional analysis, intermediate suppliers and purchasers include only those that are located in the region. Imported inputs, whether processed or not, are primary inputs from the point of view of the regional economy because they do not require locally produced inputs for their production; payments for imports are final payments because they are not used to purchase further regional inputs. Similarly, export sales, whether for intermediate or final uses, are final sales from the standpoint of the regional economy because they are not processed further within the region.

Unless the sources supplying the necessary sales data maintain exceptionally good records and are uniquely cooperative, the input-output analyst is likely to find that for many industries, total purchases will not equal total sales. It is common practice in such cases to add an additional row and column, both entitled *Undistributed*. In this row and column, residual discrepancies between the input and output totals are recorded, and the totals are thus brought into equality.

In input-output accounting, as in other forms of accounting, it is customary to attribute to wholesale and retail trade only the value of sales that represents gross margin, sales less cost of goods sold. If the value of goods sold was included in the sales figures for trade, other regional intermediate industries would show few sales to final purchasers. The bulk of sales to final purchasers would be registered in the trade industry because the larger part of the final sales of most industries reach final consumers, and many intermediate purchasers as well, through wholesalers and retailers. Sales by suppliers are recorded in accordance with the purchaser for which they are destined, whether or not the trade industry plays a role. This practice does not alter the value of total output, and it may be violated in cases where it is important to trace flows precisely and to highlight trade linkages.

Final purchasers (final sales) includes all output destinations other than regional intermediate industries; therefore, it has both local and export components. Locally, in addition to households, sales for investment and sales to government represent final sales, and there may be others. Investment includes replacement as well as growth investment. Since it is not net of depreciation, it is often called *gross investment* or *gross capital formation*. Even though investment sales may be made to regional intermediate industries, they are not considered intermediate sales because the goods purchased receive no further processing and are not resold.

Export sales, in addition to those to households, include those to businesses (whether for investment or for further processing), those to the central government, and possibly others—for example, in some cases it may be useful to distinguish between regional exports to elsewhere in the country and exports overseas. Net inventory change also represents a final purchase with respect to the regional economy for the accounting year.

Customarily, wages, salaries, profits, property income, and other sources of personal income are considered final payments to households. In some cases, it may be desirable to disaggregate these by type of payment. In addition to households, local final payments (primary suppliers) include gross business savings (including capital consumption allowances that either were made or ought to have been made to cover depreciation) and payments to government, none of which are considered to be directly connected to further regional input purchases in the accounting year. All payments for goods and services imported to the region are considered final payments in the regional transactions table. Figure 9.1 provides examples of categories of imports that might be itemized.

The transactions table format shown in Figure 9.1 is more detailed than may be necessary or feasible in the case of many regions. If only the interindustry quadrant is of real concern, the final purchasers and primary suppliers categories may be combined into a single column and row respectively; or a distinction may be made only between local and outside purchasers and suppliers.

The definition of industries, level of disaggregation, determination of final and intermediate sectors, and the like must remain matters for careful consideration in the case of each particular region. Decisions regarding these matters will reflect unique regional characteristics; the analytical orientation of the input-output study; data availability; assumptions; and perhaps even social, cultural, and political factors. There are only two ironclad rules. First, the list of regional intermediate purchasers must be identical to the list of regional intermediate suppliers. And second, accounting procedures must distinguish in a meaningful way between regional intermediate industries and final purchaser categories, on the one hand, and between regional intermediate industries and primary supplier categories, on the other.

THE REGIONAL DIRECT REQUIREMENTS TABLE

As can be seen in Figure 9.2, the regional direct requirements table format is essentially the same as that used in the island economy example (Table 9.2). As before, direct requirements coefficients are computed by dividing through

Figure 9.2
Regional Direct Requirements Table Format

		PURCHASERS					
		Industry 1	Industry 2	. . .	Industry i	. . .	Industry n
SUPPLIERS	Industry 1	X_{11}	X_{12}	. . .	X_{1i}	......	X_{1n}
	Industry 2	X_{21}	X_{22}	. . .	X_{2i}	. . .	X_{2n}
	⋮	⋮	⋮	⋮	⋮	⋮	⋮
	Industry i	X_{i1}	X_{i2}	. . .	X_{ii}	. . .	X_{in}
	⋮	⋮	⋮	⋮	⋮	⋮	⋮
	Industry n	X_{n1}	X_{n2}	. . .	X_{ni}	. . .	X_{nn}
	Total regionally produced inputs						
	Total primary inputs						
Total direct inputs		1.00	1.00	. . .	1.00	. . .	1.00

each regional intermediate industry column of the transactions table by the column total. Final purchaser columns do not appear because, by definition, their purchases are not for intermediate use from the standpoint of the region.

Frequently, primary input suppliers (final payments categories) are combined into a single primary inputs row in the direct requirements table, as has been done in Figure 9.2. But in many cases it will be desirable to retain primary inputs disaggregation in order to observe the distribution among the various categories of final payments leakages from the streams of regional interindustry purchases. This would not affect the way the direct requirements coefficients are computed.

Each data cell in the direct requirements table contains a coefficient that indicates the input required by the industry at the top from the industry at the left for each unit of output delivered by the industry at the top. Since each column must total to 1.00, there can appear no values in excess of 1.00. For any estimated or hypothesized output of any regional intermediate industry, direct input requirements from all suppliers can be computed by multiplying each of the coefficients in the appropriate column by the total output figure.

THE REGIONAL TOTAL REQUIREMENTS TABLE

The conventional total requirements table format is essentially the same as the direct requirements table format. In the case of the total requirements table, each data cell shows total sales by the industry at the left when the industry at the top delivers one unit of output to final purchasers.

It is important to remember that any coefficient in the total requirements table does not indicate which industries purchased the input supplied by the industry at the left, but only how much is required in total. The total requirements coefficients include indirect inputs sold to all intermediate purchasers as well as direct inputs sold to the industry at the top of the column.

In the total requirements table, all the cells of the *major diagonal* of the data matrix, where each regional intermediate industry's row and column intersect, will have values greater than 1.00 (in some cases equal to 1.00, but never less than 1.00). This is because these coefficients reflect not only direct and indirect requirements but also the one unit of delivery to final purchasers. All other coefficients in any other column will be smaller than the coefficient in the major diagonal. Apart from its conceptual significance, this characteristic of the total requirements table can serve as an aid in spotting data irregularities or computational errors.

In order to use the total requirements table as an estimation device, all the coefficients in each column are multiplied by the hypothesized final sales estimate for the industry at the top. Column totals will then show total outputs required from all regional intermediate industries in combination in order to enable the industry at the top to satisfy the projected final demand. Row totals will show total output required from each of the suppliers at the left in order for the regional economy as a whole to satisfy the entire set of individual industry final sales estimates.

We should now reconsider the method for developing the total requirements coefficients from the direct requirements table. Earlier, it was pointed out that if the iterative computation procedure were followed on an industry-by-industry basis for a single unit of delivery to final purchasers by each industry, it would provide the total requirements coefficients for the total requirements table.

It was also noted that an indication of nearness to limit values of the iterative process is given by the nearness of the figure for total primary inputs to the figure for final purchases. But what is to be done once it has been determined that the iterative method has been worked out far enough? In the earlier examples, the iterations were simply stopped at this point and the figures for each industry were summed for total requirements. This is not an entirely satisfactory approach; it leaves the analyst with the uncomfortable feeling that one more round would bring the computations one degree closer to actual values.

A procedure exists for estimating for each industry the total value encompassed by all the rounds that remain uncomputed after the cutoff point. There are five steps in the procedure, as follows:

Step 1: For each regional intermediate industry, compute the ratio of the increment in the last round to the increment in the next to the last round.

Step 2: Compute the average of these ratios among all the industries.

Step 3: Compute the ratio of this average to 1.00 minus this average.

Step 4: For each industry, multiply the increment in the last round by the ratio from Step 3. This gives a weighted average estimate of the sum of the remaining uncomputed increments for each industry.

Step 5: Add these quantities to the totals for the corresponding regional intermediate industries.

While this rounding-off procedure enables a form of greater precision, it also adds to the cumbersomeness of the iterative method. Clearly, when one works by hand or even with a desk calculator, the number of sectors that can be handled within reasonable limits of time and effort using the iterative method is limited. At some point it may become worthwhile, if not necessary, to employ computers to do the job.

Once a computer is doing the computations, it is possible to obtain absolute accuracy through a mathematical method known as the *matrix inverse method*. Unless the interindustry matrix covers but a handful of regional intermediate industries, the matrix inverse method can be accomplished only by computer. The method entails performing a series of mechanical mathematical operations on the direct requirements table, thereby converting it to a fully accurate total requirements table. The coefficients that appear in the total requirements table computed by the matrix inverse method represent the actual limits of the iterative process, limits that can never actually be fully attained through the iterative method. In fact, in much of the input-output literature, the total requirements table is referred to as the matrix inverse table.

It is not necessary for the regional analyst to know the operations involved in the matrix inverse method. It is a standard mathematical procedure, and can be performed on any computer with commonly available software. All the analyst need do is supply the matrix of direct requirements coefficients and request an $(I - A)^{-1}$ solution. In linear algebraic notation, this means the inverse of the matrix formed by subtracting the A matrix from the identity matrix. In this case, A is the matrix of direct requirements coefficients. Table 9.8 is the total requirements table for the island economy computed using the matrix inverse method; the reader may wish to compare it with Table 9.6.

If disaggregation of primary inputs has been retained in the direct requirements table, this disaggregation can be retained when employing the iterative method, so that the total requirements table also shows primary input detail. The matrix inverse method, however, handles only the square data matrix of intermediate

Table 9.8
Total Requirements Coefficients Derived by the Matrix Inverse Method

Requires Total Sales by \ Every Unit of Delivery to Final Purchasers by	Agriculture	Manufacturing
Agriculture	1.1594	0.8706
Manufacturing	0.0725	1.3043
Total regional intermediate inputs	1.2319	2.1749
Total primary inputs	1.0000	1.0000
Total requirements from all suppliers	2.2319	3.1749

Table 9.9
Illustrative Direct Requirements Table with Disaggregated Primary Inputs

	Regional Intermediate Purchasers	
	Agriculture	Manufacturing
Regional Intermediate Suppliers		
Agriculture	0.10	0.60
Manufacturing	0.05	0.20
Primary Inputs		
Households	0.60	0.15
Government	0.25	0.05
Total direct inputs	1.00	1.00

industries. Thus, when the matrix inverse method is used, disaggregated primary inputs must be built back in after the total requirements coefficients for regional intermediate industries have been computed.

In order to demonstrate how this can be done, we return to the island economy example for the last time. The interindustry matrix of the total requirements table has been derived from direct requirements coefficients in Table 9.2 by the matrix inverse method, and appears in Table 9.8. Now, let us substitute the direct requirements coefficients in Table 9.9 for those in Table 9.2. The only difference between the two is that in Table 9.9, primary inputs coefficients have been divided between two categories of primary suppliers, households and government.

If households and government were combined into a single primary inputs row in the total requirements table, the total requirements coefficient appearing in every data cell of that row would be 1.00. It has been decided by the island's analyst, however, that households and government should each be represented by a row in the total requirements table, so that their total requirements coefficients can be considered separately.

Each of these coefficients can be computed as the sum of products resulting from multiplying each coefficient in the primary inputs row of the direct requirements table by the interindustry coefficients for the corresponding intermediate industry in the appropriate column of the total requirements table. In effect, each row of direct requirements primary inputs is turned sideways and aligned with the appropriate interindustry column, each pair of coefficients is multiplied, and the products are summed.

Take, for example, the coefficient for households in the agriculture column of the total requirements table. This would be the sum of products that resulted from multiplying the coefficients in the households row in Table 9.9 (0.60, 0.15) by the interindustry coefficients in the agriculture column in Table 9.8 (1.1594, 0.0725). Thus, (0.60)(1.1594) = 0.6956 and (0.15)(0.0725) = 0.0109; and the households total requirements coefficient for agriculture is 0.6956 + 0.0109 = 0.7065.

The computations for the four primary inputs total requirements coefficients in the example are provided in Table 9.10. Table 9.11 shows how the results of these computations would appear in the total requirements table with disaggregated primary inputs.

The reader with a background in linear algebra will recognize the procedure described as a matrix multiplication. This operation can also be handled by computer. The correct instruction to the computer operator would be as follows: multiply the matrix of primary inputs direct requirements coefficients (the premultiplier) by the $(I - A)^{-1}$ matrix (postmultiplier) and append the product matrix to the bottom of the $(I - A)^{-1}$ matrix. The computer printout will show the complete matrix of regional intermediate and primary input direct requirements coefficients. All that will remain to be done is to write in the names of the sectors at the left; and of course, the computer can do that as well.

INTERREGIONAL INPUT-OUTPUT STUDIES

Imagine a region that exports coal and metal products. One of its principal customers for coal is the country's single steel mill, which is located elsewhere. National projections show a rapidly increasing demand for metal products. An input-output model has been constructed for the region, and it shows that in order to satisfy the greater demand for its metal products, the region will require, among other things, substantially increased imports of steel inputs. However, the input-output tables do not show that as a consequence of the regions's increased demand for steel imports, it will have to supply greater quantities of coal exports to the steel mill.

Table 9.10
Computation of Total Requirements Coefficients for Primary Inputs
(Final Payments)

	When Delivery to Final Purchasers Is Made By					
	Agriculture			Manufacturing		
Primary Inputs Are Required By	Agriculture	Manufacturing	Total	Agriculture	Manufacturing	Total
And are supplied by						
Households	(.6)(1.1594) = .6956	(.15)(0.0725) = .0109	.7065	(.6)(0.8706) = .5224	(.15)(1.3043) = .1956	.7180
Government	(.25)(1.1594) = .2899	(.05)(0.0725) = .0036	.2935	(.25)(0.8706) = .2177	(.05)(1.3043) = .0652	.2829

Table 9.11
Illustrative Total Requirements Table with Disaggregated Primary Inputs (Final Payments)

Requires Total Sales By \ Every Unit of Delivery to Final Purchasers By	Agriculture	Manufacturing
Regional Intermediate Industries		
Agriculture	1.1594	0.8706
Manufacturing	0.0725	1.3043
Primary Inputs		
Households	0.7065	0.7180
Government	0.2935	0.2829

Or imagine a region with several small craft industries. The products of these industries, as well as many agricultural products, are marketed through a trading center outside the region. Projections show a growing regional population, and the regional input-output model indicates increased imports to satisfy the growth in final demand by local households. What the input-output tables do not show is that the increase in imports, purchased in large part directly or indirectly through the trading center outside the region, will result in a substantial increase in exports, because many of the imported goods actually originate in the region.

Interregional feedback effects like these can be introduced into the input-output analysis through an interregional input-output framework. In this framework, the list of intermediate industries is repeated, for each additional region covered, at the top of the table to the right of the list for the study region and also at the left of the table below the list for the study region. Since only interregional transactions with the study region would be of interest, the table will be *dog-legged*—that is, there will be no data matrices for transactions directly among the other regions.

Thus, for each type of intermediate input that is imported to the study region, the transactions table will indicate the amount imported in the study year from each region covered in the interregional framework. Looked at from the perspective of one of the other regions, the amount of each industry's output exported to the study region will be registered. Similarly, destination regions and quantities for regional exports—or quantities imported to other regions from each of the study region industries—would be shown. In effect, the intermediate industries in the other regions are incorporated into the interindustry matrix for the study region.

For purposes of interregional analysis, the rest of the country may be considered a single "other region," or any number of other regions may be included. In either case, once the transactions data are converted to coefficients, interregional feedback effects can be accounted for—to a considerable degree if only direct requirements coefficients are computed, and completely if total requirements coefficients are computed.

In the absence of a full-fledged interregional input-output study, information on interregional linkages and feedback effects must be derived from a source beyond the framework of regional input-output analysis. Data from linkages, flows, and similar studies with an interregional orientation can provide the basis for total sales estimates that will reflect the impact of interregional production-linkage interdependence.

SUPPLEMENTARY ANALYTICAL TOOLS AND SHORTCUTS

Once the input-output transactions table is compiled, its immediate analytical value can be enhanced by reorganizing it into a *triangulated format*. Triangulation involves listing the regional intermediate industries by order of increasing structural interdependence.

The measure of structural interdependence, for purposes of triangulation, is the number of other industries to which each sells its output. A perfectly triangulated interindustry quadrant of the transactions table would appear similar to that in Figure 9.3, in which each *X* represents interindustry sales and a blank represents a zero value. Triangulation will never produce the perfectly symmetrical pattern shown in Figure 9.3, but it should produce a pattern that tends in that direction. The triangulated order of industries, listed from top to bottom in accordance with increasing structural interdependence, should conform approximately to the order of industries when ranked in accordance with final sales as a decreasing proportion of total sales.

Triangulation provides immediate insights into the role of each industry in the regional economic fabric and into the hierarchical nature of the regional interindustry structure. These insights are of major analytical value and carry over into subsequent phases of the input-output study.

It may often be found helpful to assemble a *destination of output table*. For each industry, including primary suppliers, the percentages of total output sold to regional intermediate purchasers as a group and to final purchasers as a group can be computed on the basis of data in the transactions table. Industries are then listed in the destination of output table in rank order by descending percentages of their total output sold to regional intermediate industries.

From the input-output direct requirements table, a *sources of inputs* table can be assembled. For each regional intermediate industry column, coefficients that represent regional intermediate inputs are summed. Industries are then listed in the sources of inputs table in rank order by descending percent of their total inputs from regional intermediate suppliers.

Because capabilities for collecting the relatively large quantity of transactions data necessary for input-output analysis are often limited, one of a number of

Figure 9.3
Triangulated Interindustry Quadrant, Transactions Table

		Regional Intermediate Purchasers												Final Purchasers
		Retail trade	Construction	Hotels and tourism	Personal services	Fisheries	Quarries	Agriculture	Wholesale trade	Food products	Real estate	Crafts	Utilities and transport	
Regional Intermediate Suppliers	Retail trade	X												
	Construction	X	X											
	Hotels and tourism	X	X	X										
	Personal services	X	X	X	X									
	Fisheries	X	X	X	X	X								
	Quarries	X	X	X	X	X	X							
	Agriculture	X	X	X	X	X	X	X						
	Wholesale trade	X	X	X	X	X	X	X	X					
	Food products	X	X	X	X	X	X	X	X	X				
	Real estate	X	X	X	X	X	X	X	X	X	X			
	Crafts	X	X	X	X	X	X	X	X	X	X	X		
	Utilities and transport	X	X	X	X	X	X	X	X	X	X	X	X	
Primary Suppliers														

partial input-output techniques may be preferable to the full-scale study. One such shortcut is known as the *rows only method*. It is often possible to obtain data for total shipments or sales of a regional industry, but not for their distribution among purchasers. If this is the case, the analyst might attempt to distribute total sales among the purchasing industries on the basis of information obtained from a selected sample of supplying enterprises. The surveyed enterprises need only be asked to provide information on the percentage distribution of shipments or sales among purchasing industries. Firms will generally be more cooperative in supplying the information when money values are not requested.

Following this procedure on an industry-by-industry basis provides the distribution among purchasers of the output for each row. Of course, when all the rows are filled in, the columns will also be filled in. The disadvantages in this method are that the distribution of sales is based on an indirect estimating procedure, and the benefit of a crosscheck by an independent determination of input data is lost.

Another partial input-output technique that drastically reduces data requirements is the *major-minor method*. Figure 9.4 conveys the principal idea. Regional

Figure 9.4
Major-Minor Method, Interindustry Quadrant, Transactions Table

			Regional Intermediate Purchasers										Final Purchasers
			Major Industries				Minor Industries						
			Industry 1	Industry 2	Industry 3	Industry 4	Industry 5	Industry 6	Industry 7	Industry 8	Industry 9	Industry 10	
Regional Intermediate Suppliers	Major Industries	Industry 1	X	X	X	X	X	X	X	X	X	X	
		Industry 2	X	X	X	X	X	X	X	X	X	X	
		Industry 3	X	X	X	X	X	X	X	X	X	X	
		Industry 4	X	X	X	X	X	X	X	X	X	X	
	Minor Industries	Industry 5	X	X	X	X							
		Industry 6	X	X	X	X							
		Industry 7	X	X	X	X							
		Industry 8	X	X	X	X							
		Industry 9	X	X	X	X							
		Industry 10	X	X	X	X							
Primary Suppliers													

intermediate industries are divided into groups of major and minor ones. Major industries are listed to the left and top, and minor industries are listed to the right and bottom along the interindustry quadrant. This has the effect of subdividing the quadrant into four subquadrants. The *X*s in the data matrix of Figure 9.4 represent transactions involving a major industry. These are the only data cells in the interindustry matrix for which complete data are collected.

The remaining data cells represent transactions between minor industries and other minor industries. Each column and row within this submatrix is handled as if it were a single data cell. In other words, a single sales value is derived for each horizontal (⇔), and it is not distributed among the columns spanned. Similarly, a single undistributed purchases total is derived for each vertical (⇕), and it is not distributed among the rows spanned. Thus, time and expense are reduced by minimizing detail where transactions among minor industries exclusively are concerned. If necessary, the major-minor method can be taken to the extreme, with all minor industries in combination represented by a single sales figure and a single purchases figure.

These supplementary analytical tools and shortcuts are but a suggestion of the possibilities for variations on the input-output theme. The input-output framework really is quite flexible. In designing an input-output study to serve the planning process for a region or local area, the opportunities for simplifying, modifying, and selectively applying input-output analysis will be many. They arise from known features of the structure of the local economy or limited objectives for the study, and they should be fully exploited.

CAVEATS AND OBSERVATIONS

Technical production (direct requirements) coefficients are a function of the mix of specific products being produced, supply and market price, the technology of production processes, the technology of materials inputs, external economies, input delivery time and reliabilities, binding contracts, traditional trade patterns, and more. The greater the industry detail in the tables and the rate of innovation in the region, the less reliable for long-term analysis be the technical coefficients developed in the study.

The fact that final payments are not always final and final demand is not always exogenous may also create a problem for the regional analyst. The most obvious example is labor. An increase in the demand for labor will result in increased incomes to households, which may, in turn, increase final demand and sales and therefore interindustry sales, even in the current period.

Several problems in input-output accounting are related to time concepts. Actual transactions during a single accounting year constitute the basis for the entire input-output structure. Any particular year may involve irregularities that call into question the representativeness of coefficients derived from current transactions data. Such irregularities may include major strikes, passing fads, unusually large inventories, uncharacteristic weather patterns, and other temporary conditions.

There is also the problem that stems from the fact that input purchases during one accounting year may reflect more than requirements for current output. They may be influenced as well by anticipated output in the next accounting year, and also by the level of inventories that results from sales in the previous accounting year. This problem is reduced if inputs are counted to reflect consumption in the process of production rather than purchases by producers.

To all this may be added the problem of prices. Actual sales data may be found to be incomplete or unavailable. In such cases, estimation will require the pricing of physical output. This may be quite difficult because most goods sell at one price to final purchasers and at another to intermediate purchasers. Furthermore, there is usually a gap between quoted and actual prices owing to special agreements, bulk purchasing, and so on. Moreover, prices often change during the course of a year for a wide variety of reasons.

Many of these problems can be overcome by careful backup research and analytical ingenuity. Some problems, however, remain inherent in the input-output approach. This approach involves the assumption that each industry can be represented by a single linear, homogenous production function. This means, first, that input purchases by an industry are related only to, and change in direct proportion to, the level of current output of that industry. Second, each industry is viewed as if it produced one product, and produced it uniquely and by a single production process. And third, there are no external economies or diseconomies, and therefore, the effect of simultaneous production by several different industries is equal to the sum of their separate effects.

With all this, making guesses about the future remains, after all, often an important part of the planning process. This is so not because it is really possible to know the future, but because future scenarios can be a basis for testing alternatives against the best available information. Used in this spirit, as one way of making indicative comparisons among alternatives, input-output analysis can be a handy simulation tool.

Suppose, for example, that there are two competing development project proposals aimed at increasing demand for different major regional exports (say, by reducing different types of transport costs). A regional input-output model may provide the best available means for assessing their comparative net regional effects. The one yielding the largest likely increase in final demand may or may not turn out to be the one yielding the greatest regional final payments once the full interindustry implications are revealed. An input-output model provides a reusable tool for testing a limitless number of development scenarios in a comparative way.

In general, however, the chief value of regional input-output analysis is in its descriptive analytical power. Its descriptive capabilities can be exploited to a significant degree even if the total requirements table is not computed. As a descriptive tool, input-output tables present an enormous quantity of information in a concise, orderly, and easily understood fashion; provide a comprehensive picture of the interindustry structure of the regional economy; point up the strategic importance of various industries and sectors; and highlight possible opportunities for strengthening regional income and employment multiplication.

The process of compiling the transactions table, the major task in performing an input-output study, may itself yield unexpected benefits. This activity provides the development staff with a framework for tracing through the economic structure of the region in a systematic fashion. It also reveals data gaps and provides the opportunity for finding ways of overcoming them. And the data collected for the transactions table are useful for many other kinds of studies, with regional income and product accounts and linkage investigations being the most obvious among them.

Further discussion on the use of aggregate input-output analysis in a regional planning context will be found in Chapter 10. Intraregional input-output analysis is discussed in Chapter 13.

10

Aggregate Social Accounts: A Relational Review

The term *social accounts* refers to the various accounting based methods of analyzing the economy. They are *social* in that their focus is the economy of the national or regional society rather than an economic enterprise. They are *accounts* in that they are based on the double-entry principle that every transaction is an exchange and can be represented as two flows of equal value in opposite directions. In Chapter 5 the best known of the social accounts, income and product accounts, was introduced. In Chapter 6, balance of payments statements were discussed. In Chapter 9, input-output analysis was explained. Each of these is a form of social accounting; in each case, the total of flows in one direction equals the total of flows in the other direction.

The thought may already have occurred to the reader that there must be some way to combine the three social accounts into a single system that provides a multifaceted aggregate overview of the region. The underpinning logic of the social accounts suggests linkages among them. Input-output analysis focuses on interindustry relationships, but final payments and final purchases are equivalent to income and product. One of the components of gross regional product (GRP) is net exports, or exports minus imports. It is largely these exports and imports that give rise to the financial inflows and outflows on which balance of payments statements focus. One can also think of input-output analysis as concerning itself with what goes on among the industries of the regional economy, of income and product accounts as going on from there to detail the net effect of these interactions on the region in aggregate, and of balance of payments statements as going one step further to express what this means in terms of the values of flows across the borders of the region.

The three types of social accounts can in fact be combined into a single composite *social accounting matrix*. However, this involves some rearrangement of the accounts, and an approach to income and product accounting and to balance of payments accounting that is at variance with the straightforward flexible approaches set out in earlier chapters. Moreover, in the vast majority of cases, social accounting at the level of the region is often likely to be rudimentary and indicative, and it hardly makes sense to design an elaborate composite matrix with a complex set of guiding assumptions and procedures for purposes of manipulating sketchy and relatively aggregate data.

Better, for the practical purposes addressed in this book, to think of the social accounting system as a sequence of the three types of accounts rather than as a wholly unified framework that incorporates them simultaneously. Each of the three types of accounts can help with estimating and cross-checking data for the other two. Each can provide analytical insights complimentary to those derived from the other two. Taken together, they can be a practical guide to data collection and to other types of analysis that may be needed, as well as a conceptual guide to thinking about interrelationships, analysis, and development planning for a region.

A SYSTEM OF RUDIMENTARY SOCIAL ACCOUNTS

A development planning effort has just been launched in Region R. The initial analysis framework that will provide information for it is modest and experimental, and has been designed with the knowledge that the data assembled at the outset will not be highly refined. One of the purposes of the initial analysis framework is to uncover important data gaps and provide a base of experience for the learning process that will lead over time to a finely tuned information system carefully coordinated with an ongoing regional planning process. A basic statistical compendium has been completed, and now some of the data it contains are being systematically analyzed with the help of several methods of regional economic analysis, including rudimentary forms of social accounts.

Table 10.1 shows Region R's input-output transactions table compiled for the year 19XX. Direct requirements coefficients have been included in parentheses. From this table it can be seen that only in the case of manufacturing would moderate changes in annual output have significant interindustry implications. It can also be seen that only a third of regional manufacturing production is sold outside the region, that agriculture provides the major regional interindustry input to manufacturing, and that services, the smallest of the regional intermediate industries, provides a disproportionately large share of regional inputs to manufacturing.

From a development perspective, strengthening regional manufacturing exports would appear to be an effective means of expanding the markets for regional agriculture and services. This might require greater production efficiencies to improve the competitiveness of regional manufacturing, a move that unfortunately is likely to reduce the already small proportion of local labor inputs to this industry to an even lower level. However, agriculture and services purchase

Table 10.1
Input-Output Transactions Table with Direct Requirements Coefficients, Region R, 19XX
(millions of monetary units; direct requirements coefficients in parentheses)

	Regional Intermediate Purchasers						Final Purchases		Total Sales
	Agriculture		Manufacturing		Services		Regional	Export	(outputs)
Regional intermediate supplies									
Agriculture	15	(.03)	30	(.12)	10	(.05)	145	250	450
Manufacturing	5	(.01)	20	(.08)	5	(.03)	135	85	250
Services	10	(.02)	20	(.08)	5	(.03)	105	60	200
Primary Supplies									
Regional	370	(.82)	100	(.40)	135	(.68)	45	20	670
Import	50	(.11)	80	(.32)	45	(.22)	100		275
Total purchases (inputs)	450	(1.00)	250	(1.00)	200	(1.00)	530	415	1,845

over 80 percent and 65 percent, respectively, of their inputs from local primary suppliers, so expanding manufacturing exports will probably expand overall regional employment a good bit. In fact, the availability of additional workers in regional agriculture and services is probably essential for the expansion of regional manufacturing. Regional manufacturing already imports about a third of its inputs, and if regional benefits from an expansion in manufacturing activity are to be maximized, care must be taken to assure the availability of all inputs that could possibly be supplied from within the region.

If similar analyses were made for each of the other regional intermediate industries, a package of interrelated regional development policies and activities could be derived. Such a package might include actions that would make it easier for the manufacturing sector to modernize; measures to provide indirect support in the interest of maximizing regional benefits from the modernization, such as training more workers for agriculture and the services industry; additional methods of analysis that could provide further insights, such as mix-and-share analysis; and additional studies that should be undertaken, such as one to identify the imported inputs to manufacturing for which local inputs might be substituted. Of course, Region R planners would not commit energy and scarce development resources to specific policies and activities without first considering information in the other social accounts.

Looking back at Figure 5.2 in Chapter 5, we can see that the basic idea behind income and product accounts is that the sum of expenditures (or sales) measures gross regional product on the rights side of the accounts, while the left side of the accounts reflects the distribution of costs incurred in producing the product. How is it that among the expenditures, those by businesses other than for investment are not found, and among the costs incurred in producing the product, the costs of intermediate inputs are not found? The answer is that income and product accounts count only final purchases and final payments. The logic of this becomes clear when it is recalled that in developing the input-output total requirements table, the full value of final purchase ultimately ends up, when all the rounds have been worked through, in final payments for primary inputs. The income and product accounts, then, provide a picture of the aggregate regional final implications of interindustry relationships as a consequence of the response of the regional economy to final demand.

Figure 10.1 shows the income and product accounts designed and compiled by Region R analysts for 19XX. It is somewhat ambitious for a first effort, but the fact that a number of major enterprises are government-owned makes certain information available that otherwise would be difficult to obtain; and this in turn facilitated estimates of other information based on residuals.

Owing to the particular character of Region R and the data available, regional personal consumption expenditure and investment in housing have been combined (people generally build their own shelter with the help of relatives). The analysts have separated investment data for private and government enterprises because the decision making for them comes about in different ways and because the central government owns all government enterprises, while most private

Figure 10.1
Income and Product Accounts, Region R, 19XX
(in millions of monetary units)

Regional Income and Other Charges Against Gross Regional Product		Gross Regional Product			
Regional personal income	369	Regional personal consumption and housing expenditures			376
		Regional business investment			53
		Private		41	
		Growth	25		
		Replacement	9		
		Inventory	7		
Business transfers	201	Government		12	
		Growth	0		
		Replacement	2		
		Inventory	10		
Business taxes	33	Regional government nonbusiness expenditures			101
		Capital construction	10		
		Operations	91		
		Net exports			140
		Exports	415		
Capital consumption	67	Imports	275		
Gross regional product	670	Gross regional product			670

enterprises, including farms, are owned locally. Separate figures have been estimated for growth, replacement, and inventory change because each of these types of investment has different implications for regional development. For the same reason, separate estimates have been made for government capital construction and for operations expenditures.

The first few rows of the accounts shown on the left side of Figure 5.2 are encompassed by ''regional personal income'' on the left side of Figure 10.1. Personal income represents payments to factors of production—land, labor, and capital. But, of course, people own the factors of production, so such payments are really personal income. The other items on the left side of Figure 10.1 represent other costs of regional production, the payments for which do not accrue as income to residents of the region. Statistical discrepancies have been distributed proportionally among components of the accounts.

Figure 10.1 raises some questions and highlights some areas of potential concern with regard to Region R, though the accounts would be much more instructive if they were available for several years so that comparisons over time could be made. About 45 percent of regional product does not end up as income to residents of the region. Business transfers to nonresident owners amount to 30 percent of GRP, and business taxes seem close to insignificant. While Mu 67 million is estimated to be the amount of capital used up in producing the GRP, the right side of

Table 10.2
Balance of Payments Statement, Region R, 19XX
(in millions of monetary units)

Item	Exports and Payments Inflows (+)	Imports and Payments Outflows (–)	Net
Current account			
Business sector			
Agriculture	250		
Manufacturing	85		
Services	60		
Transfers		201	
Total	395	201	+194
Government sector (nonbusiness)			
Tax revenues		33	
Capital construction	10		
Operations	91		
Total	101	33	+68
Consumer sector and unspecified	20	275	–255
Residual capital and cash movements			+7

the accounts shows that only Mu 11 million is estimated as having been spent for replacement; and, although this may not be cause for alarm in any one year, the relationship between these figures should be watched carefully over time.

Government has spent nothing to expand the productive capacity of its enterprises in Region R in 19XX, while the private sector has spent Mu 25 million. Why? Does the fact that inventories of government enterprises grew by Mu 10 million while those of the larger private sector grew by only Mu 7 million offer a clue? Replacement investment in government enterprises seems rather low. Is there a suggestion here of inefficient enterprises building up unsold inventory while plant and equipment deteriorate, a situation that could lead to collapse and unemployment in the near future? While all this is somewhat sketchy, the potential implications for the development strategy suggested by Table 10.1 are clearly major.

From the data available, Region R analysts constructed the rudimentary balance of payments statement for 19XX shown in Table 10.2. Only current account information was available, so capital and cash movements were estimated residually. Exports by regional industries were taken from Table 10.1, as were consumer sector and unspecified exports and imports. Business transfers and government nonbusiness data were taken from the income and product accounts of Figure 10.1.

The balance of payments statement seems to open up a new perspective on the economy of Region R. Looking at the balance of payments rather than just exports and imports of goods and services raises new concerns. It turns out that over 50 percent of the gains from export sales by Region R are wiped out by transfer payments to nonresident owners. It is known that the majority of transfer payments are from government enterprises in Region R to the central government treasury. This represents not only a direct loss of regional income, but in addition, through a reverse multiplier effect, the loss in terms of regional welfare is compounded. Government tax revenues are only those paid to the central government on the operations of private enterprises, which probably accounts for why they are so low. The central government spends an amount over three times this figure, but far less than half this figure combined with transfers, on capital construction and operations in the region.

Despite the fact that exports from Region R amount to nearly 60 percent of GRP, the balance of payments approaches the break-even point. In fact, the economy of Region R, which is relatively poor, subsidizes the rest of the country relatively heavily. The balance of payments statement brings further into question the viability of the manufacturing export promotion strategy suggested by Table 10.1. It now appears that progress in regional development will require not only modernization, particularly in manufacturing, and a reduction of dependence on imports; it may require as well a restructuring of effective ownership patterns or modes of central government operation in the region.

The reader is encouraged to extend the Region R exercise by expanding the interpretive analysis of the tables and figure in this chapter, identifying additional implicit linkages among them, and considering further implications for development planning.

IMPROVING THE SOCIAL ACCOUNTING FRAMEWORK

We will not be able to delve more deeply into the problems of Region R or into potential development strategies for the area at this point. There is obviously a complex of interrelated political, administrative, social, technological, and economic circumstances for which to account. We do, however, want to consider relatively modest steps the analysts for Region R might take to improve the system of social accounts for purposes of analysis for development planning. The possible improvements are of four related types: increased detail, strengthened linkages among the accounts, sharpened focus, and development of time series data.

There are many ways the amount of detail in the accounts can be increased. Factors to be considered include: sectors, industries, or issues of special concern regarding which increased detail would provide decidedly improved insights; the types of additional data that can readily be obtained; key bits of information that enable further estimates through residual calculations or other means; and types of information that can serve a variety of analytical purposes.

For example, in the case of Region R, two types of detail readily stand out as highly desirable: disaggregated regional final payments and imports (primary supplies categories in the input-output table). The former would permit more refined analysis of the actual regional benefits of expansion in any industry, and the latter would enable planners to begin to consider local inputs that could be substituted for imported inputs. The income and product accounts of Figure 10.1 suggested that a portion of the regional final payments in Table 10.1 were not ultimately regional at all, and the balance of payments statement in Table 10.2 confirmed this.

The larger portions of regional final payments and imports are generated in the agricultural, manufacturing, and service industries (rather than by direct final purchases), as Table 10.1 shows. This means that most of the desired detail can be obtained through the same sample surveys and other techniques used to obtain the interindustry data for the transactions table (most enterprises are more readily able and willing to identify sources of inputs than ultimate destinations of output). It also means that the remaining (final purchases) portions of regional final payments and imports can be estimated roughly or not at all without diminishing the value of the analysis; refinement of those portions is less urgent and can await future efforts.

If regional final payments are detailed according to the components of the ''Regional income and other charges against gross regional product'' of the income and product accounts in Figure 10.1, then the data will also enable a partial disaggregation by regional industry of origin on the left side of those accounts. And if imports are detailed according to whether they are agricultural, manufacturing, or services imports, that information will enable a partial further disaggregation of the balance of payments statement in Table 10.2.

Thus, if next year Region R analysts increased detail in the social accounts in the manner described, they not only will have done so with minimal additional effort, they at once will have generated greatly expanded insights regarding major planning issues, strengthened the linkages among social accounts and produced data useful for all of them, and sharpened the focus of the accounts. Furthermore, by building on the initial set of accounts rather than introducing wholesale revisions, consistent time series data can be built up, further enhancing the usefulness of the social accounts over time. The reader may find it an instructive exercise to introduce the improvements suggested in the transactions table (Table 10.1), fabricating the data, and then to carry the changes through the other two sets of accounts.

Of course, Region R analysts may choose to improve the accounts in other ways as well. They might expand detail considerably more, but only for regional manufacturing or government enterprises or some other industry or sector of special concern. They may decide to augment the social accounts with other methods of analysis rather than modify the accounts themselves. They may elect to undertake special studies to uncover specific information not adequately encompassed by conventional methods of regional economic analysis. Or they may select a combination of these.

III

Methods of Intraregional Analysis

11

Characteristics of Subareas and Urban Places

Intraregional analysis adds a further dimension to regional analysis by examining explicitly the differences and relationships among places within a region. Even when employing detailed industry categories, such as might be done in mix-and-share, location quotient, or input-output analysis, aggregate methods beg the question: but where in the region does it happen, and as a result, who is affected? For very small regions, like a rural town and its immediate hinterland, aggregate methods of regional analysis may suffice for planning purposes because sectoral distinctions may be fairly representative of spatial distinctions: agricultural activities and farm populations are in the hinterland, and the rest is in the town.

But most often there are several towns of different sizes with somewhat different problems, different roles in the regional economy, and possibly even different types of population groups; and there are likely to be several types of nonurban areas as well. These places interact, and together make up the regional economic organism. A full understanding of this organism, what drives it, and how it performs requires knowledge of the individual parts and their interactions.

Just as a portion of the methods of aggregate regional analysis are adaptations of analytical tools originally developed for use at the national level, so a portion of the methods of intrarregional analysis are adaptations of methods of aggregate regional analysis. The first three sections of this chapter, for example, bear headings that are reminiscent of earlier chapters dealing with methods of aggregate analysis. But in addition, there are many methods of intraregional analysis that have no counterparts in aggregate regional analysis, and it is to these that the majority of space in Part III of this book has been dedicated.

This chapter deals with several different but interrelated ways of examining and comparing characteristics of regional subareas and urban places. It is followed by chapters that deal in turn with considerations for exploring linkages and flows among places within a region; methods of assessing income and employment multiplication processes that take place as a result of trade among places within a region; and finally, methods of analyzing the settlement system of a region. For convenience, in the four chapters of Part III the term *subunit* will be used to encompass both the *subareas*, which should be thought of as largely rural, and the *urban places* of a region.

THE BASIC STATISTICAL COMPENDIUM

The basic statistical compendium can be made to serve as a powerful tool for intraregional as well as aggregate regional analysis. Apart from the wealth of information it provides about specific parts of the regional whole, the exercise of assembling it provides the planning staff with an opportunity to familiarize itself thoroughly and in a systematic way with all the geographic components of the region. Moreover, the compendium offers a framework for:

—identifying the types of disaggregated data that are available and not available;

—preliminarily identifying subregional areas, topics, and problems for which special studies should be considered;

—conducting simple types of initial intraregional analyses, such as those discussed later in this chapter, and arraying the results in a manner that highlights comparative values; and

—creating a sourcebook of data that later will be used in more formal types of intraregional analysis.

The fundamental considerations in compendium design discussed in Chapter 4 apply here as well, and will not be repeated. However, when the emphasis is on intraregional analysis, several additional considerations need to be taken into account.

The first is the heightened importance of making generous use of maps wherever possible in the compendium. It is, after all, information on differences and relations among subunits dispersed over the territory of the region that is being presented. Whenever data in the tables can be represented on maps, even in the most rudimentary fashion, doing so will heighten the understanding of their significance on the part of both the casual compendium reader and the analyst. Moreover, repeated use of a standard *base map* to display different types of information throughout the compendium imparts a cumulative "feel" for the natural, social, and economic geography of the region. This generalized appreciation of the spatial composition of the region can be an invaluable aid in grasping the significance of analytical findings.

Second, the type of data covered in the compendium—the table subjects and column headings—should include what was discussed in Chapter 4 and a good deal more. Intraregional analysis requires more processed data; that is, data that have been manipulated through at least simple methods of intraregional analysis so as to highlight the relative economic status of, and relationships among, subunits of the region.

Subjects covered in the remainder of this chapter—income measures, income and product, balance of payments, location quotients and related indicators, and natural resource characteristics—all are worthy topics for tables and column headings in an intraregionally oriented regional statistical compendium. The same is true for many of the subjects covered in Chapters 12 and 13, and especially Chapter 14, as well. Chapter 14 deals explicitly with access, relative economic functions, and market center roles with respect to settlements in the regional system. Much of the information developed through the methods of analysis discussed lends itself to presentation in both tables and maps in the statistical compendium.

The third consideration is that greater care that has to be given to the selection of subunits (table row headings) for which information is provided in compendium tables. When the emphasis is on aggregate regional analysis, the selection of subunits within the region tends to be made more casually, and more thought usually goes into selection of reference areas for interregional comparison. Within the region administrative subunits are commonly employed, because it is in terms of these subunits that data are most readily available.

But administrative subunits often are not the most analytically useful entities for purposes of intraregional analysis. Intraregional analysis generally requires a more detailed geographic breakdown, and the breakdown should be made on the basis of factors relevant for purposes of economic development. Ideally, every urban settlement in the region should be represented individually, as should every distinct agricultural, ecological, or other zone with special significance for economic development. Of course, administrative subunits do have a particular significance for development planning, because they represent an official level of decision making and of development revenue generation. So the best of all possible compendiums would list administrative subunits, and then list further territorial subdivisions under each of them.

In some cases it may be desirable to have standard table row headings, as described above, and where appropriate, to follow a standard table with a supplemental one. On the supplemental table, subunits of the region might be regrouped in a manner particularly suited to the subject of the table. For example, all urban areas and then all nonurban areas might be listed in turn, economic development zones might be shown without respect to administrative boundaries, or subunits of the region might be shown in rank order with respect to certain key data in the table.

In short, in comparison with aggregate analysis purposes, for intraregional analysis purposes:

—statistical information in the compendium should be presented graphically on maps whenever possible;

—the types of information covered in compendium tables should be more detailed and analytically oriented; and

—the subunits of the region for which data are shown in the tables should be much more detailed, and should be selected and regrouped on the basis of analytical importance.

Clearly, this is likely to make the job of data collection and presentation more difficult. Indeed, the array of data that can be presented for all the subunits listed in the tables may be rather restricted the first time an intraregionally oriented compendium is compiled. But this will serve to help identify priorities for future efforts at data collection that are part of the ongoing regional development planning process.

Regional planning staffs equipped with computers may wish to investigate the usefulness of *geographic information system* (GIS) programs now available for microcomputers. Basic data assembled for the regional compendium can be entered into a GIS program, and the program can then perform many of the desired data manipulations, statistical analyses, and intraregional comparisons. GIS programs are especially useful for analyses concerning geographic distribution, concentration, and relationships in a region. In some cases a GIS program can help establish the economic implications of actual and hypothetical geographic relationships among specific activities and resources in the regional economy. A GIS program can print out the compendium tables after processing the data, and, most important, is designed to present information on the region and its subunits on computer-generated maps. Complete discussions on geographic information systems will be found among publications listed in the third section of the Bibliography.

INCOME MEASURES AND SOCIAL ACCOUNTS

Income measures discussed in Chapter 5—gross regional product, net regional product, regional income, regional personal income, regional personal disposable income, regional personal discretionary income, and per capita and per household measures—can be estimated for individual subunits of the region. Short of reliable census data, the best ways of doing this are through studies such as those that might be undertaken in connection with methods of intraregional income and employment multiplication analysis discussed in Chapter 13, or through structured sample surveys undertaken specifically for the purpose. Where these are not possible, a method must be devised for estimating the distribution of regional values among individual subunits.

Population distribution alone cannot serve as a basis for apportioning income among subunits because this would involve an implicit assumption of per capita income equality among subunits, rendering the exercise pointless. However, if, in the course of making GRP calculations or collecting data for other types of aggregate analysis, estimates have been made of the value of output by sector or industry category, then these can be used as the basis for rough distributions of income among regional subunits.

Each sector's proportion of the value of total regional output would be computed, and in turn, each subunits's proportion of the output of each sector would be estimated. In their coarsest forms, these estimates would be made using the assumption that each subunit specializes in a single sector, the one that is in fact dominant there. In their more refined forms, surveys—even minimal "quick-check" varieties—can serve as a basis for allocating proportions of the output of several sectors to each regional subunit.

In any case, these proportions can then serve as a basis for apportioning various types of regional income among subunits of the region. Dividing each subunit's estimated portion of a regional income measure by its population would yield unique per capita income estimates for each subunit. These estimates would admittedly be only indicative insofar as absolute levels are concerned, but would have considerable validity for comparative purposes.

Simplified forms of income and product accounts and balance of payments statements, the social accounts discussed in Chapters 5 and 6, can also be prepared on an intraregional basis (input-output, a third type of social account, is discussed in Chapter 13). Again, the best ways of doing this are with the help of reliable census data, through special studies undertaken in connection with methods of analysis discussed in Chapter 13, or through structured sample surveys undertaken specifically for the purpose. Alternatively, estimation techniques like those described above can be used.

Of special interest for intraregional analysis is not only the gross product, exports and imports, and net payments flows of subunits of the region, but also how these express themselves as economic relationships with other subunits in the region as against places outside the region. Thus, for each subunit for which a rudimentary income and product account or balance of payments statement is prepared, columns should be added on the right side representing areas within the region and areas outside the region.

Viewing the matter realistically, this could involve an effort of enormous proportions for regions with any amount of complexity in settlement composition. Therefore, the best course is to undertake income and product accounting and/or balance of payments accounting not for all subunits of the region, but only for two to four of them. These two to four subunits should be defined, however, to encompass the entire region. For example, the region may be divided into urban areas and nonurban areas; or into the central city, other urban areas, and nonurban areas; or into the central city, other urban areas, agricultural zones, and other nonurban areas. Ideally, in the case of the accounts for each subunit, columns would appear to the right for each of the other subunits and for the rest of the world outside the region.

Intraregional social accounts prepared at regular intervals can provide invaluable planning information on trade and development trends within the region, including changing terms of trade among regional subunits, as related to patterns of change for the region as a whole.

ECONOMY COMPOSITION ANALYSIS

The data for intraregional methods of economy composition analysis (discussed in their aggregate forms in Chapter 7) can be developed using very minimal surveys to estimate values for employment or production in the various sectors or industrial categories of each subunit, or by using extensive surveys. In the latter case, these same surveys can be used to collect information also for other types of intraregional analysis, including income and product and balance of payments accounting, extended commodity trade systems analysis (Chapter 12), and economic base and input-output analysis (Chapter 13). Naturally, the number and nature of subunits defined for purposes of the analyses will very much affect the magnitude of the data collection effort necessary.

But even if conducted on a relatively rudimentary basis, the different forms of economy composition analysis offer the easiest means for beginning to expand aggregate regional analysis into intraregional analysis. And the analytical output of methods of economy composition analysis lends itself readily to inclusion in the statistical compendium.

The means for adaptation of mix-and-share analysis to subunits of the region are self-evident. Just as mix-and-share analysis can be undertaken for the region relative to the nation, so it can be undertaken for regional subunits relative to the region. When the results of intraregional mix-and-share analysis are viewed next to aggregate mix-and-share analysis, a much more informative picture emerges. This picture reveals not only the components of relative change that add up to net regional change in employment by sector or industry category, but also how these have expressed themselves in turn on employment in different types of economic activities in different subunits of the region. This represents a major step—one that will be augmented by other methods of intraregional analysis—toward understanding not only what sorts of actions might be taken to strengthen the regional economy, but where they should be focussed geographically.

Obviously, time series data are needed for mix-and-share analysis, so unless census data or data from prior studies are available, the method cannot be used intraregionally the first time an effort is made at intraregional analysis. Data collected for intraregional location quotient and related computations the first time can serve as base year data for a second analysis effort.

Although the simplicity of mix-and-share analysis means that it could in principle be conducted for all subunits in the region listed in the statistical compendium, in most cases disaggregating to this extreme will not be a useful exercise. Subunits for mix-and-share analysis could be defined in terms of the two to four specially defined subunits encompassing the entire region mentioned in the social accounts discussion above.

Alternatively, regional subunits might be defined for purposes of mix-and-share analysis on the basis of the locations of major concentrations of activity in different sectors, or on the basis of the locations of large enterprises (large factories, mining operations, plantations) on the one hand, and small ones, on the other. In some regions a useful approach might be to define subunits for mix-and-share analysis on the basis of concentrations of particular population groups of special concern.

Computation and use of the location quotient has received attention in two previous chapters. Generally, what has been said above regarding mix-and-share analysis for regional subunits applies to use of the location quotient for intraregional analysis as well. Location quotients computed for regional subunits would employ regional data as reference variables. However, unlike mix-and-share analysis, location quotients for many types of specialization variables can provide useful comparative information at even the most highly disaggregated levels of intraregional analysis. In addition, there are a few indicators related to the location quotient that are frequently used in intraregional analysis.

The *index of concentration* indicates the degree to which selected activities or characteristics are geographically dispersed or concentrated in the region. Commonly, subunits are taken in terms of square kilometers or other geographic measures, and for this purpose urban places would be incorporated into surrounding subareas. To compute an index of concentration, first the proportion of total regional territory represented by each subunit is calculated; we can refer to this proportion as the reference proportion, Rp. Then, each subunit's proportion of the regional total for the activity or characteristic being explored (number of farms, employment in a certain sector, irrigated farmland, gross product, and so on) is calculated; we can refer to this as the concentration variable proportion, CVp.

Next, for each subunit, CVp is subtracted from Rp; the result may be positive or negative, depending on whether the concentration variable proportion is lesser or greater than the reference proportion. Then, (Rp − CVp) for all the subunits are added together, but are added as if they were all positive numbers. The result is divided by 2 and, by convention, this result in turn is subtracted from 100 to produce the index of concentration for the region. In other words:

$$\text{Index of concentration} = 100 - [\text{sum of (Rp} - \text{CVp) as a positive number for all subunits}]/2$$

Since the sum of positive (Rp − CVp) values will equal the sum of negative (Rp − CVp) values, an alternative formulation is:

$$\text{Index of concentration} = 100 - [\text{sum of positive (Rp} - \text{CVp) values}]$$

Thus, the index of concentration can range between 0 and 100, and the higher the value, the more even (roughly speaking) is the distribution of the concentration variable over the territory of the region.

Any single index of concentration has little value in its own right, but when indexes of concentration using the same reference proportions are computed for several different concentration variables and then compared, important information may be revealed. For example, comparing indexes of concentration computed for number of farms, irrigated farmland, farms above a certain size, employment in farming, and farm income would reveal a great deal about the relationships among these variables within the subunits of the region.

Also, indexes of concentration can be computed using different reference proportions, like arable land area, rural area, and urban area, in order to address different analytical concerns. Again, when indexes of concentration using the same concentration variable proportions are computed on the basis of different reference proportions and then compared, the intraregional analytical usefulness of the indexes is vastly increased.

Moreover, the calculations leading up to the index of concentration are of comparative value. These calculations can be displayed as a table showing Rp, CVp, and (Rp − CVp) as a positive or negative number for each subunit, offering instructive intraregional comparisons. To make the relative significance of the figures for each subunit a bit easier to grasp at a glance, an indicator called a *distribution quotient* can also be computed for each subunit and displayed next to the (Rp − CVp) value in the table. This quotient is simply:

$$\text{Distribution quotient} = \text{CVp/Rp}$$

In other words, the distribution quotient is the concentration variable proportion as a percent of the reference proportion. If the concentration variable shows less proportionate concentration than the reference variable in a particular subunit, the distribution quotient for the subunit will be less than one; if it shows a greater concentration, the distribution quotient will be greater than one. The amount lesser or greater than one is an indication of how far apart the two proportions are.

It may already have occurred to the reader that an index of concentration–type calculation could be made using subunit reference proportions based on other than geographic measures. Rather than viewing the region's subunits as territorial units, they can be viewed as population units, and relative degrees of concentration of selected activities or characteristics can be explored relative to the distribution of population, rather than territorial, mass. For this purpose, measures like population, working-age population, or the like could be used as the basis for reference proportions.

Indeed, what is commonly referred to as the *index of association* is an index of concentration calculated for any two variables in order to explore the degree of association between them throughout the region. For example, if consumer goods wholesale trade is used for Rp and consumer goods retail trade is used for CVp, patterns of concentration in one type of trade or the other, and implicit consumer goods intraregional trade patterns, would emerge from the calculations.

Needless to say, the usefulness of these indicators is heightened when data are available that allow them to be computed for two points in time, so that relative trends among regional subunits can be revealed. In fact, if time series data are available, a further indicator, the *shift index* can be computed. The shift index is based on one of the types of calculations done in connection with mix-and-share analysis. It is used for the explicit purpose of exploring the relative shifts among subunits of the region in employment, income, output, and related variables, either by specific sectors or in aggregate, over a period of time.

The shift index for each subunit for any selected variable is calculated as:

$$\text{Shift index} = 100 \times \frac{\text{value of the variable at the end of the period}}{\text{value of the variable at the regional rate of change}}$$

In other words, if employment in services were the selected variable, then for each subunit, service employment at the end of the period would be divided by

[(service employment at the beginning of the period) × (the regional rate of change in service employment over the period)]

and, by convention, the result would be multiplied by 100. Multiplying by 100 merely shifts the decimal point two places to the left, so that an index below 100 indicates a rate of change less than for the region as a whole, and an index greater than 100 indicates a rate of change greater than for the region as a whole.

The shift index can easily be computed for all subunits of a region, and can serve as a partial alternative to a full set of mix-and-share computations for them. Shift index computations are most informative when indexes are computed for several related variables, like employment in several different sectors, and the results are compared. Shift indexes provide insights into the way regional totals have been shifting among subunits, and therefore can be good complements to the findings of aggregate mix-and-share analysis.

NATURAL RESOURCE ASSESSMENTS

Natural resource assessments are necessary to assemble information about the full array of opportunities offered by the region's environmental resources. They are also necessary in order to enable planners to evaluate the environmental sustainability of development project proposals. Thus, no matter how rudimentary the means by which they are accomplished—including nothing more than conducting conversations with people knowledgeable about the natural resources in each subarea—natural resource assessments should be thought of not as extras in the regional planning process, but as essential and integral components of it.

Natural resource assessments, like other methods of regional analysis, serve as input to the processes of project identification, evaluation, and design.

Natural resource assessments are sometimes thought of as a form of aggregate regional analysis. But even more than many other types of economic resources—skills, capital, and information, for example—natural resources are firmly rooted to specific locations, and can only be properly appreciated for regional development purposes in terms of where they are, and where they are not, located. A discussion of technical methods of natural resource assessment is beyond the scope of this book. Presented below, however, are a number of methodological approaches and frameworks for natural resource assessment that have been used in regional analysis exercises.

Generally, natural resource assessments are conducted on the basis of regional subunits, normally rural subareas, but together encompassing all of the regional territory. However, the most appropriate subunit designations for natural resource assessment purposes in any particular case depends on the characteristics of the subareas, urban places, and major natural resource systems, and the way they are used in the region.

Resource suitability classification is an approach to natural resource assessment that focusses on the suitability of each major resource in each subarea for one or more specified uses. The uses considered would include major ways the resource is already being used and other uses under discussion. Each major resource in each subarea is classified with respect to its suitability for each use in terms of four aspects of suitability, as follows:

1. *Basic Suitability*. In light of its current status in the subarea, is the resource suitable or not suitable for this use?
2. *Order of Suitability*. If suitable for this use, is the resource highly suitable (HS), moderately suitable (MS), or only barely suitable (BS)? If not suitable for this use, is the resource only currently not suitable (CN), or permanently not suitable (PN)?
3. *Limitations of Suitability*. What are the basic reasons for the order of suitability (moisture, erosion, chemical composition, pollution, disease, hazard risk, minimal quantity, competing higher use, and so on)?
4. *Opportunities for Improving Suitability*. What measures (management practices, production methods, and so on), if any, might raise the order of suitability?

A resource suitability report can be prepared for each subarea, covering all major resources and suitability classifications for major uses considered, with a resource suitability summary for the subarea as a whole. Alternatively, a report can be prepared on a region-wide basis for each resource. In this case, each report would show results of suitability classification exercises in each subarea and provide a regional summary for the individual resource. In either case, the four aspects of suitability would be covered by verbal description. However, for quick review purposes, or to enable inclusion of information on resource suitability classification in the basic regional compendium, the options under each aspect of suitability can be coded: for example, as indicated above, HS, MS, and BS for the three orders of suitability; and CN and PN for the two orders of unsuitability.

Resource depletability analysis characterizes the major resources of each subarea of the region in terms of categories of depletability. One system that has been used includes five such categories:

1. *Depletable: Maintainable Renewable*. Resources, such as some fishing grounds, that renew themselves or can be maintained with proper management practices or, after depletion, will renew themselves if left unexploited for a period of time.
2. *Depletable: Maintainable Nonrenewable*. Resources, such as soil susceptible to erosion, that can be maintained with proper management practices, but that if depleted will be lost forever.
3. *Depletable: Nonmaintainable Reusable*. Resources, such as mineral ores, that become depleted with exploitation, but can be reused through product recycling.
4. *Depletable: Nonmaintainable Nonreusable*. Resources, such as oil, that become depleted with exploitation, and after use cannot be recycled.
5. *Inexhaustible*. Resources, such as solar energy and wind power, that are not affected by exploitation.

Other approaches to depletability categorization that are more or less extensive can be devised as suitable to the types of major resources, and their uses, prevailing in a particular region. Here, too, reports can be prepared that discuss the depletability status of major resources by subarea for all resources or by individual resource on a region-wide basis. And again, a coding system for resource depletability can be devised so that the basic information can be included in the basic regional compendium.

A *resources/sectors situation report* is a report that covers the status, uses, problems, and opportunities associated with each major resource in each subarea. Conventionally, one such report covering all major resources is prepared for each subarea, and a consolidated report briefly covering all resources region-wide is also prepared. All these may be organized as chapters in a single report. The unique aspect of the resources/sectors approach is that the information concerning each resource in each subarea is considered and presented in relation to specific major sectors of economic activity, including public services.

Conceptually, the reporting framework for each subarea, and also the summary for the region as a whole, can be thought of as a matrix. Along the top of the matrix would be listed the several resources of major concern covered by the situation report. Under each resource would be columns for status, uses, problems, and opportunities. Along the left side of the matrix would be listed the designated sectors of economic activity. Each cell of the matrix would contain an analysis of the resource characteristic at the top of the column as related to the sector at the left of the row. Figure 11.1 shows this schematically for the region as a whole, highlighting one resource and one sector.

Figure 11.1
Framework of the Resources/Sectors Situation Report

Sectors	Subareas	Farmland				Water...etc
		Status	Uses	Problems	Opportunities	...
Public Services	Subarea A	____	____	____	____	...
	Subarea B	____	____	____	____	...
	Subarea C	____	____	____	____	...
	Subarea D	____	____	____	____	...
	Subarea E	____	____	____	____	...
	Subarea F	____	____	____	____	...
	Region-wide	____	____	____	____	...
Agriculture : : : Etc.						

The several resources of major concern are usually designated as such because of recognized problems or opportunities associated with them in a subarea. Thus, at the regional level, every resource of major concern in any subarea will be covered. The sectors are designated on the basis of their importance in each subarea; hence, again, at the regional level any sector of importance in any subarea will be covered. This means that, conceptually speaking, the matrix at the regional level will have a number of blank cells, where the interactions of some resources with some sectors in some subareas are not of significance. A matrix framework like the one shown in Figure 11.1, without the subarea listings, can be used in the basic regional compendium to present a concise summary of the resources/sectors situation for each subarea and also for the region as a whole. For this purpose no more than a brief descriptive sentence, phrase, or even a code, would appear in each matrix cell.

In 1987 the United Nations Centre for Human Settlements (UNCHS/Habitat) and the United Nations Environment Programme (UNEP) jointly published *Environmental Guidelines for Settlements Planning and Management*. Volume 3 of the three-volume publication is titled *Environmental Considerations in Regional Planning and Management*, and contains practical approaches and methods for incorporating environmental considerations into regional development planning. Its basic orientation is one that promotes sound management of environmental resources as a tool of regional development. Among other things, it offers full descriptions of the following additional natural resource assessment tools.

—''Natural resource/hazard inventory'': an inventory of the quantities, qualities, sources, and spatial distribution of key natural resources and hazards in the region and its subareas in a form useful for purposes of economic development analysis.

—''Resource utilization capacity and hazard risk analysis'': a framework for developing characterizations of each major resource in the region and its subareas in terms of qualities and quantities that give rise to the ''goods and services'' derived from it, and of each major hazard in terms of the threat it poses.

—''Environmental sensitivity analysis'': an assessment of the capacity of regional natural resource and hazard systems to sustain different intensities and types of development activity.

Readers are encouraged to refer directly to the UNCHS/UNEP publication for details on these and related methods of natural resource assessment in a context of regional analysis.

If time, money, and staff are sufficient, ideally two or more of the approaches discussed above would be combined into a natural resource assessment package tailored to the unique requirements of the study region.

12

Intraregional Linkages and Flows

The discussion of linkage investigations, flow studies, and friction analysis in Chapter 6 emphasized the importance of understanding actual and potential interactions between the region and other areas, and of understanding also the factors that inhibit such interactions. If the essential equation for regional economic growth is increasing returns from regional exports and multiplying the income earned within the region, then economic interactions between the region and other areas have major analytical importance, particularly because they are the source of export returns.

Linkages among subunits in the region, their associated flows, and factors inhibiting flows have major analytical importance, particularly because they are the mechanisms through which regional income and employment are multiplied. The essential questions addressed by intraregional linkage, flow, and related investigations are: What are the major types of linkages, and their natures and magnitudes, among subunits of the region? What volumes of economic goods flow among major points of origin and destination in the region? What are the major factors inhibiting productive economic interaction among subunits of the region? How do intraregional linkages and flows of different types fit together as components of trading chains important to regional economic growth?

The basic methods for conducting linkage investigations, flow studies, and friction analysis were discussed in Chapter 6, and are applicable to intraregional analysis as well as aggregate and interregional regional analysis. Some of the discussion in Chapter 11 concerning social accounts, economy composition analysis, and natural resource assessments is also directly relevant to the subject of this chapter. Chapter 13 discusses intraregional income and employment multiplication, and therefore also bears directly on the subject of intraregional linkages, flows, and friction. Finally, Chapter 14, dealing with analysis of the regional settlement system, introduces a number of methods for exploring the roles and relationships among urban places in a region. This chapter presents some considerations additional to those discussed elsewhere in this book that come into play when linkages, flows, and friction are investigated intraregionally. The reader concerned with the full story on the subject of this chapter will want to consult the other chapters mentioned as well.

LINKAGES, FLOWS, FRICTION

The introduction to Chapter 6 begins:

> There is a multitude of interregional linkages—physical, social, technological, political, institutional, and economic—through which regions interact with each other. These interactions, in turn, generate impulses that work their way through the regional economy by means of an equally complex intraregional linkage system.

It may be more accurate to describe the intraregional linkage system, from the point of view of regional development analysis, as considerably more complex than the interregional linkage system. For purposes of aggregate analysis, the regional analyst has the luxury of viewing the region as a single entity that interacts with the rest of the world. All interregional flows originate or terminate as if at a single point, "the region," or a large urban place within the region that serves as a proxy for the region as a whole. The primary challenge is to figure out which interactions to explore and then to assemble the relevant data.

The same challenge confronts the analyst exploring intraregional interactions. But in this case the challenge is complicated by the fact that a wider variety of types of interactions may be immediately relevant to regional economic growth processes and are therefore of greater analytical importance than would be the case in aggregate analysis. Moreover, regional development planning can influence a larger number of interaction factors internal to the region than external to it; for this reason also more needs to be known about more types of intraregional linkages than interregional linkages. Figure 12.1 summarizes major categories of linkages among subunits of the region that may need to be explored in the course of intraregional analysis.

As suggested in Chapter 6, experimentation with location quotients and related indicators can help point out the types of linkages and flows that warrant further investigation. But in the context of intraregional analysis, the linkages and flows highlighted by preliminary exploratory techniques have to be understood as possibly only single dimensions of types of interaction systems that are important for purposes of regional development analysis. For example, an intraregional location quotient computation may reveal that a certain regional subarea markets a much smaller proportion of its maize, relative to the amount of its land in

Figure 12.1
Categories of Intraregional Linkages

Category of Linkage	Elements and Flows Included
Transportation	Road, water, rail, and air transport routes, infrastructure and fleet stock including condition), major types of cargo, patterns of use, ownership and control, services offered.
Communication	Telegraph, newspaper, and other communication media networks, types of infrastructure (including condition), patterns and types of use, ownership and control, services available; other important formal and informal methods of information dissemination, including locations and types of principal dissemination points and audiences.
Natural resource	Natural resource systems, such as rivers, drainage systems, wind currents, agro-climactic zones, and also interventions in these systems such as irrigation networks, that create interdependencies among subareas of the region.
Economic	Final and intermediate market chains and goods flows; production linkages; consumer shopping patterns; patterns of economic ownership and control; income flows, including transfers and remittances; capital flows; formal and informal financial systems; commutation; seasonal employment migration.
Social	Ethnic and religious affinity group patterns; kinship patterns (especially rural-urban or among subareas); class linkages.
Public service	Utility networks; education and training networks; specialized research and information dissemination systems; personal transportation services; health service linkages; voluntary association networks.
Institutional	Public administration linkages; budget allocation systems among different administrative levels; political decision chains; authority-approval-supervision patterns.

maize, than would be expected on the basis of region-wide proportions. Does this suggest the potential to expand a marketing linkage that would at once raise regional exports, increase employment in agricultural marketing, increase farm household incomes in the subarea, and increase income multiplication as a result of increased spending by these farm households? The matter would seem worthy of further investigation.

But this may not be simply a maize marketing linkage question. Examples of important linkages at work or not at work in this case may be affinity group trade patterns; market information communications; financial services networks and consumer trade patterns (in some areas farm commodities are used as a form of cash reserve for acquiring daily household needs); other commodity trade linkages (the maize may be used for livestock feed and the livestock in turn traded through unregistered channels); and more, including, of course, transport linkages. How does the analyst know where to begin?

And then, the intraregional analyst does not have the luxury of viewing the region as a single entity, as a single point at which flows originate or terminate. In most regions there is a relatively large number of subunits among which economically beneficial interactions occur or could occur. Which interactions among which subunits should be explored?

There is a tendency among regional analysts, especially those inclined to structural spatial analysis, to want to "document intraregional linkages" and then analyze the linkages as a means of identifying worthwhile development projects. But it is easy to see that documenting even just one major type of linkage or flow from among each category shown in Figure 12.1 among all subunits in a region would be a task requiring a major commitment of analytical resources (time, money, and staff). Much of the data collected would provide little more than a numerical representation of basic information that is already known. Furthermore, the question to be addressed in intraregional analysis for development planning is not where are there and where are there not different types of linkages and flows; rather, it is which are the linkages and flows that serve or could serve as important generators of regional income and employment, and how can they be improved or encouraged?

In addition to using preliminary exploratory analytical methods, the challenge of determining the types of interactions that should be investigated among selected subunits of the region can be met by formulating a series of leading questions. The questions should be organized under regional exports, intermediate imports, and consumer goods market categories; and they should be structured in hierarchical patterns that lead analysis from general to more specific issues. Figure 12.2 provides a sample list of leading questions that can be used as a starting point for developing a similar list for a particular region. The appropriate set of questions for any region will depend upon the composition of the region's economy, its interactions with other areas, and other unique characteristics.

Each level of question is addressed for all market categories before moving on to questions at the next level. As the answers to questions at each level are developed, the significance of the answers for purposes of development planning is assessed; the implications for reformulation of questions at the next level in more specific terms (or possibly for their elimination) are considered; the relationship of questions at each level to counterpart questions in the other categories is appraised; the usefulness of data in hand as against data that needs to be collected in the field is evaluated; and the types of linkages, flows, and friction factors that need to be investigated in progressively more detail on a priority basis can be determined.

In other words, the purpose of the leading questions is to move thinking through a process that systematically narrows and consolidates analytical focus on the actual and potential types of interactions among specific subunits in the region that are of priority concern. Generally, it will be found that this approach tends to direct analysis to a limited number of linkages and interactions among a limited number of places that figure significantly in all three types of markets. Once the linkage, flow, and friction studies have been completed, their results should be represented on maps as well as in other forms to the extent possible.

Figure 12.2
Sample Leading Questions to Help Guide Intraregional Interaction Investigations

Exports	**Level 1:** What are the regional exports actually and potentially very important in regional income and employment generation? **Level 2:** What are the major locations of production and points of exchange? **Level 3:** How and by whom are goods transferred among these points; through what mechanisms, with what information, and by whom are trade agreements reached; and on what infrsatructure, support service systems, and official administrative mechanisms do the exchanges depend? **Level 4:** What are the major bottlenecks and cost elements, for both buyers and sellers, between and at major points of exchange; and what are the major factors sustaining cost-inflating friction and otherwise threatening markets?
Intermediate Imports	**Level 1:** What are the regional imports representing a significant cost element in production processes that directly and indirectly account for major amounts of regional income and employment? **Level 2:** What are the locations of major points of exchange within the region? **Level 3:** How and by whom are goods transferred among these points; through what mechanisms, with what information, and by whom are trade agreements reached; and on what infrastructure, support service systems, and official administrative mechanisms do the exchanges depend? **Level 4:** What are the major bottlenecks and cost elements, for both buyers and sellers, between and at major points of exchange, and what are the major factors sustaining cost-inflating friction and the absence of cheaper sources of supply?
Consumer Goods	**Level 1:** What are the three imported and three locally produced types of consumer goods that account for the largest volumes of consumer sales in the region? **Level 2:** What are the locations of major intermediate and final points of exchange within the region? **Level 3:** How and by whom are goods transferred among these points, and on what infrastructure and support service systems do the exchanges depend? **Level 4:** What are the major bottlenecks and cost elements, for both buyers and sellers, between and at major points of change; and what are the major factors sustaining cost-inflating friction?

EXTENDED COMMODITY TRADE SYSTEMS ANALYSIS

The leading questions approach discussed above points the way to priority types of interactions among subunits of the region that should be investigated. There is an alternative approach that differs subtly yet significantly: extended commodity trade systems analysis. This approach is particularly well suited to regions with economies dominated by household agricultural production and related rural activities like fishing and the manufacture of wood products from local forest resources. Extended commodity trade systems analysis is based on the assumption that within major existing extended commodity trade systems are the critical linkages, flows, and friction factors that can be encouraged or overcome so as to increase regional multipliers, and perhaps returns from exports as well.

Extended commodity trade systems analysis does not aim at identifying general types of intraregional linkages and interactions that should be investigated. Rather, it is a method of intraregional analysis that involves documenting and analyzing specific intraregional extended commodity trade systems, defined in terms of their linkages, flows, and the factors impinging upon them. That is, under this method, intraregional linkages and flows are examined only in the context of and in relationship to specific extended commodity trade systems.

An *extended commodity trade system*, as the term is used here, refers to a concept that is somewhat different from that represented by the term *commodity marketing system*, which is used by agricultural marketing specialists, and with which it is sometimes confused. The latter encompasses the flows and functions from producer (most often a farm household) to final consumer in the marketing chain for a particular agricultural commodity. An extended commodity trade system covers the same flows and functions, but for the most part examines the marketing chain only as far as the first transaction that takes place beyond the borders of the region. And in addition to the marketing of a commodity, an extended commodity trade system covers input supply and uses of net income linked to production and sale of the commodity (hence, ''extended''). There are four basic steps in the analysis of extended commodity trade systems.

1. *Selecting key commodities*. Typically, extended commodity trade systems are explored for three to six key agricultural or other rural commodities in the region. Generally, *key* means these are the commodities from which the largest amounts of direct regional income are earned. A *commodity* may be an individual commodity or a group of closely related commodities grown and marketed by the same people in the same way (such as beans and maize in some cases) that only together constitute a major source of income.

Analysts may choose to designate a commodity as key for reasons other than the volume of direct income it generates in the region. For example, they may designate as key a commodity that predominates in a subunit of the region that would not be represented in trade system analyses for the other key commodities. Also, a commodity may be designated key that is not now a major income earner in the region, but that has significant growth potential; this would lead to examination of the linkages and flows that will have to expand and possibly become more efficient for the potential growth to be realized. Most often, key commodities can be designated on the basis of common knowledge about the region's economy, information already gathered for the basic statistical compendium, and/or published information from government statistical bureaus, extension services, marketing boards, cooperatives, and the like.

2. *Determining the essential outlines of the extended trade systems of the key*

commodities. As suggested earlier, an extended commodity trade system has three principal components:

—the commodity marketing chain in the region (including bulking, grading, storing, processing and other marketing-related functions);

—the marketing chains in the region for inputs to production and marketing of the commodity; and

—regional patterns of expenditure from net income associated with producing and marketing the commodity (these would be expenditures primarily for consumer goods and services, including daily household needs, public services, and consumer durable goods).

In this step, through discussions with appropriate people (farmers, traders, transporters, extension workers, and so on), the basic outlines of the principal trading chains and significant secondary chains in each of the three components are determined for each of the extended commodity trade systems.

The most important aspects of the basic outlines of trading chains determined in this step are;

—the major *transaction points* in the chains—locations where significant amounts of exchange (of commodities, inputs, and consumer goods) take place;

—the approximate relative volumes (of key commodities, inputs, and consumer goods) flowing between and through these locations in a typical year; and

—the people and institutions involved in these transactions.

Obviously, judgement needs to be exercised in figuring the appropriate level of detail for the basic outlines of the trading chains. For example, in terms of places, they cannot be taken to the level of individual farm households, and probably not to the level of individual villages, either. In terms of flows of goods, only major inputs and consumer goods categories can be considered.

A special word is in order concerning tracing the outlines of trading chains for consumer goods. The consumer goods trading chains to be traced in principal represent regional patterns of expenditure from net income associated with producing and marketing each of the key commodities. Quite commonly, consumer goods purchases are made from a general pool of household income, and cannot be associated with farm net income from one commodity or another. If this is the case in the study region, then consumer goods can be treated separately and generally, and need not be linked to individual extended commodity trade systems. In this case consumer goods might be categorized as food, personal items, personal services, public services, and consumer durables, and the basic outlines of their principal trading chains in the region determined.

But it is important that significant trading chains for major types of consumer expenditures be accounted for, because studies have shown that it is often in consumer goods trade that the larger part of regional income multiplication takes place. For this reason, too, it is important to determine if net revenues from certain kinds of farm commodities do in fact tend to be used for certain kinds of consumer purchases, and if so to link them to the extended commodity trade systems with which they are associated.

For example, in many countries women are traditionally responsible for certain crops and have control as well over the uses of net income from those crops. Frequently, expenditures by women have a higher regional income multiplication effect than expenditures by men because women tend to concentrate their expenditures more on food and small household goods and services made locally. As a result, the net income from the crops for which they are responsible will have the potential to generate more overall regional income; and the efficiency of the links in the trading chains for the types of goods they buy may have greater significance than others.

As another example, payment for certain types of farm commodities tend to be made in a small number of large payments over the course of a year, while payment for others is received in small regular increments. Often, so-called "lumpy" receipts are used for lumpy expenses like school fees and consumer durables, which may have low regional income multiplication effects. Hence, it is important to determine whether significant linkages exist between types of commodities and types of consumer expenditures, and to treat consumer expenditures in the manner most appropriate.

In any case, when the basic outlines of the several extended commodity trade systems have been determined, and if possible, mapped, an interesting—and convenient—finding is almost certain to be observed by the analyst. It is likely to be found that to a significant degree the same locations and routes, and many of the same institutions and categories of producers and traders, figure prominently in many, if not all, the extended commodity trade systems. This vastly simplifies the job of data collection and analysis.

3. *Documenting the extended trade systems*. On the basis of the trading chain outlines developed in the second step, the links to be documented are selected and studied. The links are the trading chain segments between and including transaction points. Surveys, public and private records, interviews, road counts, and other devices can be used for this purpose. The documentation should encompass as many of the categories of linkages shown in Figure 12.1 as possible and appropriate. The aim is to establish, for each important link, how it functions in terms of volumes and values of flows, people and institutions involved, capacity of infrastructure and capital equipment, administrative systems, and major friction factors and inefficiencies; and also, why it functions as it does. Because so many of the locations, routes, and other elements of the extended commodity trade systems will be shared, most of the data for all the systems can be gathered at the same places.

4. *Representing and analyzing the trade systems in terms of linkages, flows, and inhibiting factors*. Once the data are collected they are reordered and processed into descriptive analyses of the extended commodity trade systems (re-

ferred to as *horizontal* analysis). Again, to the extent possible, the systems should be documented on maps as well as in other forms. Finally, the data are reordered again into descriptive analyses of individual links (referred to as *vertical* analysis). These links are described in terms of the principal linkages, flows, bottlenecks, and inefficiencies that characterize them; and in terms of the implications of these for the operation of each extended commodity trade system.

The reason for first ordering the data as individual commodity trade systems (horizontal analysis) is to be able to detect the ramifications of the quality of one link on the performance of other parts of each system. This, in turn, provides important input to the vertical analysis. Indeed, at this last point in the analysis of extended commodity trade systems, observed close interdependencies among adjoining discrete links may make it appropriate to consolidate some of them into larger linkage segments for further analytical and planning consideration.

Chapter 13 contains additional discussion regarding extended commodity trade systems analysis. There the emphasis is on ways of analyzing the data for insights into regional income multiplication associated with the performance of specific links in trading chains as expressed through events at the transaction points that define them.

13

Intraregional Income and Employment Multiplication

Having considered methods for dealing with the characteristics of subunits of a region in Chapter 11, and then methods for dealing with the connections among those subunits in Chapter 12, we turn now to methods for analyzing how income and employment are multiplied through trade within and among regional subunits. In general, the more intraregional trade, the higher the regional income and employment multipliers; and the more dispersed that trade over the territory of the region, the more broad-based the income earning opportunities created by it.

This chapter deals first with intraregional economic base and accrual analyses. The main purposes of these types of analysis are to enable comparison of multipliers of different regional subunits and to improve the analytical understanding of how regional multiplier effects associated with different types of subunit export activities disperse themselves throughout the region. The second section of this chapter rounds out the input-output analysis discussion of Chapter 9 by introducing some additional considerations for using this type of analysis to explore intraregional interindustry effects. The final section introduces an analytical method called rural-urban exchange analysis, which builds on extended commodity trade systems analysis (discussed in the previous chapter) and also incorporates accrual analysis (discussed in the first section of this chapter). In combining two simpler methods and adding to them, rural-urban exchange analysis produces otherwise unobtainable insights into regional income multiplication associated with the operations of extended commodity trade systems.

ECONOMIC BASE AND ACCRUAL ANALYSIS

Economic base multipliers (discussed in Chapter 8), and especially the simpler varieties, can be computed for all of a region's subunits. For this purpose, the basic sector is considered to be composed of all exports from a subunit, including exports to other parts of the region. Economic base analysis can serve the same analytical functions for regional subunits as it does for the region in aggregate.

In addition, basic sector employment, nonbasic sector employment, and the base multiplier for all subunits can be arrayed in a table for intraregional comparison. Some regional analysts have even computed a *base multiplier location quotient* for each subunit, and included that in the table as well. The formula for this location quotient would be:

$$\text{Base multiplier location quotient} = \frac{\dfrac{\text{total employment in the subunit}}{\text{basic employment in the subunit}}}{\dfrac{\text{total employment in the region}}{\text{basic employment in the region}}} = \frac{\text{base multiplier for the subunit}}{\text{base multiplier for the region}}$$

A base multiplier location quotient less than 1 means that the base multiplier of the subunit is less than that of the region in aggregate; a base multiplier location quotient greater than 1 means that the base multiplier of the subunit is greater than that of the region in aggregate; and the distance from 1 in either direction is an indication of the discrepancy between subunit and regional base multipliers.

Comparing subunit base multipliers, or comparing estimates of subunit changes in total employment based on them, can be useful exercises in regional analysis. They can help highlight possible ''problem'' subunits of the region that should receive special attention because of weak internal multipliers. Comparison of subunit base multipliers with the regional base multiplier—that is, using the regional base multiplier as a standard of comparison—can also be a useful exercise. For example, the analyst might look for commonalities among all subunits with base multiplier location quotient values less than 1, and among all those with values greater than 1, in an effort to identify major factors that contribute to stronger or weaker localized employment multiplication effects.

Using base multipliers this way, however, should be done with great care and for preliminary indicative purposes only. It may have already occurred to the reader that the basic sector of a regional subunit has a different composition than the basic sector of a region. If subunit exports include exports to other parts of the region, then some of a subunit's basic sector is in the nonbasic sector of the aggregate regional economy.

Moreover, the economies of at least some regional subunits are likely to be even more open than the regional economy as a whole. As a result, subunit base multipliers can be quite misleading. For example, suppose a subarea of a region specializes in export crops, most of which are collected directly from farms by trucks that come from the country's central city outside the region. Farm households in the subarea spend most of their income in a relatively nearby regional town outside the subarea that specializes in servicing the consumer demands of surrounding agricultural zones. The base multiplier for the subarea would be very low, since total employment and basic employment would be nearly equal. The base multiplier for the town would also be relatively low, since there too total employment and basic employment (servicing farm households from outside the town) would be nearly equal.

True, problems of export definition could be addressed by conducting studies that allow for differentiation of multipliers associated with exports that go directly to markets outside the region, exports that go to markets outside the region but are traded through other subunits of the region, and exports to markets in other parts of the region. It is true also that problems of meaningful subunit definition for purposes of economic base analysis could be remedied by undertaking studies of intraregional commutation and spending patterns and using them to adjust boundaries of regional subunits for purposes of the analysis. But even then, there is no practicable way of linking up base multipliers among subunits to see how they interact, short of collecting the type of data needed for intraregional input-output analysis.

As a result, if the nature of the region, its subunits, and available data require these types of studies in order to compute meaningful subunit base multipliers, many analysts opt for a different approach to intraregional multiplier analysis. One approach is, of course, intraregional input-output analysis, discussed in the next section. An approach that usually involves less extensive data collection and processing is *accrual analysis*. Accrual analysis examines what types of income accrue and where within the subunit and elsewhere in the region in association with final sales of major subunit exports. It thus provides rough indications of income and employment multiplication effects associated with these exports.

Imagine that in Subarea S of Region R coffee beans are a major export ("basic") industry. The coffee is grown by farmers who deliver the beans to processing stations outside the subarea, from where it eventually moves to final market destinations. Farmers typically are able to keep 50 percent of their coffee sales revenues as net income; the remainder covers input costs. The 50 percent that pays for inputs breaks down into 35 percent for labor from other households in the subarea to help at picking and other critical times in the annual cycle; 5 percent for locally purchased implements and implement repair; and 10 percent for chemical inputs purchased elsewhere in Region R. This could be represented as shown in Figure 13.1.

The accrual summary gives an indication of the intraregional income and

Figure 13.1
Illustration of First Round Accruals: Coffee, Region R, Subarea S

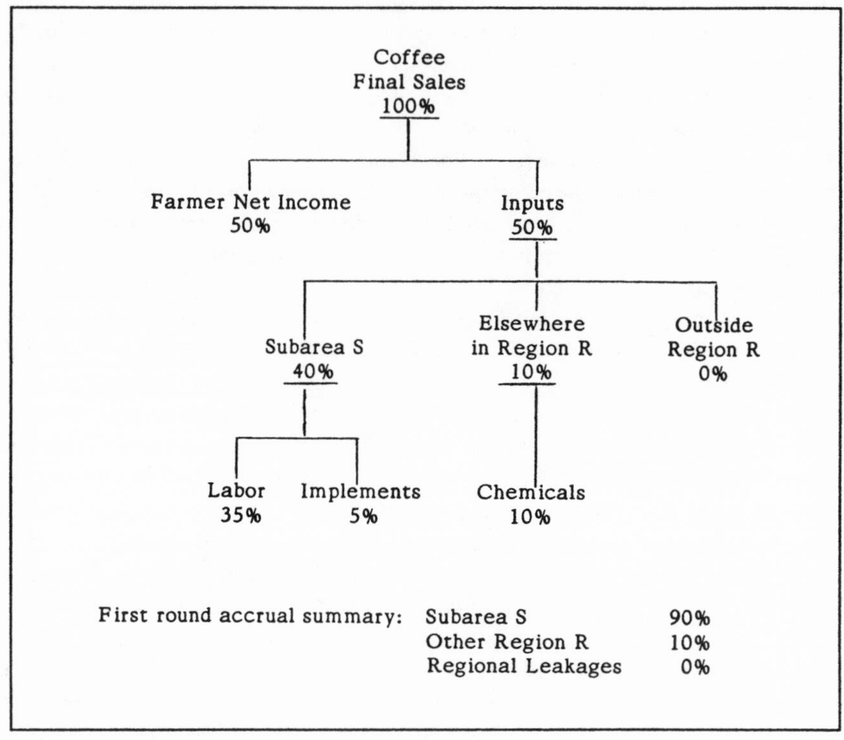

employment multiplication effects in terms of the distribution of first round income accruals from every unit of final sales of the export; but the distribution proportions should not be confused with actual multiplier ratios. The term *final sales* refers to final sales from the perspective of the subunit; in the case of the example, the final sale occurs when the coffee is delivered and the farmer is paid at the processing station outside the subarea. Even though Figure 13.1 appears to cover three rounds of distribution of final sales revenues, the three tiers in fact only represent breakdowns by location and type of expenditure of the first round of the distribution of revenues from final sales.

The accrual concept can serve as the basis for a structure of intraregional accrual analysis that can be either very simple or very extensive, in accordance with what is appropriate and possible in any regional situation. In its simplest form, a first round accrual analysis like the one illustrated in Figure 13.1 can be carried out for the single most important export in each subunit of the region. Alternatively, a larger number of significant subunit exports can be covered. In that case, the first round accruals could be weighted to reflect each export's proportion of total exports and then added together to produce summary figures for subunit export sales in aggregate.

Using the same sort of weighting technique, first round accruals could be tabulated separately for export sales directly to markets outside the region, sales to markets outside the region but that are traded through other subunits of the region, and sales to markets elsewhere in the region. This would allow intraregional accrual analysis to be linked with aggregate regional export data so that intraregional diffusion of first round accruals from regional exports can be determined.

On the input side, instead of "elsewhere in the region," inputs can be traced to other specific regional subunits. And of course, documentation could be carried out to the second round of inputs. Stopping at the first round will tend to overstate the significance of accruals relative to actual income earned in the region. In the illustration of Figure 13.1, for example, it is a good guess that some of the implements sold in the subarea were imported from elsewhere, and that most or all of the chemicals originated outside the region. Carrying documentation to the second round of inputs brings accruals closer to actual income earned. Field experience suggests that in most regions after two rounds, accruals are extremely close to actual income; and given the usually rough nature of the data in any case, going beyond two rounds is hardly ever warranted. All this is not to suggest, however, that limiting the analysis to one round of inputs (a more challenging task) is not a worthwhile exercise, especially for intraregional comparative purposes.

Rough as it appears in comparison with input-output analysis, for what it is intended to provide, accrual analysis (if taken to the second round of input supplies) is more accurate. That is because input-output analysis uses only first round data (direct inputs, or requirements) as the basis for computing what in effect are the multipliers for total interindustry transactions, as illustrated in Table 9.3, whereas in accrual analysis, proportions of inputs from different sources are documented directly as associated with the export sales of particular industries in particular regional subunits.

The results of accrual analysis can be displayed in tables and maps such that discrepancies in subunit and intraregional multiplication effects among different subunits, and also among different types of exports, are highlighted. Analysis of these discrepancies leads to an improved understanding of factors that play and can play central roles in income and employment multiplication within and among subunits of the region, and in turn, an indication of measures that would enhance those factors. An important quality of accrual analysis is that it can be a relatively simple method of analysis that produces very informative findings. But as much complexity can be built into it as desired. Indeed, at some point the data collection and processing involved can equal and even exceed that associated with intraregional input-output analysis.

INPUT-OUTPUT ANALYSIS

The material in Chapter 9, including interregional input-output analysis and supplementary analytical tools and shortcuts, applies here as well, and the fol-

Figure 13.2
Intraregional Input-Output Interindustry Quadrant Format

		Intermediate Purchasers															Final Purchasers
		Subunits															
		A					B					C					
Intermediate Suppliers		Industries					Industries					Industries					
Subunits	Industries	1	2	3	4	5	1	2	3	4	5	1	2	3	4	5	
A	1																
	2																
	3																
	4																
	5																
B	1																
	2																
	3																
	4																
	5																
C	1																
	2																
	3																
	4																
	5																
Primary Suppliers																	

lowing discussion deals only with additional considerations for intraregional input-output analysis.

For intraregional purposes, the input-output interindustry quadrant is set up with regional subunits adjacent to each other from left to right along the top, and in the same order from top to bottom along the left side. The list of intermediate industries is repeated under each subunit along the top, and in the same order for each subunit along the left side. The intraregional interindustry quadrant is illustrated in Figure 13.2. Unlike in interregional input-output analysis, the intraregional interindustry quadrant is not dog-legged. In intraregional analysis the analyst is interested in transactions and interdependencies among all subunits.

To the right of the interindustry quadrant along the top, final purchaser categories within each regional subunit are listed in turn. To the right of these are columns for consolidated regional final purchases and for export final purchases. Similarly, below the interindustry quadrant along the left, primary supplier (final payment) categories within each regional subunit are listed in turn; and these are followed by rows for consolidated regional primary suppliers and for import primary suppliers.

Clearly, collecting transactions data for intraregional input-output analysis could be an enormous task. In most cases, neither the quality of data that can be obtained nor the purposes for conducting the analysis make it appropriate or necessary to deal with all industry categories in all subunits individually. The best course is to define, for purposes of the analysis, two to four regional subunits that together cover the entire region. One common approach is to subdivide the region into only two "subunits": urban areas and nonurban areas. If there is a major city in the region, it might be separated out into a third subunit. If there are two rural zones with very different economic bases, they might also be treated separately.

Also, in most cases it is sufficient to aggregate intermediate industries into three to six principal categories, using the major-minor method to aggregate minor categories of economic activity. Alternatively, the analysis can be performed on a partial basis, covering only industries of particular analytical interest. For example, the analysis might include only the three major industries (or agricultural commodities in rural areas), plus another that is not now major but appears to have considerable growth potential. Moreover, transactions estimates for the study year can be based on key informant, published, and sample survey information rather than universe surveys.

Intraregional input-output data are processed essentially the same way as aggregate input-output data. Although geographic subdivisions have been introduced into the analysis, the tables don't "know" this; they "view" the columns and rows of the interindustry quadrant as though they represented a long list of individual industries, the same as in aggregate analysis. Still, the effort is usually worthwhile even if the analysis is carried no further than the computation of direct requirements coefficients.

Input-output analysis can provide insights into the intraregional interindustry and income multiplication ramifications of final demand for the region's products, which are extremely valuable for development planning. It should not be precluded only because the associated effort of data collection appears overwhelming. The job of the analyst is not so much to find the data to perform the analysis "properly" as it is to adapt the analysis to the needs of the regional planning situation and the data that can be obtained with reasonable effort.

RURAL-URBAN EXCHANGE ANALYSIS

Rural-urban exchange analysis builds directly on extended commodity trade systems analysis (discussed in Chapter 12) to provide indications, through accrual analysis (discussed in the first section of this chapter), of how income earned directly through extended commodity trade systems is multiplied further in the region.

Rural-urban exchange analysis is best suited for rural areas where most of the population is engaged in agricultural production and other rural industries. It is called rural-urban exchange analysis because, while the production of key commodities is rural-based, usually on farms, most of these commodities are marketed in or through towns. Also, most inputs to rural industries (other than harvested commodities in the cases of nonfarm industries) and consumer goods originate in towns or are marketed through them. Thus, the essence of the extended commodity trade systems and the income multiplication associated with them is rural-urban exchange, or trade. But of course, extended commodity trade systems can go beyond just rural-urban trade to include urban-urban trade as well. Urban-urban trade is also encompassed by rural-urban exchange analysis, as appropriate to the extended commodity trade systems being explored.

The first two steps in rural-urban exchange analysis are the same as for extended commodity trade systems analysis: selecting key commodities and determining the essential outlines of their extended trade systems, as described in the previous chapter.

But there are important differences starting with the third step, documenting the extended commodity trade systems. In rural-urban exchange analysis too, because so many of the locations, routes, and other elements will be the same for all the extended commodity trade systems studied, most of the data for all of them can be gathered at the same places. These places are primarily the principal *transaction points* that articulate each significant trading chain associated with each extended commodity trade system. In the case of rural-urban exchange analysis, however, the emphasis is not on gathering information to document linkages between transaction points as such. Instead, at each transaction point, types of information are collected that will enable measurement and understanding of the commodity trade system incentives and responses at work. Under ideal circumstances, this would include information on:

—the location and its physical qualities;
—frequency of trading;
—sellers;
—buyers;
—prices;
—price margins (value added);
—typical form of payment;
—uses of income;
—quantities typically traded;
—quantity traded annually; and
—other factors influencing the character and efficiency of exchange.

A price margin is an important key to how much "new" income is earned and how much income is multiplied as a result of the activity that takes place at a transaction point. A price margin is the increase in price between one transaction point and the next: the difference between cost of goods sold and selling price, or the markup or value added. The price margin at each transaction point is made up of the cost of inputs (other than the commodity itself) for the trade, processing, bulking, storing, onward transportation, or whatever the seller does at the transaction point; and the seller's net income, or profit.

To assess income multiplication effects, income represented by the price margin at each transaction point would ideally be documented as to its distribution between inputs and net income; and in turn, among expenditures from net income; and then, for inputs and expenditures from net income, among expenditures in the various regional subunits and expenditures outside the region. In other words, ideally, data would be collected enabling documentation of first round accruals, including accruals from consumer expenditures associated with net income generated in the commodity trade system at the transaction point. If at all possible, research should be extended to second round accruals from these first round expenditures.

The fourth step, analysis of the data, is similar to the fourth step of extended commodity trade systems analysis in that first *horizontal*, and then *vertical* analysis is undertaken. But in this case, the vertical analysis focusses on the transaction points rather than the links between them. The basic question guiding vertical analysis is this: What opportunities are there for increasing returns to producing and marketing the key commodities through improvements in rural-urban exchange systems, and what opportunities are there for expanding regional income multiplication from agricultural marketing, purchasing agricultural inputs, and spending net income from production and marketing?

In addressing this question, the analyst looks for indicators of possible development intervention (project) opportunities. Such indicators at any transaction point would include:

—low productivity;

—high input prices;

—low producer prices;

—high price margins;

—high differentials between the price at the last transaction inside the region and the price of a commodity in its final form at its final market outside the region; and

—low income multiplication effects, as indicated by first and preferably second round accruals.

The indicators are uncovered by comparing quantities of product, prices, price margins, and income accrual at different transaction points within an extended commodity trade system and among extended commodity trade systems. If possible, they may also be compared with similar measures prevailing elsewhere in the country and with other standards.

As with other methods of regional analysis, rural-urban exchange analysis should be adapted to the situation of a particular region and the development planning process being pursued. This is done by carefully considering and selecting commodities, places, the extent of the trading chains, and the level of detail for which information is collected. Properly adapted to regional circumstances, analytical needs, research time and money available, and data that can be obtained with reasonable effort, rural-urban exchange analysis can lead, more than many other methods of analysis, directly to indications of potential opportunities for development projects.

14

Settlement System Analysis

We turn now to methods for analyzing the components of a region's settlement system and the system as a whole. Literally speaking, the settlement system of a region includes farms and villages as well as urban places. But by convention, the term has come to refer to the network of regional towns, their functions, and their relationships to their hinterlands; and that is what is meant in this case.

Chapter 11 discussed methods for exploring and presenting characteristics of regional subunits, including urban places. Chapter 12 concerned itself with the linkages among those subunits, which express themselves largely as linkages among the urban places in those subunits. Chapter 13 dealt with methods for exploring income and employment multiplication that result from trade among places in a region—trade between rural and urban places, and trade among urban places. So a great deal relevant to the subject of this chapter has already been covered.

What remains are methods aimed at analyzing urban places in terms of their unique functions and links as urban places, not just as regional subunits like other regional subunits. In Chapter 2 there was a discussion of the special roles of towns in regional economies and in regional economic growth. That discussion emphasized town roles in terms of demand, supply, and trade. This chapter echoes that theme through the organization of its three sections.

The first section presents methods for analyzing access to urban places and the functions found in them; that access is essential if the need for urban economic activities is to be translated into effective demand. The second section presents methods for analyzing the functions—the supply of activities—currently found in towns of the region's settlement system. The third section introduces market center studies, methods that explore the roles of towns in regional trade. Although the sections are organized to reflect different aspects of a region's settlement system, the reader will quickly find that the intertwining of these aspects reflects itself in strong connections among the methods of analysis presented.

The methods of settlement system analysis in this chapter in fact represent but a small portion of the full catalog of such methods in common use. This is because many of those in common use result in findings that are interesting to spatial analysts and scholars, but not very useful for the sort of practical, locally based regional development planning with which this book is concerned.

Examples of types of methods of settlement system analysis not covered here include those comparing the regional settlement hierarchy with normative models; those that develop overall regional indexes of settlement dispersion; those that second-guess market forces by, for instance, estimating population concentrations necessary to support certain economic functions; and those that assess settlements by degree of modernization or another arbitrary standard. These types of methods are of use only if the essential question being addressed is, how far removed is the settlement system from the way it "ought" to be? They contribute little, if anything, to addressing the practical development questions of the nature of the settlement system, how it works, and what modest interventions would allow it to better fulfill its role in the regional economy.

Some of the methods discussed in this chapter require the use of maps. Even when this is not the case, the findings of the methods presented generally lend themselves to display on maps as well as in other forms. Map displays always enhance communication of the development messages embodied in the findings of intraregional analysis.

ACCESS STUDIES

Perhaps the simplest way of creating a description of relative levels of access to towns, or "central places" in a region, is through use of a *connectivity quotient*, computed as follows:

1. For each urban place, determine the shortest transportation distances to every other urban place in the region, and add them together;
2. Sum the totals for all urban places, and divide by the number of urban places, producing a regional average; and
3. Divide the total for each urban place by the regional average—a quotient less than 1 implies better-than-average connectivity between that town and other towns, a quotient greater than 1 implies worse-than-average connectivity, and the distance from 1 indicates the severity of the deviation from average connectivity.

A connectivity quotient computed for each urban place as described above is of little value. To convert the quotient to an analytical tool that provides insights into relative levels of access of regional towns, it should be computed in several different ways.

The first question the analyst must address is which "urban places" to include in the analysis. The answer, of course, depends on the regional situation and what the analyst is seeking from the analysis. One can select places to be included on the basis of population size; one can include only known market centers; one can include only major towns with significant connections to larger cities outside the region (thereby concentrating on the access of smaller towns to those "export centers"); and so on.

The analysis could also be restricted to certain types of settlement system relationships. For example, one could limit it to the distances between lower-order farm produce collection centers and higher-order agricultural bulking centers. Or, the region could be subdivided for purposes of the analysis into subunits, each representing approximate spheres of influence of one larger town, and the analysis could be carried out for distances between each larger town and the smaller towns surrounding it. Likewise, the analysis could be carried out for each regional market town relative to the agricultural villages surrounding it.

The second question the analyst must address is how to measure distance. The answer is, connectivity quotients should be computed using several different measures of the shortest transportation distance. There is distance in kilometers along paved roads, along paved or all-weather roads, and along any road. There is distance in terms of time, in terms of cost, and in terms of other measures of the level of transportation service available, such as a combination of frequency and cost. There is time, cost, and level of transportation service as relates to the transportation of people, the transportation of small lots of produce, and the transportation of bulked produce; also, as relates to perishable produce, nonperishable produce, and manufactured goods.

After the connectivity quotient has been computed in several different ways as appropriate for the situation, the totals as well the quotient for each place, computed in each of the different ways, can be arrayed in a table for comparative analysis. Supplementary tables can be developed that display the rankings of urban places under the different connectivity quotient approaches. The ranking scores can be adjusted to reflect not just the order but also the approximate degree of variance among the places. For example, if there are five towns, the difference between the lowest and the highest can be divided into a scale of 20 standard units; then, the least connected can be given a score of 1, the most connected a score of 20, and the other three would have scores between in accordance with their standing on the scale.

Connectivity quotients for each town can be added together and divided by the number of different kinds of quotients computed to produce average quotients for each place. Weights reflecting importance for various analytical purposes can be assigned to connectivity quotients computed on different bases, or to the rankings associated with them, so that composite quotients or ranking scores can be derived for each town.

The ultimate aim is to use the simple connectivity quotient as a basis for

Figure 14.1
Simple User Origin Analysis Table Format

Town	Percent of Users from Outside Town	Maximum Distances for Outside Users			
		Nearest 25%	Nearest 50%	Nearest 75%	100%
Town A Town B Town C Town D Town E : :					

developing meaningful indications of relative access among urban places in the region. These indications take on more analytical usefulness when considered in light of the principal functions of each urban place and of other places to which it is connected, and also in light of the principal economic activities of the rural area surrounding each urban place. The basic question being addressed is the extent to which difficulty of access appears to inhibit trade among certain places within the region because it results in costs that offset the economic efficiencies normally provided by networks of urban centers.

Another approach to developing indications of access to central places in the regional settlement system is to conduct a *user origin analysis* based on selected functions provided by each town. This involves selecting one to four key types of functions for each town—food retailing, produce bulking, consumer dry goods retailing, farm equipment repair, small-scale manufacturing, education, medical care, and so on, as appropriate for the town and the principal analytical concerns; and then conducting surveys of users of these functions to determine how far they travel to avail themselves of the services.

The surveys are conducted in the towns at the shops, stalls, workshops, and public buildings where people come for the services. Care needs to be taken to survey a representative sample of users by accounting for market and nonmarket days, perhaps seasonal variations, and other factors bearing on travel and shopping patterns. When user origin analysis is done in its simplest form, all the survey data are combined for each town and arrayed in a table like the one illustrated in Figure 14.1.

The first column to the right of the list of towns provides a clear indication of the extent to which people outside the towns make use of the functions relative to their use by people who live in the towns. The next column to the right shows the maximum distance traveled to make use of the service among the 25 percent of out-of-town users surveyed who come from points nearest to the town.

Again, the basic data can be manipulated in a variety of ways to assist comparative analysis. Finer gradations of percentage categories can be used; median or average distances can be derived for each town and for each percentage category; quotients based on regional averages can be calculated; weights can be assigned to different functions, and the weighted average distances shown in the table; and unweighted and weighted rankings can be developed. Most important, a companion table can be assembled in which the columns represent distance gradients—say, 5 kilometers, 10 kilometers, 15 kilometers, and so on—and shown in the body of the table would be the proportions of out-of-town users coming from within each gradient.

Even with enhancements, this simple approach can be somewhat analytically unsatisfying for several reasons. Undertaken as described above, different functions serve as the basis for user origin surveys in different urban places, raising questions of comparability. To address this, the analysis can be undertaken for different size or general functional categories of towns, using the same functions as the basis for analysis of all towns in each category. Separate tables and maps would be prepared for each category.

Still another approach would be first to determine major functions to serve as the focus of analysis. Functions would be characterized by both nature and scale: major consumer marketplaces and secondary consumer marketplaces, for example. User origin surveys for each function would be conducted in urban places where the function is found. Tables and maps would be prepared for each function, showing the distance ranges for towns where the function is found.

The surveys described so far relate user distance traveled to a particular town function. But we know that people do not necessarily travel from their homes solely to take advantage of a particular service in a particular place, and that ease of access is not the only factor in their travel and shopping patterns. They may avail themselves of a service offered in a certain town because they needed to visit the town anyway for other services offered there; they may take advantage of services offered in a town because they are passing through as part of a longer journey with other principal objectives; they may incur extra access costs as a tradeoff for better prices; and so on. Moreover, *access* means different things to different people, depending on the transportation routes and services available to them; alternative sources of the town service they seek; household sizes and gender and age roles, and therefore how much labor can be spared from other duties for travel to urban places; and other factors.

These sorts of considerations can be accounted for through more extensive user origin survey questionnaires and analysis of the data they produce. For purposes of development planning analysis, it is especially useful to collect information not only by distance, but also by cost and time as related to specific routes of travel. Maps and tables can then be compiled reflecting access along specific routes to specific places and functions, and these, in turn, can be evaluated in light of connectivity quotient computations. The ultimate aim of the analysis is to compare relative levels of access to each urban place and its functions, and also to determine if there are important gaps in access to places and functions that impede intraregional trade in ways that may be cause for development concern.

FUNCTIONAL ANALYSIS

In some cases the urban places in a region may never have been looked at as a *settlement system* before, and a relatively simple analytical starting point is needed. Developing a *settlement typology scheme* can serve as that starting point. A settlement typology scheme is nothing more than a characterization of the urban places in a region according to their principal economic functions. The simplest approach is to identify the three to five types of activities—retail trade, crafts, manufacturing, transportation services, mining, agricultural marketing, personal services, and so on—that represent the top categories of employment in each town. Codes are assigned to each type of activity. On a map of the region the three to five codes for each town are placed over its location, in descending order of amount of employment. The map can be accompanied by a table showing actual employment figures and location quotients for the top activities in each urban place, or it may be possible to show them directly on the map.

If the top activities in a particular place are of an administrative (government, cooperative center, headquarters offices) or public service (health, education, extension) nature rather than what may be commonly thought of as an economic activity, that should be indicated. Anomalies like a major economic activity with little employment should be represented and explained in a footnote. Population figures should accompany the other data as an indication of the size of each urban center.

The principal aim of this simple exercise is to characterize the regional settlement system in terms of the dominant functions and their orders of magnitude in its central places. But having gone this far, one could take the next step and develop a more informative picture of the region. This more informative picture would begin to point more clearly to actual and potential systemic linkages and relationships, and suggest to the analyst matters that need to be pursued through other methods. For this purpose the map could be further developed by highlighting key transportation routes connecting the urban places, indicating zones of dominant crops or other rural activities in the areas surrounding each town, and perhaps showing connectivity quotient and user origin ranges derived from access studies for each town.

The most common method employed in settlement system functional analysis is the *settlement function scalogram*. This is a matrix, as illustrated in Figure 14.2, in which the urban places of the region are listed along the left in descending order of population; typically, the population of each town is shown along with its name. The array of functions found in urban places is shown along the top of the matrix. An *X* is placed in each matrix cell where the function represented by that column is found in the urban place represented by the intersecting row.

Figure 14.2
Illustration of a Settlement Function Scalogram

Urban Places	Urban Functions												
	1	2	3	4	5	6	7	8	9	10	11	12	13
Town A	X	X	X	X	X	X	X	X	X	X	X	X	X
Town B	X		X		X	X	X		X		X		X
Town C	X				X		X			X			
Town D		X		X		X	X	X	X				
Town E	X						X		X				X
Town F			X				X						
Town G	X				X		X	X	X				X
Town H	X						X						

Figure 14.3
Illustration of a Triangulated Settlement Function Scalogram

Urban Places	Urban Functions												
	7	1	9	13	5	3	6	8	10	2	4	11	12
Town A	X	X	X	X	X	X	X	X	X	X	X	X	X
Town B	X	X	X	X	X	X	X					X	
Town D	X		X				X	X		X	X		
Town G	X	X	X	X	X			X					
Town C	X	X			X				X				
Town E	X	X	X	X									
Town F	X					X							
Town H	X	X											

Information for the scalogram is obtained by surveys or key informant interviews if not available from published sources.

The settlement function scalogram is normally triangulated to facilitate interpretation. This involves shifting columns and rows until the *X*s form a pattern as close as possible to a triangle extending out from the "northwest" corner. The result of triangulation is to reorder the list of urban places in descending order of numbers of functions, and simultaneously to reorder the list of functions in descending order of frequency of appearance in urban places. Figure 14.3 shows the triangulated form of the Figure 14.2 matrix.

The order of towns in the triangulated scalogram suggests a rough settlement hierarchy pattern. The pattern that emerges overall will probably not surprise anyone familiar with the region. Of special concern, however, are the linkages among the urban places in relation to their relative functional roles, access to functions at different levels, and gaps and "stray" Xs in the triangular pattern. The first can be explored by comparing and analytically combining the settlement function scalogram with the results of linkage and related studies; the second can be explored by comparing and analytically combining the scalogram with the results of access studies; and the third can be addressed by special investigations to determine the reasons behind the gaps and strays, and the implications, if any, for the efficiency of intraregional trade.

While the settlement function scalogram produces an overall picture of the region's settlement system functions that is informative in its own right, its ultimate analytical use is in the context of analysis to determine whether there is a supply of services most efficiently provided in urban areas that is adequate, sufficiently dispersed, and sufficiently accessible; and if this does not appear to be the case, why not. Adequate, sufficiently dispersed, and sufficiently accessible means that the functions support exploitation of the comparative advantages of the region's subareas, and in doing so provide a network of services that fosters intraregional trade and multiplication of income and employment.

Extracting the full analytical value from settlement function scalograms may require constructing them in several different ways, and in any event using an approach somewhat more complex than described above. For one thing, as described above, an X represents a function or service, without regard to the number of establishments in a place that provide the service or the scale of the service. A modest farm implement supply shop in a lower-order town is granted the same X for "farm implement supply" as the concentration of a dozen larger implement supply shops in the major regional urban center. Yet the nature of the functions in the two places would be significantly different, and the differences would be important for regional analysis purposes.

For this and other reasons the regional analyst needs to give careful consideration to the list of functions used in the scalogram. The functions covered can be defined in terms of scales within functional categories, with different scales of the same activity appearing as separate "functions" in the scalogram. Scales of activity may be differentiated by type of structure (shop or market stall) or other objective characteristic, or on the basis of judgement as to whether they are "large" or "small." In the body of the matrix, instead of an X, the number of establishments or employment can be shown in the cells; and this can be taken into account in shifting the rows and columns to form a hierarchical pattern.

Scalogram functions obviously can be defined broadly or in terms of very discrete activities. In fact, the very concept of *function* needs to be carefully considered for scalogram purposes. The analysis would naturally cover what are commonly understood as economic activities, but public service and administrative activities could be included as well. Different types of infrastructure could also be considered functions, as could individual aspects of what are often thought of as single functions: deposit and credit services instead of just financial services, for example. The more detailed the list of functions, the more cumbersome the processes of assembling and analyzing the scalogram. But also, the more detailed the list of functions, the more insight can be gained concerning functions that tend to appear in clusters or to be associated with certain types of infrastructure or public services at different levels of the settlement hierarchy.

On the other hand, the analyst may choose to limit the scalogram to a small number of functions reflecting special analytical concerns. For example, in a rural region, scalogram functions might be limited to different types of agricultural extension, input, and marketing services. Or the scalogram might be employed to analyze the distribution of different types and scales of transportation services in the region. Or a small number of key functions representative of basic types of services determined to be needed at all levels of the settlement hierarchy might be selected for scalogram analysis.

Further specific focus can be brought to scalogram analysis through the selection of urban places. Separate scalograms using different lists of functions can be assembled for towns of different size classes or towns with known different overall characters—local market towns, warehousing and transport centers, administrative centers, and manufacturing centers, for example. Or a first broad scalogram analysis can be used to categorize towns into groups representing different levels of functional diversity, and then more detailed analyses can be undertaken for each of these groups.

Since so many variations are possible on the settlement function scalogram theme, it is a good idea to consider in advance just how this method will be used in conjunction with other intraregional analysis methods. In other words, careful thought should be given to the specific analytical need that can best be served by scalogram analysis, and to how the analysis should be designed to serve that need.

MARKET CENTER STUDIES

Places in a region that serve as significant marketing centers will likely already be known to local regional analysts and planners. If not, they can be identified through other methods of intraregional analysis, such as the functional analysis methods presented above. Assessing the commodity, spatial, and institutional trading patterns associated with market centers provides important information on trade efficiencies and on trade-inhibiting inefficiencies in the region, and therefore can suggest possible measures for facilitating greater intraregional trade.

In what follows, two different approaches to market center studies, both based on field survey work, are described. The presentations are made in general terms, and it is left for the analyst to select and adapt from these approaches in accordance with the regional situation and analytical needs. At the risk of repetition it is emphasized yet again that careful forethought should be given to the number and levels of market centers encompassed in the study, the level of detail regarding traded goods and other market center characteristics, and the specific objectives of the study in relation to principal analytical concerns and other methods of intraregional analysis employed.

The first approach is the more common one. It goes by many different names, but is essentially a *market center trade* study. In this type of study, the emphasis is on the overall characteristics of the market center, of the goods traded there, and of participants in the trading conducted there. The approach is best described in terms of the five broad types of information collected and analyzed for each market center included in the study.

1. *Overall market characterization*. Whether the market is periodic or permanent; if permanent, whether there are certain types of trade that only take place on certain days; if periodic, the schedule of market days. Land area of the market; portion paved; portion under cover; number of open air trading enterprises, number of stalls, number of shops; vehicle access and parking facilities; quality and nature of access roads; overall physical character; physical deficiencies. Entity administering and managing the market; personnel assigned and their duties; fees, licenses, and fines; annual public revenues generated. Whether the market is in a town; if so, name of the town, its size, and general character. Dominant types of trade (wholesale, retail, and major categories of each); associated bars, restaurants, and hotels; associated social facilities (parks, religious institutions, entertainment places, etc.); associated porterage and transportation services. Other features uniquely characterizing this market center.
2. *Trade volume*. Volumes of major goods and categories of secondary goods traded in a standard week, in both physical and money measures. Periodicity and seasonality of trade in certain goods or categories of goods, and associated deviations from standard week volumes.
3. *Inbound trade*. Points of origination of major goods and categories of secondary goods traded; routes and means of transportation; costs of transportation; major difficulties and cost factors in movement and trade; linkages to lower and higher order markets.
4. *Outbound trade*. Points of termination of goods traded for onward marketing; routes and means of transportation; costs of transportation; major difficulties and cost factors in onward movement and trade; linkages to lower- and higher-order markets.
5. *Buyers and sellers*. Typical number of sellers of different types of goods, in different types of structures, and retail or wholesale; number of retail and wholesale customers in a standard week; periodic and seasonal variations; types of people and institutions buying and selling; origins and access routes of buyers and sellers; linkages to other markets; major obstacles and costs of doing business in this market; nonmarket reasons for being at the location of this market.

The second approach involves *market center commodity linkage* studies, and is especially appropriate for regions where production and marketing of rural commodities predominates. This approach differs from the first in that it concentrates on flows and linkages through the market center, and also on income accruals associated with them. In other words, the focus in this case is more on how the market center fits into larger marketing chains and their patterns of income multiplication than it is on the characteristics of the center and the trade conducted there.

The surveys for market center commodity linkage studies are conducted with respect only to a small number of key commodities or types of goods traded in the center. *Key* means that these commodities or types of goods are the major ones traded, or are representative of major classes of commodities traded. As the reader may have guessed, this approach incorporates elements of extended commodity trade systems analysis, linkage and flow studies, accrual analysis, and rural-urban exchange analysis. Market center commodity linkage studies involve the following six steps for each of the market centers studied. The details of these steps are found in corresponding sections of other chapters of this book.

1. Identify the three to six key commodities or types of goods (for example, food or consumer dry goods) traded at the market center.
2. Track each commodity forward to the next transaction point and backward to the prior transaction point, even if they are outside the region.
3. For each commodity, collect market chain linkage data for the two market chain links, as described for extended commodity trade systems analysis.
4. For each commodity, collect transaction point data at the three transaction points, as described for rural-urban exchange analysis.
5. For each commodity, perform first round, and if possible second round, accrual analysis based on the three transaction points.
6. Combine the data on the separate traded commodities and analyze for an overall assessment of how the market center fits into larger marketing chains and their patterns of income multiplication; analysis should concentrate especially on market functions and inefficiencies, and on trade-inhibiting frictions and transaction costs embodied in forward and backward trade linkages.

Clearly, elements of the two approaches can be combined. Tables and maps can be developed from the survey data that show commodity flows, relative volumes of trade activity, linkages with other market centers, and other information, depending on the specific approach used. From these can be developed regional maps showing region-wide systemic relationships and friction factors among market centers in general, and also for many specific commodities. The information collected should fit in neatly with, and enhance the findings of, other methods of intraregional analysis being used.

IV

Methods of Project Identification and Evaluation

15
Project Identification

Analyzing the region in aggregate and intraregional terms has value in its own right. Whether or not there is a formal program of regional development planning, decisions are made daily by both the public and private sectors that influence the course of regional economic development. Regional analysis findings can provide politicians, government agencies at local and higher levels, regional representatives to provincial and national legislatures, trade organizations, businesses, educational institutions, and others in the area with information important to their work. The findings can also be used in documents providing basic information for potential new businesses in the area.

When there is formal regional development planning, structured regional analysis sometimes goes no further than the application of analysis methods like those described in Parts II and III of this book. On the basis of the insights provided by those methods, participants in the planning process simply "figure out" the specific regional development projects that need to be undertaken. Regional development planning is art, and no matter how accurate the data and how careful the analysis, in the end there must be a great deal of figuring out. But the figuring out can be done with more or less analytical structure. This chapter is for those who want more analytical structure.

What are the indicators of possible opportunities for project interventions provided by regional analysis findings? How do we move from indicators of possible project interventions to ideas for specific projects? How do we systematically examine these project ideas and refine them into an initial list of project proposals worthy of more detailed evaluation? The three sections of this chapter respond to each of these questions in turn. The following chapter is concerned with means for more fully evaluating and refining the initial list of project proposals.

Thus, the two chapters together offer suggestions for a single process of project identification and evaluation. The specific details of that process, of course, have to be tailored to the situation in each particular region and the nature of the planning exercise at work there. The last chapter in Part IV discusses benefit-cost analysis, which could be incorporated into the project identification and evaluation process as desired. In any case, the ultimate aim of the project identification and evaluation process is to end up with a limited set of practicable, high-priority project proposals that as much as possible represent a strategically considered package of development measures.

FORMULATING INDICATORS OF INTERVENTION OPPORTUNITY

The term *intervention opportunity* means *development project*. Although the former term is more cumbersome, and for that reason will not reappear hereafter, it has been used to introduce this discussion because it carries a message that the latter term does not. An intervention is any measure that introduces a new element into the physical, institutional, or policy environment of the region. The aim of a development intervention is to improve that environment so that human initiative and creativity can function to better advantage, and thereby create more employment, income, and wealth within the bounds of equity and long-term growth considerations.

Such measures represent opportunities—opportunities for increasing broad-based opportunities. To be properly identified, evaluated, and prioritized, development projects have to be seen and seized as intervention opportunities, not as "solutions to problems." The implicit question behind project identification and evaluation is, what measures are most likely to expand economic opportunity and democracy, and thereby to result in widespread improvements in human welfare in the region?

While the specifics of what this means will vary from region to region, most development opportunities will be found in the broad areas of increasing returns to regional exports and increasing income (and thereby employment) multiplication within the region. Returns from regional exports can be increased by measures leading to expanded volumes of exports or higher returns per unit of export—or, of course, both. Income multiplication can be increased by measures resulting in more local value added to goods traded in the region or more intraregional trade—or, of course, both. As it turns out, measures that promote increased returns from regional exports also often create opportunities for expanded regional income multiplication, and the other way around.

To identify opportunities for expanding returns from exports and increasing income multiplication, a framework of possible indicators of such opportunities needs to be formulated for the region. Let us take, as an example, a region in

Figure 15.1
Illustrative Project Opportunity Indicators for a Rural Region

Indicator of Project Intervention Opportunity	Opportunity to Expand	
	Returns from Exports	Income Multiplication
Low farm productivity	X	
High farm input prices	X	X
Low producer prices for agricultural commodities	X	
High trader price margins for agricultural commodities	X	
Large differences between the prices of agricultural commodities at the last transaction inside the region and their prices in their final forms at their final markets	X	X
Low levels of first round income accrual from farm household spending		X

which the major export earners are agricultural commodities. In this case, development planning would focus initially on projects that would create opportunities for increased farm production, for improved net revenues from farm products, for increased nonfarm value added to agricultural commodities, and for expanded trade between farms and towns and among and within towns of the region.

As the development planning process continues, all this will be increasingly translated into more specific terms, and other types of opportunities might come to light. But these broad categories are a reasonable starting point. Figure 15.1 shows what some of the indicators of these types of opportunities might be in the region. The indicators are key analytical findings that suggest possible opportunities for development projects that would improve them: that would raise indicators that are low and lower indicators that are high. Again, the list of indicators might be expanded as the planning process continues, but those shown represent a fair starting point. Figure 15.1 also shows whether the indicated opportunities are related to expanding returns from regional exports, to increasing regional income multiplication, or potentially to both.

Obviously, in regions that are more diversified, urbanized, or industrialized than the example, the starting list of indicators might be rather different. Whatever the case, a preliminary set of indicators of possible project opportunities should be formulated before regional analysis has been carried very far. The set of preliminary indicators can help determine the types of analysis most needed, their specific purposes, and how they should be adapted to the needs of the regional planning effort.

As regional analysis proceeds and more is learned about the region and its economy, the list of indicators is likely to undergo alteration, and certainly elaboration and refinement. When the analysis is complete, the set of project opportunity indicators provides a framework for effectively and succinctly summarizing key analysis findings and linking them directly to possible development project opportunities. While debate is always a part of the planning process, the use of explicit indicators of project opportunity helps introduce a measure of ordered reason, if not true objectivity, into the project identification process.

Sight should not be lost, however, of the fact that methods of regional analysis serve purposes that go beyond providing project opportunity indicator data. They are a means for developing an understanding of the overall operations and performance of the regional economy as a complex system of interconnected places, populations, and economic activities. Without an adequate grasp of this complex, the meaningful interpretation and use of specific indicators is not possible.

GENERATING PROJECT IDEAS

Having identified possible project intervention opportunities with the help of the indicators, the next challenge is to identify possible projects that would lead to the improvements in the indicators. This entails carefully considering the results of regional analysis to explore relationships such as those among sectors, between income and product, between income and exports, among all these in different places, and so on, to help determine the true origins of indicator values. It also entails considering factors in the *conditioning environment*. This is the environment of *externalities*, *nonquantifiables*, and *noneconomic factors* (such as were mentioned in Figures 1.2, 2.1, and 3.1 in Part I of this book) that condition the overall environment in which people make economic decisions.

Following are examples of eight types of factors in the conditioning environment that may not have been covered by common methods of regional analysis.

1. *Social structure and cultural characteristics:* social relations in which certain groups, through tradition, wealth, or political power, control access to key resources or economic functions in a region; cultural heterogeneity that may result in rivalries precluding constructive economic relations between certain groups in the region; and local cultural practices such as those regarding gender and age roles, kinship ties, occupational limitations, and religious values that influence the way people respond to economic incentives.
2. *Natural resource access and management:* practices and institutional mechanisms and relationships related to use, access, and management of natural resources, that bear on the ability of farmers and others to respond to economic incentives and to continue responding in a way that generates increased income on a sustained basis.
3. *Infrastructure:* attributes of the physical system that facilitate town-based activity and intraregional trade, and thereby influence the possibility and costs of trade.
4. *Available technology and skills:* technology and production processes, and associated

skills, employed by rural and town enterprises as they affect the nature and latitude of capabilities for response to economic incentives.

5. *Availability of inputs and consumer goods:* access to inputs, including labor, that affect the ability of rural and town enterprises to respond to economic incentives; and access to household goods and services that affect the desire to respond to incentives.
6. *Institutional arrangements:* a strong or weak government system that maintains roads and provides public services or does not; the structure of marketing operations that influence possibilities for income multiplication and the latitude for altered price incentives; operations and capabilities of nongovernmental and financial institutions; and the overall organization of different types of production.
7. *Macropolicies:* national commodity pricing, exchange rate, inflation, taxation, land tenure, enterprise, industrialization, parastatal, financial, regional development, and related policies that affect the latitude for prices to change and for production to change in response.
8. *Final market characteristics:* price elasticity, efficiency of market administration and management, current and expected world market conditions, and related factors in the final markets for important regional exports.

Generally, development projects will be aimed at altering factors in the conditioning environment. These alterations will be designed to expand economic opportunities. Response to these expanded opportunities will change the values of the indicators. The development planning effort will have been successful if future regional analysis shows the indicators to have changed for the better.

Project identification involves establishing the causal relationship between key factors in the conditioning environment and the values for the indicators of possible project opportunities, in light of what regional analysis suggests to be the true origins of those values. There is no fixed formula for doing this. In some cases, the causal relationships will be readily apparent and the needed development projects obvious. In other cases, specific investigations will clearly be needed to link the correct factors in the conditioning environment with indicator values. Quite often the collective wisdom of analysts, planners, and other participants in the planning process is sufficient to identify the principal factors at work, the changes in them that are needed, and the types of project activity required to bring those changes about.

However, in trying to identify the types of changes needed and the projects that might bring those changes about, it is helpful to bear in mind considerations that lend concreteness to the exercise. These considerations are spelled out in the second section of Chapter 3. They can be summarized as follows: The purpose of most regional development projects is to improve and expand the economic options available to the people of the region. This implies, above all, projects leading to improved efficiency in the operations of regional producer and consumer markets, including production for those markets. This, in turn, means an emphasis on projects, and on linked packages of projects, that reduce the costs of buying and selling in regional markets in which people participate, and that reduce barriers to entry, such as outright restrictions or lack of access to resources or technology, into markets in which people could be participating. This covers a very wide range of possible physical, institutional, policy, and other types of interventions in the regional economic environment.

In a spirit of brainstorming, a large number of project ideas should be invited. These should be placed in an unrefined starting list without judgement whether they are too large, too small, or too outlandish. Their practicabilities and relative utilities will be evaluated in due course.

CONDUCTING INITIAL PROJECT EVALUATIONS

Project proposals in the large starting list need to be evaluated initially through a process that is relatively quick and easy to carry out. This process should involve not just professional analysts and planners, but the broadest possible participation by members of the public, if possible acting through a structure of topical committees. The aim of the process is to develop and analyze information about each of the project proposals that will at once enable sorting out the highest-priority dozen or so proposals on the basis of both practicability and likely consequences. A secondary aim of the initial evaluation is to generate data needed to begin more detailed evaluations and initial project planning. Many proposals are likely to be eliminated at this stage because no one is willing to invest effort in their initial evaluation.

The best way to conduct the initial evaluation is to prepare, for each project proposal, an *initial project brief* describing:

—the proposed project;

—the requirements for its implementation and management

—the expected effect, preferably in terms of the indicators of project opportunity as well as other measures; and

—the mechanisms—the sets of linked places, activities, actors, incentives, and responses—through which the proposed project is expected to have its effect.

The project briefs should be prepared without extensive research, but based on the soundest estimates technically possible without such research.

The different types of project briefs that have been prepared in connection with regional development planning exercises cover a wide spectrum. In general, especially when there is a good deal of public participation in the planning process, they are found most useful when limited to a maximum of six pages, following a standard format to simplify comparison.

An easy way to structure the format is to formulate a list of standard initial evaluation questions to serve as headings for the text of the brief. Each question is answered briefly, including in most cases a cursory explanation. The text of the brief should not exceed five pages; if necessary, supplementary information

Figure 15.2
Illustrative Questions for the Initial Project Brief

Project Proposal Questions	Descriptors (as relevant)
1. <u>The Proposed Project</u>	
a. Working name of the project?	Name
b. How would you describe it in two sentences?	
c. Into what category does it fall?	
• infrastructure and other physical capital;	PC
• public and private institutions;	Inst
• public sector policies;	Pol
• other?	Other
d. Proposed location?	Place name
e. Overall scale?	Size measure
f. Areas, activities, groups targeted?	Names
2. <u>Implementation and Management Requirements</u>	
a. Formal feasibility/design study required?	Yes/no
b Amount of implementation funding required?	Money amount
c. Likely funding source?	Institution name
d. Source of implementation management?	Institution name
e. Source of operation management?	Institution name
f. Expected to be financially self-sustaining?	Yes/no
g. Adequate environmental resources available?	Yes/no
h. Complementary measures needed to ensure project success or reinforce intended effects?	Yes/no
3. <u>Expected Effects</u>	
a. Indicator of project opportunity addressed?	Indicator
b. Lower transaction costs?	Type, place
c. Reduced barriers to market participation?	Type, place
d. Increase returns to exports?	Type, place
e. Increase regional income multiplication?	Type, place
f. Public expenditure/revenue impacts?	Money amounts
4. <u>Mechanisms of Effect</u>	
a. Other places affected; how?	Names, how
b. Economic activities affected; where, how?	Names, places
c. Prices affected; where, how?	Names, places
d. Other incentives affected; where, how?	Names, places
e. Expected responses to the changes?	Types of behaviors
f. Project relationships to other planned or ongoing activities?	Names, locations

can be included in an appendix. The first or final page is reserved for summary *descriptors*—words, phrases, or numbers—representing the answers to each of the questions that lend themselves to summary in descriptor form. Figure 15.2 provides examples of questions that might be used to structure the initial project briefs, and also indicates the kinds of descriptors that might be used for the summary page.

In the course of assembling information for the initial project briefs, it is likely to be found that the most fundamental requisites for viability of some proposed projects do not exist. As a result, additional project proposals will be eliminated during the course of this work, and project briefs will not be completed for them.

The final step of initial project evaluation involves debate. For ready reference during this debate, descriptors for remaining proposed projects are assembled in a single matrix listing the questions along left and remaining project proposal names along the top. Proposals should be organized in groups representing infrastructure and other physical capital; public and private institutions and institutional performance; public sector policy reform; and other types of projects. While facilitating planning debate, the matrix, supported by the more complete information in the project briefs, helps perceive the possible relationships among project proposals. That is, it promotes considering potentials for putting together strategic project packages and encourages evaluating individual project proposals in this light.

The outcome of the debate is a much shorter list of project proposals to be subjected to the full project evaluation process discussed in the next chapter.

16

Project Evaluation

Project identification exercises, like those described in the previous chapter, clearly go somewhat beyond simply generating project proposals. These exercises conclude with a relatively short—that is, manageable—list of proposed regional development projects that have survived initial winnowing. The proposals now need to be further evaluated and the list further refined. Some of the proposed "projects," already at this early stage, may in fact be strategic packages of linked activities originally proposed as individual project ideas.

Just as project identification is more than just identification, so project evaluation is more than just evaluation. The final product sought from project evaluation exercises is a limited set of priority practicable proposed projects representing interventions in the regional economy. These are interventions that, based on the best information available, appear most likely to lead to important improvements in the way the economy operates and in the ability of the region's population to achieve a fitting living through that economy. As much as possible, the proposed projects should be justified within a framework of current regional economic relationships and strategic priorities. The projects should not only represent seizing the best opportunities for expanding the near-term economic options available to people, but as much as possible should be aimed at improving the fundamental economic dynamics of the region, so that continued expansion is self-sustaining.

In an effort to achieve this, project evaluation has three fundamental elements, represented by the three sections of this chapter. The first is individual project evaluation, which carries work begun in the project identification phase a good bit further. The second is comparative evaluation, which is also an extension of a type of work undertaken in a very preliminary manner in the project identification phase. The third is combined evaluation, which explores interrelationships within and the combined effects of the entire program of development activity represented by the project proposals that have survived to this point. Project evaluation stops short of final project technical and financial planning.

The elements of project evaluation need to be understood not just as different aspects of assessing the merits of project proposals, but also as a process of refining project proposals. It should not be surprising if the process results in a program of development activity only reminiscent of the starting list of project proposals.

INDIVIDUAL PROJECT EVALUATION

Individual project evaluation carries the work of initial project evaluation that was part of the project identification exercise into far greater precision and detail. If we refer back to Figure 15.2, dozens of subquestions come to mind regarding each of the initial evaluation questions: What would be the implementation timetable? Precisely who will do it? Where will the staff come from? How will it be paid for? What is the precise location? Is land needed, is it in hand, or is it available for sale? What are the precise cost components? What are the projected annual costs and revenues? How will the proposed project be maintained? Is there political support? What is the basis for estimates of transaction cost reductions? What is the basis for price change estimates? What is the basis for estimates of response to cost or price changes? And so on.

Obviously, one part of this is more extensively researched technical, financial, economic, and management analyses. In order to carry out these analyses each proposed project requires more precise definition than in the project identification phase. In turn, the precise specifications of each project will be further detailed and refined in the course of the analyses. For institutional and policy reform projects, and others that do not involve hardware (construction, machinery), the natures of the analyses will be somewhat different from those that do involve hardware. In all cases, detailed analysis should be undertaken not only with regard to implementing the activity, but also with regard to the expected economic performance consequences.

Owing to the different natures of project proposals, at this level of specificity the project analysis reports cannot be prepared according to standard formats, as was possible in the project identification phase. However, the reports can be organized on the same broad pattern. The best pattern is the one suggested by the discussion in Chapter 3: technical feasibility; financial and economic viability; environmental sustainability; and social, administrative, and political acceptability.

Moreover, certain elements of the analyses can be standardized, at least when relevant to the nature of the project. For example, in Chapter 11, several different approaches to natural resource assessments were presented. From the assessments

Figure 16.1
Example of an Employment Assessment Checklist:
Creating Opportunities for Local People Currently Unemployed

1.	Number of new local jobs expected to be directly associated with operation of the project:	________
2.	Number of new local jobs estimated to be created indirectly as a result of purchases connected with operation of the project:	________
3.	Number of new local jobs estimated to be induced by consumer purchases of the new employees:	________
4.	Estimated total number of new local jobs created (1+2+3):	________
5.	Number of local jobs estimated to be eliminated, directly and indirectly, by the project:	________
6.	Estimated net number of new local jobs created (4-5):	________
7.	Number of new jobs estimated to be seasonal:	________
8.	Number of new jobs estimated to be temporary:	________
9.	Number of new jobs estimated to be part-time:	________
10.	Number of new jobs for which current unemployed are qualified:	________
11.	Number of new jobs for which displaced workers would be qualified:	________
12.	Number of new jobs likely to be filled by current local residents (rather than newcomers or commuters):	________
13.	Number of new jobs likely to be filled by women:	________

can be developed an *environmental resources and hazards checklist*, specifying development-related concerns with regard to each major natural resource and hazard in the region as a whole and in each of its subunits. All project proposals can be evaluated against this checklist using standardized reporting procedures. This, of course, would not substitute for more extensive analysis of environmental sustainability which is needed for some project proposals.

Also, there may be special concerns in the region for which standard *special purpose assessment checklists* can be developed for use with all project proposals. More and more, for example, development projects are being closely scrutinized for their impacts on energy consumption, traffic congestion, public service provision, and waste generation. Sometimes the special concerns may be directly related to the nature of economic expansion. Figure 16.1 is an example of a special purpose assessment checklist that has been used in several regional development planning efforts in the United States. In regions where it was used, the major concern was expanding employment opportunities among local people who were currently unemployed.

As detailed analyses of individual projects are being carried out, careful consideration has to be given to financial, physical, technological, institutional, and human resources that can be made available for project implementation and management in the region. Careful consideration needs also to be given to special development concerns and opportunities, and to associated overall regional development objectives and strategic thrusts for the current planning cycle.

While many of these matters will have been addressed during the course of regional analysis, and again implicitly in the course of project identification, in many cases final conclusions concerning them will be influenced by findings of investigations undertaken in connection with individual project evaluation. This should not be surprising, since many of these investigations will be undertaken at a level of specificity previously absent from the regional planning process; they are likely therefore to uncover new resources, the absence of resources where they were thought to exist, new concerns, and new opportunities.

The outcomes of explorations and deliberations regarding development resources and priorities can be translated into an additional standardized project evaluation tool, the *summary project evaluation checklist*. This checklist has two major sections: a set of *project eligibility criteria* and a set of *project preference criteria*. The first reflects primarily development resources that can be made available, and the second reflects primarily development priorities.

The eligibility criteria represent permissible limits, if there are any, on the financial, locational, natural resource, technological, management, technical skills, energy, and other requirements of a development project. In the eligibility criteria section of the checklist, the value limit for each requirement is shown, and next to it is entered the amount required for the proposed project. In principle, if the requirement of a proposed project exceeds the limit, it is ineligible for further consideration.

The preference criteria represent preferred characteristics of development projects. These might be based on the sorts of questions listed in Figure 15.2, but they might also be based on factors related to ease of implementation and development resource requirements. In the preference criteria section of the checklist, questions about these characteristics are listed, and next to them are entered the estimated values for the development project. In principle, projects with better "scores," are preferred.

However, the ratings for the different preference criteria are not additive, and no overall preference score can be assigned in a truly meaningful way. One way to deal with this partially is to have two or more levels of importance among preference criteria. Better scores among the more important criteria would stand for more than good scores among the less important criteria.

As was the case in the project identification phase, some projects are likely to be eliminated in the course of individual project evaluation and full evaluation reports will not be completed for them. But the purpose of the evaluation reports is not just to determine the full requirements, and the benefits and costs, associated with each project proposal. They also are meant to provide recommendations for project design, including changes from the original proposal, that would result in improving their practicability, enhancing the benefits they would produce, and lowering their costs: in short, for making them more doable and efficient.

This suggests that individual project evaluation, in the best case, is a somewhat iterative process of investigation, assessment, modification, detailing, additional investigation, and so on. The outcome is a further reduced list, but one that contains project proposals that have been fairly well investigated, elaborated, and refined.

COMPARATIVE EVALUATION

The next task is to evaluate these proposals in relation to each other. For the most part, this is done on the basis of the findings of individual project evaluations. Project evaluation reports for all the projects are, of course, studied and carefully compared. A *summary comparative evaluation* report can be prepared that in a single paragraph summarizes the findings for each proposed project regarding technical feasibility; financial and economic viability; environmental sustainability; and social, administrative, and political acceptability. Data from summary project evaluation checklists can be combined into a single matrix enabling comparison of eligibility and preference criteria information for all remaining project proposals. In a similar fashion, comparative evaluation matrices can be assembled for special purpose assessment checklists.

In addition, many analysts like to employ models for comparative evaluation purposes. Income and product accounts, balance of payments statements, economic base analysis, input-output analysis, and rural-urban exchange analysis, if they have been undertaken for the region, all can serve as comparative evaluation models. The expected effects of each proposed project in turn are introduced into and worked through the accounts, statement, or analysis, and the resulting changes from the original findings of these methods of analyses are compared. This sort of exercise should not be confused with actual simulation or projection exercises. The results have no actual predictive value. The models merely offer a means for testing alternatives against data in hand for purposes of relative, not absolute, comparison. In other words, the approach is based on the assumption that the same degree of unreality inherent in using the models for prediction will apply fairly equally to all the proposals tested.

Comparative evaluation can obviously involve absorbing and mentally comparing a large amount of information. That is why it is important as much as possible to employ summary matrices. The matrices may not contain sufficient detail for full comparative evaluation, but they are backed up by source documents that can be referenced, and their entries serve as reminders to the reviewer of the full story that may appear elsewhere.

Another device that can help ease the labor of grappling with a large amount of comparative evaluation data is a list of a half-dozen or so leading comparative evaluation questions. These questions should be agreed on by participants in the planning process in advance of the comparative evaluation exercise; indeed, the effort to reach agreement on them is likely to help clarify development objectives, strategies, and project priorities. The few leading questions cannot encompass all the factors, or even all the important factors, to be taken into account in the course of comparative evaluation. But they can help assure that all participants in the process are at least asking a few identical questions as they pore over the information in hand. Examples of possible leading questions are:

—Does this project contribute directly and significantly to one or several of the principal current objectives or strategic thrusts of the regional development effort?

—Can this project be fully and effectively implemented in a relatively short time?

—Does this project build on known resource strengths and comparative advantages of the region?

—Will this project be environmentally sustainable over the long run?

—Will this project result in permanent improvement in the basic intraregional growth dynamics, the diversity of economic opportunity, and the resiliency of the regional economy?

—Will the benefits of this project accrue to a large number of people in the region, either directly or indirectly?

—Does, or can, this project have a mutually reinforcing link with another proposed project?

All the devices used in the process of comparative evaluation ultimately serve planning debate. The outcome of this debate is a still shorter list of proposed projects that are yet more fully elaborated and refined, more clustered in strategic groupings, and concerning the importance of which there is considerable consensus.

COMBINED EVALUATION

Individual, and even comparative, project evaluation, like environmental impact statements, do not reveal the combined effects of individual projects. In order to develop an adequate appreciation for the potential conflicts and complementarities among the remaining proposed projects, and their net effects, combined evaluation is necessary. This represents the final step of refinement in the current program of regional development projects before detailed project planning begins. Several different devices can be employed for combined evaluation that emphasize potential conflicts among projects, complementarities among them, combined effects, or a combination of these.

The reader may have already concluded that the easiest devices to employ are the various comparative evaluation matrices. Once the data for eliminated projects are deleted, rows or columns of these matrices can be added for the combined impacts of remaining project proposals. Caution and prudence need to be brought to this, however, because data for different projects may not be strictly additive. That is, the estimated requirements, benefits, and costs for two projects undertaken together may not be equal to the sums for these things when the projects are undertaken individually. The combined sums may be less, owing to shared resources or other reasons, or they may be more, owing to competition for resources or other reasons.

It is often helpful, as one of the first steps in combined evaluation, to assemble a *conflict/complementarity/compatibility matrix*. This is simply a matrix that lists all remaining project proposals along the top and left. In each cell of the matrix (only half the cells need be used) a symbol is entered representing conflict, complementarity, or simply compatibility between projects represented by intersecting columns and rows. The matrix is based on information in the individual project evaluation reports or comparative evaluation documents, on debate, or if necessary, on additional investigation. Whatever the case, the matrix serves to help focus the further process of combined evaluation, and serves as well to help identify needed modifications in project design to remove conflicts or enhance complementarity.

A major arena for potential conflict, and in some cases for complementarity, among regional development projects is the arena of environmental resources and hazards. Using the environmental resources and hazards checklist described earlier as a starting point, a *project/resource matrix* can be assembled. In this matrix each column represents a significant natural resource or hazard, listed first for the region as a whole and then for regional subunits, and each row represents a proposed project. Each cell of the matrix contains a statement indicating the nature of the relationship, if any, between the intersecting columns and rows. At the end of each row and the bottom of each column, the relationship of a project to all environmental resources and hazards, and the effects of all projects in combination on each environmental resource and hazard, are summarized respectively.

Factors in the conditioning environment can also serve as a basis for combined project evaluation. These factors were explored, and the most important ones among them were identified, in the course of the project identification phase. The project proposals now being evaluated all represent interventions to bring about changes in some of these factors. A *matrix of conditioning environment impacts* can be prepared, listing key factors in the conditioning environment along the top and the remaining project proposals along the left. In each cell of the matrix is entered a brief statement of the change the project represented by the row is intended to achieve in the conditioning environment factor represented by the intersecting column. The matrix is reviewed for intended changes that are in conflict, intended changes that are mutually reinforcing, key factors that have been ignored, and overconcentration on certain key factors that imply more change than can realistically be expected.

As with comparative evaluation, it can be helpful for participants in the planning process to agree on a short list of leading questions for reviewing information in hand during combined evaluation. Examples of possible leading questions that could serve combined evaluation purposes are:

—Does this project appear to be, or could it be, pivotal in the sense that several other projects do, should, or could tie into it?

—Does or could this project, together with certain others, form a complex of core activities representing a major strategic component of the regional development program?

—Is this project of a nature that suggests it should be sequenced in relation to one or more other proposed projects in order to derive maximum developmental benefit from it?

—Is this project of a nature that suggests it should be undertaken in concert with one or more other proposed projects in order to derive maximum development benefit from it?

—Is this project mutually exclusive with any other proposed project?

—Does this project appear to duplicate the purposes of any other proposed project?

—Can this project be combined with another proposed project into a single activity?

In preparation for the planning debate that is the final step in combined project evaluation, the development planning staff can be assigned responsibility for preparing a number of *alternative implementation scenarios* that include different combinations of proposed projects. Each scenario would be presented in a few pages that describe the requirements, necessary actions by various organizations and individuals, implementation timing, costs, consequences, and other elements associated with different project combinations.

The debate, based on the alternative scenarios and other combined evaluation devices mentioned, leads finally to an agreed, limited number of priority projects that are fairly well researched, evaluated, proven practicable, and strategically combined. These, together with a program of preparatory actions that include detailed project planning, constitute the current regional development plan. This plan may be further refined in terms of implementation action after detailed project planning has been done.

17

Benefit-Cost Analysis

All regional analysts should know how to perform benefit-cost (or cost-benefit) analysis. The reason is not just because they have to be able to work with people whose job it is to do benefit-cost analyses, nor is it the fact that sooner or later even regional planners have to do a benefit-cost analysis of something. The reason, rather, is that through familiarity with the concepts of benefit-cost analysis, regional development practitioners can better express regional issues in benefit-cost terms understandable to others, and can ensure that regional development implications are incorporated into benefit-cost analyses.

There are three aspects to benefit-cost analysis: deciding what to count as benefits and what to count as costs, deciding how to count them, and calculating the benefit-cost ratio and internal rate of return. In what follows they are presented in order of increasing conceptual complexity, the reverse of the order in which they were just listed.

BENEFIT-COST RATIO AND INTERNAL RATE OF RETURN

Any project can be conceived as a stream of yearly benefits and a stream of yearly costs over its life. In the simplest case, a project takes one year to build (or to implement in some other way); all investment costs are accounted for in that year; and thereafter it has annual benefits as measured by revenues and annual operating costs over, say, a 20-year period representing its effective life. A local marketplace could serve as an example.

We might want to calculate a benefit-cost ratio for the marketplace to be sure the relationship of its benefits to its costs is above some minimum standard, to

Table 17.1
Hypothetical Data for a Proposed Marketplace: Streams of Revenues and Costs

Year	Revenues (benefits)	Option A		Option B	
		Cost	Net Benefits	Costs	Net Benefits
0	0	1,000	-1,000	0	0
1	300	200	100	420	-120
2	350	200	150	408	-58
3	400	175	225	371	29
4	400	125	275	309	91
5	400	100	300	272	128
6	400	100	300	260	140
7	400	100	300	248	152
8	400	100	300	136	264
9	400	100	300	224	176
10	400	100	300	212	188
11-20	400	100	300	100	300

compare it with that of an alternative design, or to compare it to that of a competing project. And we might want to calculate the internal rate of return to be sure it meets an acceptable standard, or that it compares favorably with the rate of return on money invested elsewhere, or to compare it with the rate of return on a competing project or with an alternate way of financing the marketplace.

Suppose the data for the streams of revenues and costs for the proposed marketplace were as shown in Table 17.1. The revenues are estimated income from the rental of stall space. Rental revenues rise to a constant yearly amount reflecting full occupancy. The construction cost is Mu 1,000. Operating costs decline to a constant yearly amount reflecting peak efficiency. Under Option A, the local government pays for construction out of its current budget and does not amortize the investment. Under Option B, the construction funds are borrowed at 12 percent per year for ten years.

Mu 1.00 is worth less if received next year than it is today. It is worth even less if it is received in two years. This fact expresses itself through the interest rate. If you have a choice between Mu 1.00 now and Mu 1.00 next year, you will take it now because, if nothing else, you can invest it and get Mu 1.00 plus interest next year. This means that even though annual revenue from the rental of marketplace stalls in Table 17.1 is Mu 400 for years 3 through 20, each year the Mu 400 is worth less as we view it from the perspective of today. And the same is true for costs. Benefit-cost analysts would say that the streams of revenues and costs cannot be properly summed without first converting them into terms of equal value: specifically, into terms of value that make sense in the present, since it is now that the financial commitment must be made.

To convert the streams of future revenues and costs into terms of present value, a

Table 17.2
Hypothetical Data for a Proposed Marketplace: Present Value at Discount Rate of 15 Percent

			Option A		Option B	
Year	Discount Factor	Revenues (benefits)	Costs	Net Benefits	Costs	Net Benefits
0	1.000	0	1,000	-1,000	0	0
1	.870	261	174	87	365	-104
2	.756	265	151	114	308	-43
3	.658	263	115	148	244	19
4	.572	229	72	157	177	52
5	.497	199	340	1,022	135	64
[5-20]	[3.404]	[1,362]				
6	.432	173			112	61
7	.376	150			93	57
8	.327	131			44	87
9	.284	114			64	50
10	.247	99			52	47
11-20	1.242	496			124	372
Total		2,380	1,852	528	1,718	662

rate for discounting future value must be selected. In Table 17.2, a discount rate of 15 percent was used. Although the Option B loan had an interest rate of 12 percent, let us suppose that this was through a special central government program, and that on the commercial market a 15-percent interest rate prevails. Using a discount rate of 15 percent answers the question, how much would have to be invested today at the market rate of interest in order to yield each of the annual revenue or cost figures in each of the 20 future years? In other words, future values are converted to present values on the assumption that the value of money deteriorates each year in accordance with a 15-percent discount rate.

The present value of an amount A due or available in n years at discount rate r can be computed as:

$$\text{Present value} = \frac{A}{(1 + r)^n}$$

In table 17.1, for example, it can be seen that revenue from the rental of marketplace stalls in the third year will be Mu 400. Using a discount rate of 15 percent, the present value of that revenue would be:

$$\frac{400}{(1 + .15)^3} \text{ or } \frac{400}{(1.15)^3} \text{ or } \frac{400}{1.521} \text{ or Mu } 263$$

This is the amount that appears in Table 17.2, in the revenues column for year 3.

Normally, however, the conversion to present value is done with the help of a table called *Present Value of One*, *Table of Discount Factors*, or something similar. It will be found in any book containing the most basic algebraic tables, including business manuals and high-school algebra textbooks. It will have interest rates along the top and years numbered 0 through 25 or more along the side. Each cell of the table contains a *discount factor*, the fraction by which 1.000 should be multiplied to determine its present value for interest rate and number of years represented by the intersecting column and row.

If you were to look at the column for 15 percent in such a table, the numbers shown for years 0 through 10 would be those appearing in Table 17.2. Take the discount factor for year 6, which is 0.432. Investing Mu 0.432 today at 15 percent per year would yield Mu 1.000 in six years. Or, Mu 1.000 in six years is worth Mu 0.432 today. The present value amounts in Table 17.2 were produced by multiplying revenues and costs for each year from Table 17.1 by their respective discount factors.

Mercifully, most projects are estimated to develop a fixed pattern of annual costs and benefits after a period. In Tables 17.1 and 17.2, annual data for Option A become fixed starting in year 5. Annual data for Option B become fixed starting in year 11. There is a handy formula for dealing with situations like this: (1) sum the discount factors for all the years with constant annual data, and then (2) multiply this sum by the constant annual figure. This yields the sum of the present values for all the years with constant annual data. In the case of Option A, for example, the sum of discount factors for years 5 through 20 is 3.404. Multiplying 400, 100, and 300 from Table 17.1 in turn by this number yields 1,362, 340, and 1,022 as shown for years 5 through 20 in Table 17.2.

Once all the data have been converted to present value terms, the streams of future revenues and costs can be summed. From Table 17.2, the total net benefits, or net present value, and the benefit-cost ratio using a 15 percent discount rate can be seen to be as follows:

	Option A	*Option B*
Net present value	528	662
Benefit-cost ratio	1.23	1.39

Under Option B, with borrowed money, the net present value of the profits from the marketplace over 20 years are higher; for every Mu 1.00 spent, Mu 1.39 will be returned at present value, as against Mu 1.23 for Option A. This makes sense, since under Option B the investment cost is spread into future years, diminishing its present value; and the interest rate paid is below the discount rate used, which reflects the current commercial interest rate.

The internal rate of return is the discount rate at which benefits and costs are equal in present value terms. In other words, it is the discount rate at which the benefit-cost ratio is 1.00. It is the effective interest earned on the investment in the project.

Table 17.2 showed that the benefit-cost ratio under Option A was 1.23, using a discount rate of 15 percent. We are looking for the discount rate at which the benefit-cost ratio is 1.00. It makes sense that this would be a higher discount rate, since a higher rate would further reduce the present value of net benefits in later years, and it is in the later years that the largest net benefits accrue. If we experiment with a discount rate of 25 percent, the benefit-cost ratio under Option A will turn out to be 0.93: costs exceed benefits. If we try a discount rate of 24 percent, the benefit-cost ratio will be 0.95: costs still exceed benefits, but by less. If we try a discount rate of 22 percent, the benefit-cost ratio is 1.03: benefits exceed costs. The internal rate of return, then, is roughly 23 percent. This is rather good performance, considering that the rate of return on the commercial market is only 15 percent. The reader may find it a useful exercise to figure the internal rate of return for Option B.

As a final step, benefit-cost analysts may undertake sensitivity analysis. This entails assuming that revenue or cost estimates are inaccurate over some range, say ±20 percent. The future cost and benefit streams would each be adjusted up 20 percent and down 20 percent, and the impact on the benefit-cost ratio and internal rate of return would be calculated. The idea here is to see how sensitive benefit-cost analysis ratings of a proposed project are to the range of possible revenue and cost estimation errors. How would Options A and B in Table 17.1 work out if actual costs were 20 percent higher than estimated? And what if actual revenues were 20 percent lower than estimated?

Sensitivity analysis might be performed on only one component of a benefit or cost stream. For example, under Option A it may make sense to assume that construction cost estimates are accurate, and that operating costs alone could vary by ±20 percent.

HOW TO COUNT

Clearly, a great deal turns on the discount rate used. In the past, one international lending organization required that 12 percent be used as the discount rate by all its borrowers when doing a benefit-cost analysis, because as a matter of policy it was prepared to lend for projects with an internal rate of return of 12 percent or better. Put otherwise, the organization was ready to lend for projects with a benefit-cost ratio of 1.00 or better at a discount rate of 12 percent.

In some cases it may be appropriate to use the average rate of return on other projects as the discount rate. In some cases the commercial market rate of interest may be appropriate. Often there are a number of discount rates that could legitimately be used, and this is frequently the source of a great deal of debate when proposed projects are being selected and evaluated for funding. Of course, it is always possible to run the benefit-cost calculations over a range of discount rates.

For an enterprise intended solely to produce a money profit, benefits and costs are easily counted, as they were in the marketplace example. But suppose in that example the government took a broader view and recognized that other benefits would accrue to the public treasury from the new improved marketplace. As a consequence of increased market activity, a higher volume of business and personal tax revenues would be generated. Or, suppose the government took an even broader view and decided that because the marketplace was meant to be a regional economic development project, the increased market activity, reflecting more production, trade, and income in the region, was itself a benefit. While both tax revenues and market activity can be measured in money, it may not be entirely clear or unarguable which money to count.

One could argue that the only benefits deriving from the marketplace project that should be counted are those that are additional (economists would say *marginal*) to those that would obtain without the project. As a general rule, before-after comparisons are made when a project is perceived as *curative*—that is, meant to solve (cure) an existing problem or improve an existing situation. With-without comparisons are made if a project is perceived as *preventive*—that is, meant to prevent an anticipated problem from arising.

If the old marketplace that the new one will replace had witnessed declining trade that eventually stabilized at a low level of activity, the project could be viewed as curative. If the old marketplace were now adequate for local needs, but trade activity showed signs of declining owing to advancing dilapidation of the marketplace, the project could be viewed as preventive. Yet, one can see that reasonable arguments could be made for a with-without comparison even in the former case; and that the dividing line between curative and preventive can be vague.

There are other counting problems. If a project is to be a public investment, many economists would argue that *economic costs* rather than just financial costs should be counted. The economic cost reflects *opportunity costs* to the economy rather than actual money paid. The opportunity cost of a thing is the price it would command on the open market in its best alternative use. According to economists, this price represents the value of opportunity foregone, what is given up, in order to use a resource for the proposed project.

Perhaps the two most common situations that benefit-cost analysts run up against where economic costs and financial costs differ are those in which there is high unemployment or fixed foreign exchange rates. In the case of high unemployment, the wages paid to workers constructing the project may be higher than they would earn in other employment, if any could be found. In other words, though the construction workers are paid a certain wage that represents a financial cost to the project, their opportunity cost in terms of the economic benefits foregone owing to their unavailability for other employment are probably much less, possibly zero. To compute the economic cost of the proposed project, *shadow prices* for construction labor would be estimated to reflect its opportunity cost.

If there are fixed foreign exchange rates, the shadow price of imported construction materials might be based on the higher black market foreign exchange rate, thought to be a better measure of the true value of domestic currency than a rate fixed by the government. If a central government agency pays duty on imported construction materials, the duty should be deducted from the economic cost, because it is only an interagency transfer rather than an actual expenditure of public resources.

All this has been but a sampling of the counting problems in benefit-cost analysis. The more the perspective on benefits and costs is broadened, the more difficult the counting problem becomes. The easiest case is that in which the project is viewed as a single profit-making enterprise. But economic development projects seldom can be viewed so simply. Because the notion of quantified benefit-cost analysis derives from business planning, and because what is good for a single private business may be bad for private enterprise or the economy collectively, there are frequently situations in which the appropriateness of the conventional benefit-cost analysis approach is arguable. Equally frequent are situations in which the interpretation of the results of a benefit-cost analysis is entirely in dispute.

In the case of the marketplace, for example, it could be argued that the internal rate of return of 23 percent, far from representing good performance, is scandalously high for a public project. Perhaps stall rental fees should be reduced, which would stimulate full occupancy at an earlier date and leave more money in the hands of vendors and others in the private sector, though the benefit-cost ratio might be less than one. Perhaps, through the workings of the income multiplication process, the economic development benefits of such an alternative course of action would be even greater.

WHAT TO COUNT

It is almost impossible to contemplate how to count without touching on the issue of what to count, as was the case in the foregoing discussion. If we estimate conventional shadow prices for construction labor, is this not a statement that we consider the laborers only in terms of their values in the open market? One could argue that the financial cost of labor for the project should be set at a level higher than its economic cost because creating jobs is a principal purpose of development activity, and doing so constitutes a benefit that to some extent offsets costs. We might tabulate reduced public assistance expenditures, increased personal taxes, multiplier effects from putting money in the pockets of construction workers hired for the project, and increased future earnings that some workers will receive owing to on-the-job training, and deduct these from the construction costs.

International lending agencies often wag their fingers at benefit-cost analysts in borrower countries who fail to include the cost of government land in project investment costs. The land belongs to the government, so government analysts may view it as a free good with respect to the public cost of the government development project. But the land has economic value; some measure, like the price it would bring on the open market, represents opportunity foregone, effectively an additional cost, and should be added to other investment costs.

It could be argued, however, that to do so is to attempt to account for economic efficiency at a level of abstraction so far removed from operating reality as to make it irrelevant for evaluating a proposed project. Suppose local analysts know, as does everyone, that the land is part of a government preserve that, as a matter of policy, will never be for sale. Its market value is zero because it is not in the market. From the perspective of the international lending agency, the policy of the government to withhold its land from the market, or not to value it as if it were on the market, is economically unsound. But is it appropriate to require that the implications of that perspective be imposed on a project benefit-cost analysis that as a practical matter must be viable within a different operational reality?

It should be clear by now that the issue of what to count, as well as how to count, has no absolute resolution. The problem with benefit-cost analysis is that it has an air of authenticity, quantified precision, and objectivity about it that gives it an importance somewhat out of proportion with its technical usefulness. There is no right way and no wrong way to do a benefit-cost analysis, there are only different benefit-cost perspectives. That is why such a simple notion as comparing benefits and costs has spawned such a vast body of literature.

Imagine again the proposed marketplace project. Consider a benefit-cost analysis from the perspective of a private owner; it would probably be similar to Tables 17.1 and 17.2. Now consider it from the perspective of a banker: perhaps the initial investment should be larger under Option B to cover operating losses in the first two years. Now consider it from the perspective of the government budget, from the perspective of cost per increment of improvement in the welfare of intended beneficiaries, from the perspective of regional income and product, from the perspective of long-term development dynamics, from the perspective of efficiency in the use of environmental resources, and from the political perspective.

Obviously, the guidelines for benefit-cost analysis differ in accordance with the perspective. Stated otherwise, any set of benefit-cost guidelines defines a unique perspective. However technical the terms used, the issue is almost always the appropriate benefit-cost perspective. Good project evaluation would entail benefit-cost analysis from several perspectives.

To the regional planning practitioner, the notion of a regional development benefit-cost analysis is suggested. The findings of many of the methods of regional economic analysis described in Parts II and III of this book, especially when available in time series, lend themselves to presentation in a benefit-cost framework. Short of this, many of the tools of regional analysis can be used to develop data for conventional types of benefit-cost analysis. In fact, it is through regional economic analysis, including the tools of project identification and evaluation, that benefits and costs of potential projects can be linked to broader regional economic development planning.

V

Approaches to Regional Development Planning

18

An Idealized Planning Model

We all plan. And the basic planning process is the same whether for personal planning, corporate planning, or regional planning. That process involves setting goals, examining options for reaching them, and selecting a course of action. What distinguishes one way of planning from another is not so much the fundamental logic of the process as the way the process is elaborated and the tools and procedures that are used for the particular planning job to be done. If planning is done in a dynamic context rather than a limited, controlled, and finite one, it must be a continuing process that incorporates implementation of a course of action, evaluation, and new information into new cycles of setting goals, examining options, and so on. Regional development is just such a dynamic context.

In this chapter, first an idealized planning model is presented as adapted to the regional planning context, and then some basic considerations for designing an actual regional planning process are reviewed. The following chapter describes alternative approaches for launching regional development planning and for the overall nature of a regional planning routine, both based on working experience around the world. The final chapter combines elements presented earlier in this book into a general framework that can serve as the starting point for designing a planning process specifically suited to a particular regional situation.

BASIC PLANNING STEPS

Figure 18.1 is a schematic representation of an idealized planning model. Other models, using different terms, different numbers of planning steps, or a

Figure 18.1
Schematic Representation of an Idealized Planning Model

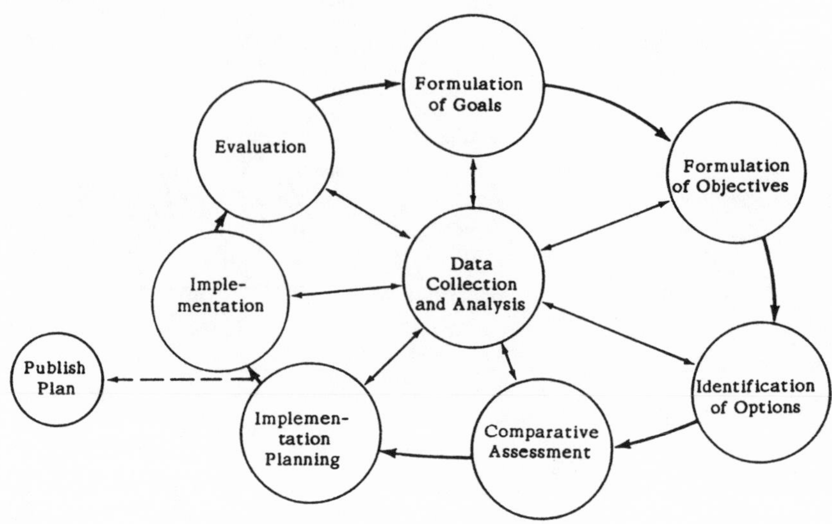

different schematic framework could be equally valid. The scheme in Figure 18.1 has three special features:

1. Data collection and analysis is not a sequential step in the process, but a function that continuously supports all others and receives information from them;
2. All the steps of the process are part of a continuing cycle in which goals are periodically reconsidered, objectives reformulated, and so on; and
3. A published plan is not the end of the process, but one is produced from time to time for practical reasons.

The planning support information system, ''Data Collection and Analysis,'' ideally encompasses five broad subject areas:

1. Evaluation of the previous planning cycle;
2. Performance of development projects previously undertaken in the region and in similar regions elsewhere;
3. Assessment of development resources external to the region, but available or potentially available to it (public and private funds that might be invested in the interest of local economic development, special talents or capabilities of individuals and institutions that can be tapped, and so on);
4. Characteristics and dynamics of the regional setting, including especially data on the economy, infrastructure, physical and social characteristics, resources, and institutions; and
5. The relationship of the local setting to other areas important to its future development.

Evaluation of the previous planning cycle and the projects that have been implemented is shown as the last sequential step in Figure 18.1, even though it is an integral component of data collection and analysis. This has been done in order to emphasize the evaluative review of previous activity that ideally precedes a formal reformulation of goals. However, like other data collection and analysis activities, aspects of evaluation may be going on at all times. Methods of regional economic analysis covered in chapters 4 through 14, and some covered in chapters 15 and 16, can be used to good advantage in four of the five data subject areas mentioned, the exception being assessment of external resources.

It useful to establish a set of analytical rubrics to structure data collection and analysis. This subject is fully discussed in Chapter 4. The analytical rubrics selected can carry over from data collection and analysis to formulation of goals, formulation of objectives, identification of options, and even to the committee organization of those involved in the planning process. This introduces clarity and consistency along with overall structure into planning activity.

Formulating goals is often given short shrift in regional development planning, probably because it is believed that everyone knows what the goals are: expanded employment opportunities, higher incomes, diversification, prosperity, stability, and economic growth. Goals formulated this way really provide very little guidance as to what is desirable or undesirable. Each can be interpreted in many and contradictory ways.

Ideally, a regional development goal provides sound and unequivocal planning guidance. To do this, a goal requires three qualities:

1. It should reflect a future self-image of the region that is a long-term one, relating not only to a static state (for example, more jobs) but also to a regional economic dynamic (for example, an increased rate of new job creation);
2. It should derive from an intimate knowledge of the region based on formal quantitative and qualitative analysis as well as on information deriving from experience in the region; and
3. It should adhere to the what-which rule—that is, it should say what is sought with respect to which individuals, organizations, activities, or locations, so that it provides real guidance to the preferable courses of economic development activity, though the goal should be expressed in nonnumerical terms.

The term *objectives* is used here in a formal sense that distinguishes objectives from goals, rather than in the broader sense in which it was used in earlier chapters. Objectives are the standards by which progress toward the achievement of goals is measured. They are quantified and time-framed performance targets. Every goal should be expressed in terms of at least one quantified and time-framed objective. In addition to quantified and time-framed objectives, a goal can be expressed in terms of objectives that are only time-framed; but in such cases the condition to be achieved within the given time should be as explicit and clearly discernible as possible. There should be both near-term objectives and longer-term ones. The latter will, of course, be reconsidered in the coming planning cycle.

If a goal must adhere to the what-which rule, it must be amplified by at least one objective that adheres to the how much–when rule. The aims of regional economic development activity will thereby be articulated in a set of statements that say clearly how much of what is supposed to be the case with which individuals, organizations, activities, or locations, and by when this should occur. And there you have the basis for determining the best courses of action.

If a goal is to "increase the rate of small enterprise formation in the towns of the region," a related objective might be "establishment of 50 new enterprises each employing five people or less in the three largest regional towns within two years." The number of new small enterprises has thus been quantified for an explicit time frame, the term "small" has been defined, and target locations have been specified. This is indeed a performance target for the regional planning and development process.

Occasionally, a given objective will suggest a unique course of action. Occasionally, there will clearly be a limited few options for achieving a particular objective, and these will readily suggest themselves. But most often there will be a number of relevant options, many of which will not readily suggest themselves. The aim of the next step in the planning process is to increase the range of known options—that is, to identify all potential courses of action that might contribute to achieving performance targets and, in turn, goals. This step roughly coincides with what was encompassed under "project identification" in Chapter 15.

The search is for ideas regarding strategies and projects that will contribute to achieving the goals and objectives. Strategies represent broad approaches, and projects are specific measures related to physical capital, human and institutional capital, and policies undertaken as the applied expression of a strategy. Several projects related to a single strategy are often referred to as a program.

Finalization of strategies, and of goals and objectives as well, can take place only in association with identification and evaluation of project possibilities, because the process of identifying and evaluating projects generates additional planning information. For example, projects originally proposed independently of each other may be found to have a strategic relationship suggesting a new strategic alternative that may, in turn, provide a context for identification and consideration of additional project ideas.

Comparative evaluation of alternative courses of action, which here is meant to encompass the various aspects of "project evaluation" covered in Chapter 16, can be carried out in many ways. In general it entails first eliminating strategies and projects that are undesirable, infeasible, or impracticable, and then for the remainder selecting those that are preferred. The outcome of this step in the planning process is a limited number of priority projects that are fairly well researched, evaluated, proven practicable, and strategically combined.

Implementation planning in the idealized model, which coincides roughly with the final step in "project evaluation" as presented in Chapter 16, can also be undertaken as a two-phase step. The task here is to refine the package of strategies and projects into specific integrated activities. First a long-term economic development program or *strategic plan*, can be prepared that identifies major activities over several years and links them to specific expected results, specific objectives, and, through these, to specific goals.

Then an action program, or *near-term implementation plan*, is prepared covering the next planning cycle and detailing how the first part of the long-term plan is to be carried out. The near-term implementation plan identifies discrete tasks associated with major activities, including detailed project planning. It shows when each task is to be carried out, the responsible individual or organization, the intended result, the cost, the source of funds, and so on. Formal plan documents may be published at this point or after a certain amount of detailed project planning has been completed. In any case, the process moves on to implementation, evaluation, and eventually to the next cycle.

The reader may already have protested that the world does not work this way. What has been described is an idealized model—a regional development planning process in theory, if you will—not a prescription. Reality differs indeed, but the function of a model of this sort is to provide an ordered frame of reference as we grapple with that reality. Certainly at times we find ourselves starting with projects, returning to carry out the justifying analysis, jumping to implementation, and then writing a plan. But as we find need to do these things, a model like this helps us to sow a seed here and there that may contribute to emergence of a proper regional planning process.

The reader may also have noticed that even the idealized model described here is not as neat and tidy as might at first appear. It is circles within circles within circles. For example, in the discussion on identification of project options, mention was made of a circular interplay between strategies and potential projects. Similar circular interplays, or iterations, take place between the two stages of comparative evaluation and possibly the two stages of implementation planning. The outcomes of these iterations in turn may cause a rethinking of goals and objectives, and in turn a search for new options, and so on to another round of iterations. This means that in practice, as will be seen in the next chapter, the process could start with projects, or with goals and strategies. In any case the outcome of the starting step will be refined through the iterative process.

Implementation, of course, is actually going on all the time. Elements of evaluation are always active. So in fact, most of the steps of the planning process are active to some degree at all times, and it is only their relative intensities, or perhaps their final determinations for the current planning cycle, that follow a sequential pattern.

The formal planning cycles themselves represent overall planning iterations at intervals shorter than that covered by the strategic plan. This means that economic development goals may never be achieved, objectives may be altered before being realized, and long-term economic development programs may never be fully implemented. Many are likely to change long before that. And they should change, because the national and international environments are changing, the regional economy is changing, and people are changing. The function of the long-term goals, objectives, and development program is only to provide a cohesive and coherent working framework for development decisions for the near term.

REGIONAL PLANNING CONSIDERATIONS

One of the built-in features of the idealized model described is that it is a learning-based process. This makes it particularly appropriate for development planning, because regional development is itself a learning-based process. It is possible to start with a very rudimentary planning process and build up from there as each cycle is succeeded by the next over time.

Following are a few central questions that should receive attention during efforts to design a realistic economic development planning process for a region:

1. What are the interrelationships and interdependencies among development policies as they are formed at different administrative levels and in the private sector? What mechanisms for policy coordination are needed to enable regional development policies to have effect?
2. What are the sources of data and where are the analytical capabilities relevant to different levels of policy formation and decision making? What sort of information system is needed to support the development planning process? What framework of aggregate regional and intraregional analysis is best suited to the region, to the available data and analytical capacity, and to the nature of the development planning process?
3. What instruments of development policy implementation are available at different administrative levels? These instruments include regulation; economic incentives and penalties; public investment; public procurement; and information, training, and education. What mechanism is needed to unite authority to use these instruments in a manner consistent with the regional development planning process?
4. How can coordination among economic development activities, among places, and over time be incorporated into the planning process, and through it into the development process?
5. How can aggregative (bottom-up) and disaggregative (top-down) planning be balanced?
6. How can technical and participatory planning be balanced?
7. What mechanisms are needed to ensure that the development planning process remains an open learning-based process at all levels? How can the fear of "mistakes" be replaced by an appreciation for what is learned from every development planning decision?

Regional economic development is a public, collective decision-making process. It is a proper complement to private decision-making processes. It should be designed and understood as a public decision-making process and not as a professional exercise apart from that. Those who will be called on to help implement development planning decisions, and those expected to alter their behavior in response as a result of those decisions, must be parties to the decisions, and therefore to the regional planning process. This is not just good ethics, it is also regional development planning that can be most effective.

19

Applied Regional Approaches

Formal regional development planning was first undertaken about 30 years ago. The main body of applied experience has been accumulated in the past 20, and especially the past 10 years. The time has come to ask, what does this experience teach us about how to approach regional development planning?

In an effort to answer that question the United Nations Food and Agriculture Organization (FAO) in 1989 undertook a review of 30 of the most promising cases of regional development planning cited in formal and informal literature. These cases represented all continents except Europe. Most of them reflected work done in the 1980s, and none reflected experience more than 20 years old. Most of the cases were from present or former developing countries. The full report of the study is published as *Rural Area Development Planning: A Review and Synthesis of Approaches*, and is available from FAO headquarters in Rome. What follows in this chapter derives largely from cases reviewed during the FAO study.

Upon examination, some of the 30 ''cases'' turned out to be fiction. That is, what had been presented in the literature as a process being used for regional development planning was in fact a proposal or plan for planning that had never really been put into effect. Some of the cases turned out to be nothing more than procedures for project review and approval among administrative levels of government. Some of the cases represented strictly top-down planning; the planning had been undertaken for a region by central government experts or outside (often expatriate) consultants, with little or no involvement of anyone who lived in the region.

Indeed, in some cases what had been called regional planning was in fact a central government national planning exercise, with the country divided into regions as a matter of administrative convenience. And some of the cases represented sincere grass-roots efforts at regional planning, but amounted to little more than series of community meetings in the villages and towns of a region, each to debate the projects in its locale that the central government should be pressed to fund. In the end, only 10 of the 30 cases were found to be largely locally controlled regional planning aimed at identifying, evaluating, and strategically combining development projects through an ordered process that involved some minimum analysis of the regional economy.

What was learned from the 10? First, it is safe to say that there is no one generally accepted approach to regional development planning. The regional planning process seems constantly to be reinvented, emerging each time in different form in accordance with the current and changing capabilities, philosophies, needs, cultural and social characteristics, and administrative imperatives of the country context. And on reflection, what could be more sensible? The lesson is that those who would design, or help to design, regional planning processes should not look elsewhere for planning processes that they can transplant. Rather, they should examine the experiences of others, identify elements appropriate to their own contexts, and then use that as a basis for building a planning process uniquely suited to the situation of the region in which they are working.

Second, despite enormous and basic differences, when reduced to their most fundamental elements, the planning processes can be seen to hint at a general framework for regional planning that bears a discernible relationship to the idealized model discussed in Chapter 18. However, they reflect two distinctly different approaches to launching a regional planning exercise: beginning with projects, and then reassessing and clustering projects in a strategic framework; or beginning with a strategic framework (which may or may not include explicit goals and objectives), and then identifying projects for pursuing the strategies.

The first two sections of this chapter discuss in turn the *projects to strategies* approach and the *strategies to projects* approach to launching a regional development planning process. The third section discusses the *nested plans* alternative to a unitary planning process for the overall planning routine. The discussions are not meant simply as reports on findings from the cases reviewed in the FAO study, but are cast in terms meant to be helpful to planning practitioners contemplating one approach or another. In this way the present chapter is meant to provide information with which, together with ideas introduced in Part IV and Chapter 18, the reader can build on the general framework for regional planning presented in the next chapter.

FROM PROJECTS TO STRATEGIES

It is often the case that at the time it is decided to undertake a formal regional development planning process, a number of project proposals generated by sectoral agencies of the national government stand ready for final review or implementation. Seldom is it possible, even if desirable, to forestall these until a first cycle of planning can be completed.

Another common situation is that different groups of people in the region have been pressing for years for certain projects that "everyone knows" are critical. While launching a regional planning process promises to introduce order and reason into the welter of competing demands for projects, there is no patience for "more studies and plans." People see the planning process as nothing more than a mechanism for formally submitting their demands, a bureaucratic obstacle to be turned to advantage as quickly and with as little effort as possible.

It is also sometimes the case that a regional development planning endeavor is launched that is designed to be extremely participatory, and this requires a "bottom-up" approach with heavy public involvement at the village and town levels. As planning begins, the expertise, experience, and procedures for integrating local and regional level knowledge and concerns are lacking. As planners at the regional level contemplate this problem, they find themselves presented with lists of local projects sent up from "the bottom."

It is for reasons like these that many regional development planning processes are launched using an approach that begins with assembling project proposals, and then proceeds to reassess and cluster the proposals in a strategic development framework. The emphasis when this approach is used seems to be twofold: moving quickly through the first planning cycle to preparation of a first regional plan, and in the process introducing a modicum of strategic discipline, and perhaps even some analysis, to lay the groundwork for the next planning cycle and a continuing planning routine.

Project proposals may be generated by any of many possible means: some may already be on the table, others may be identified by local politicians, others may be generated by local groups or through local-level consultations, others may be the suggestions of the regional planning staff, and others may originate with central government sectoral agencies. Whatever the case, despite the fact that the proposals were not preceded by regional analysis, many of them are bound to have merit.

The overall orientations of the project proposals initially generated in any region will tend to be one of three types, depending on their sources. They may be primarily sectorally oriented projects, reflecting the sectoral agencies or special interest groups that put them forward. They may be primarily locale-oriented, if generated through political or community participation means. Or they may be a mixture that is predominantly neither sectorally nor locale-oriented.

The next task after assembling project proposals under the projects to strategies approach is to organize the projects into programmatic groupings. The idea here is, without threatening the validity of any proposal, to introduce an element of structure by merely grouping the proposals into subject areas related to regional development. This allows them to be seen in some form of relationship to each other, and also helps the proposers to define the intended purposes of their project proposals.

If possible, the programmatic grouping should promote a different way of looking at the region than is reflected in the prevailing orientation of the project proposals. If the projects tend to be sectorally oriented, they can be grouped into programs for regional subunits or locales; if they tend to be locale oriented, they can be grouped into sectoral programs; alternatively, or if they do not have any clear orientation, they can be grouped into strategic subject areas. Ideas for programmatic groupings will be found in the discussion of analytical rubrics in Chapter 4. These groupings implicitly constitute a strategic framework for development planning; they make almost inescapable observations about what is duplicative and what is missing in each program area.

If there is opportunity for regional analysis, observations on each of the programmatic groupings suggest priorities for it. Generally, if the project proposals had a sectoral orientation and have been organized into programs by regional subunits, the emphasis should be on intraregional analysis, accompanied by some aggregate analysis that employs sectoral distinctions. If the project proposals had a locale orientation and have been organized into sectoral programs, the emphasis should be on aggregate regional analysis, accompanied by some intraregional analysis to establish connections, if any, among proposals from different locales. Otherwise, the mix of aggregate and intraregional analysis will depend on the nature of the programmatic framework and the overall character of the project proposals.

Whether or not there is opportunity for regional analysis, from the perspective of general participants in the planning process (rather than the planning staff), there are only three elements in the planning exercise: submitting proposals, organizing them into programmatic groupings, and deciding which ones are to be included in the plan at this time. For purposes of the last element, some of the tools described in the last section of Chapter 15 and in chapters 16 and 17 would prove useful.

As a consequence of what emerges from this first planning cycle, priority analytical needs should be quite clear to the planning staff. In the time between cycles, they can undertake regional analysis and lay the groundwork for a greater degree of structure in the next planning cycle. The idea of a programmatic or strategic framework should now be widely understood, and new project proposals can be developed with reference to that framework.

The work between cycles is designed to promote the idea of the planning process as a continuous one, with each cycle really only being an exercise carried out at intervals when participants in the process interact intensively to go through the ordered steps necessary to reach consensus and produce a plan. Because of the routine planning work that continues between formal planning cycles, project ideas tend to be generated more and more in association with the planning process, including its regional analysis elements.

FROM STRATEGIES TO PROJECTS

To a surprising degree, cases reviewed in the FAO study reflected approaches in which first a framework of goals, objectives, strategies, or a combination, in some form, was developed, and then an exercise was undertaken to identify specific projects in specific places or sectors for meeting the goals or carrying out the strategies. These cases tended to be ones where the regional development planning effort was introduced with a strong hand. That is, these tended to be cases where the central government or another outside agency supported the planning exercise, required a strategies to projects approach, and often equipped regional staffs with the necessary capacity.

When this approach was required as a condition of outside support for planning and implementation, it led to a variety of responses, at least in the first planning cycle. In all cases the formal planning process indeed proceeded from strategies to projects in the orderly fashion suggested by the approach. In some cases, the result was a set of strategically packaged project proposals, or strategic programs, arising to a greater or lesser degree from methods of regional and project analysis such as those described in parts II, III, and IV of this book.

In other cases, however, the procedural formalities of formulating goals, determining strategies, and even conducting regional analysis were dutifully carried out, and then project proposals waiting in ''back pockets'' of participants were placed on the table and arranged into a ''strategic'' plan. In several cases, project decisions arising from the regional planning process were overridden or ignored by central government sectoral agencies with their own development agendas.

The principal differences among the various forms of the strategies to projects approach seem to be of three types: where and how regional analysis fits into the approach, the means for formulating a strategic framework, and the relationship of project identification and evaluation to strategy refinement.

In a few cases, regional analysis was undertaken as a first step in the planning process, based on the logic that one needs information before contemplating goals and strategies. But that logic derives from planning texts written by and for professionals who go into a region to plan or help with planning, and indeed need basic information before they can get started.

In most cases regional analysis was viewed as something that could be considered only after at least an initial set of goals or strategic framework was formulated. In these cases the function of regional analysis was seen as helping to refine the strategic framework and in the process to generate information that could be used for project identification and evaluation. Hence, the methods of regional analysis used, how they were adapted, and the relationship between aggregate and intraregional analysis all were initially determined by the nature of the framework of goals or strategies.

While all this is suggested by case documents, further investigation, including discussions with planning participants, leads to the conclusion that reports of careful thought given to a framework of methods of regional analysis reflect sincere intent more than practice. It appears that as a practical matter, in the first planning cycle precious little regional analysis was done in most cases. The emphasis in the first cycle was often on more traditional types of analysis, and especially sectoral analysis. Methods of regional analysis tended to come later, with the establishment of a continuing planning routine.

In a few cases goals and strategies were taken as necessarily highly formalized, structured, and even quantified—that is, "from strategies to projects" was interpreted as "from targets to arrows." These were always cases that began with quantified analysis, though not necessarily regional analysis as described in this book. The regional development planning process was seen as something close to a mathematical problem: on the basis of analysis, target levels of income, product, and employment were set on the theory that projects could be identified and mathematically tested so as to ensure that targets were met.

In most cases, however, goals and strategies were not quantified. In general, they tended to be loosely defined, at least initially, and most often reflected a concern with solving problems that had been annoying people for some time. In many cases the approach to strategy formulation was a traditional sectoral one. Sectors served as the organizing framework (the *analytical rubrics*) for the planning process, research was carried out with respect to each sector, and although sectoral strategies were formally formulated before projects were formally identified, both were based on this research. In these cases, goals or strategies were generally defined in terms of sectoral problems that needed to be solved, and there was little regional cohesion to the strategic framework.

In a small number of cases, a matrix approach to strategy formulation was employed. In Chapter 11 reference was made to a *resources/sectors* approach to natural resource assessment. In one regional development planning case, essentially the same matrix approach was used to formulate development strategies by sectors, based on the efficient utilization of resources. The matrix made it possible to coordinate the sectoral strategies so that as a regional package they reflected the best sustainable use of regional resources.

A matrix approach used in another case involved listing sectors along the top and regional subareas along the left, and investigating issues suggested by each of the column and row intersections. In turn, as appropriate, objectives were formulated and refined in the same matrix framework, enabling a continuous relational perspective on them all. Other variations on the matrix theme include listing economic variables like production, personal income, employment, value added, sales, exports, and so on along the top, and either sectors or subareas along the left.

From the foregoing it should be clear that in certain cases, strategies to projects was seen as a rigid procedural dictum. After strategies or goals were formulated, the job was done and the matter closed, and the planning process moved on to the next step. In these cases, whatever the initial intent, the planning process tended to evolve into an increasingly closed exercise. The public became discouraged and excluded by degrees owing to lack of planning sophistication and an increasingly technical and inflexible (and some claimed intolerant) orientation on the part of the planning staff. What could not be fully determined from the cases was the nature of the reward system under which the staffs operated and who controlled that reward system.

At the other extreme were cases where the strategic framework may or may not have been taken seriously, but in any case was viewed as infinitely flexible. Sometimes this flexibility was taken to the point of reserving final goal or strategy formulation until after the final list of projects was agreed on. The function of a strategy in these cases was apparently to imply a context of higher aims for proposed projects. In one case, the term "strategy" was even defined as the list of preferred projects. The trouble with this sort of flexibility is that it removes effective structure from the planning process, which in turn results in two related problems.

First, it denies any real regional focus to the planning exercise. Indeed, in these cases there was no discernible relationship among the proposed projects, nor was there any perceivable regional development context reflected in the strategy statements. Second, it promotes contention at the final stages of planning. An important advantage of moving from strategies to projects is that consensus is achieved by degrees, so that debates about the final list of projects concentrate more on issues of practicability and relationship to regional development strategies than on narrow interests.

In most cases, a middle path appears to have been taken. Flexibility was retained, and the right reserved to adjust the set of goals or strategic framework at any time. But as far as can be determined from case documents and interviews, once these were determined, they were changed only out of necessity. In other words, the planning process was characterized by a willingness to let new knowledge alter conclusions based on earlier perceptions. Especially since in general little formal regional analysis had been undertaken in the first planning cycle, new hard information was frequently generated in connection with project identification and evaluation.

Overall, the transition from the first planning cycle to a continuous regional development planning activity appears to be smoother when the first cycle is based on a strategies to projects type of approach. In several cases a gradually building body of directed regional analysis and periodic, formal, broadly participatory cycles are reported to have followed nearly routinely from the first experience. However, this may be accounted for in part by the more extensive outside support often associated with planning processes that were launched with this approach.

NESTED PLANS

In many cases planning was carried out as a single process beginning either with projects or strategies and proceeding through a sequence of steps ending up with a more or less refined list of priority projects for near-term implementation. But in a number of cases—and, significantly, in all of them in which a continuing regional planning routine had been introduced—an alternative overall approach, nested plans, was adopted.

Nested plans are plans within plans. An example of nested plans is the combination of a longer-term strategic plan and a near-term implementation plan mentioned in Chapter 18. The general pattern seems to be that strategic plans are oriented to three- to five-year intervals, and the short-term implementation or *tactical*, plan is oriented to one- to three-year intervals.

As the name implies, strategic planning emphasizes goals, objectives, and strategies based on a cumulating body of information about the regional economy. The strategic plan document often includes findings from methods of regional analysis and a full explanation and justification of a strategic regional development framework and its associated packages of projects for the coming period. Tactical planning involves refining the list of proposed projects for near-term implementation and developing a schedule of associated actions to realize them.

There are four important advantages to a nested plans approach to regional development planning. First, because strategy and overall program formulation is separated from final evaluation and selection of projects for near-term implementation, planning participants can focus on each in turn more thoroughly and without distraction. Participants from the general public can give real thought and energy to matters related to the broader view of the region's future on the one hand, and to activities aimed at serious project identification and evaluation for near-term implementation purposes on the other. Likewise, professional staff can map out and undertake a long-term program of regional analysis, and also give more attention to gathering detailed information for project identification and evaluation.

Second, the tactical planning effort can be coordinated with the budgetary cycles and changing budgetary circumstances of local and central government, and even outside funding sources. This helps regional authorities to position themselves to seek funding for the highest-priority projects at the most opportune times, and yet to always be able to present project proposals in a context of formal regional development strategies.

Third, the nested plans approach allows greater flexibility. If necessary, as a result of major events, special planning sessions can always be convened out of cycle to adjust strategic plans. More important, tactical plans are reconsidered at relatively short intervals. Thus, they are regularly updated and adapted to altered circumstances, including the results of project implementation, changed institutional relationships, changing national and world markets, new findings regarding resource sustainability, new technologies, and so on.

Finally, a nested plans approach generally promotes broader participation in the regional development planning process, and therefore better regional planning, on several counts. When members of the public participate, they normally do so outside of work; a nested plans approach tends to reduce the time and energy burden of participation. A nested plans approach enables the planning staff to provide more complete factual information to planning participants, which helps reduce contention and the associated disheartening interpersonal and interinstitutional tensions. Also, because the tactical plan is regularly and frequently revised, participants supporting a particular project that has not been chosen for implementation in connection with one tactical planning cycle know that it can be included in the next near-term implementation plan. This tends to encourage continued participation rather than disappointed retreat from the planning process.

Perhaps most important, a nested plans approach usually shortens the time between the determination of current priority projects and the implementation of at least some of them, without sacrificing attention to a broader view of the region's economic development. Few phenomena more encourage planning participation than witnessing implementation of projects that emerge from the planning process.

Where a nested plans approach is not suitable to prevailing regional planning circumstances, practitioners might consider alternate ways of achieving similar benefits through a unitary planning process design. Whether a unitary or nested plans approach is employed, these benefits—full attention to a strategic framework and its associated regional analysis as well as near-term implementation planning, adaptability to budgetary cycles and targets of financial opportunity, responsiveness to changing circumstances, and promotion of broad participation by minimizing the workload on unpaid participants and the time between planning and implementation—are important for an effective regional planning process.

20

A General Framework for Regional Planning

In the introduction to Chapter 19 it was mentioned that worldwide, despite their enormous and basic differences, practical regional development planning experiences suggest a general framework that bears a discernible relationship to the idealized model discussed in Chapter 18. It is the purpose of this chapter to set forth that general framework, and to do so in a way that incorporates the ideas presented in the previous chapter and also links the framework to material presented in the other chapters of this book.

What is presented here is a general planning framework, not a planning process. Designing a planning process requires determining detailed planning steps to be taken and procedures to be followed. That can be done only with respect to the operative circumstances of a given regional planning situation. The general framework is meant to offer a starting point for determining first an overall approach, and then the breadth and nature of planning focus, detailed planning steps, points and mechanism of public participation, administrative structure, time frame, and methods of aggregate and intraregional analysis that make up an explicit planning process leading to effective project interventions in the regional economy on a routine basis.

LAUNCHING THE PLANNING PROCESS

A regional planning process is generally launched by first identifying projects and then refining them into a strategic framework, or by first developing a preliminary strategic framework and then identifying projects through which strategies can be pursued, as described in the last chapter. Once a planning process has been launched, the first planning cycle has been completed, and a continuing regional development planning routine establishes itself, the differences in these approaches fade. To one degree or another, regional analysis, a rethinking of goals and strategies, new project identification, implementation, and evaluation go on all the time, though discrete formal planning cycles that produce written plans are undertaken periodically.

The formal planning cycles can be structured as single exercises in which strategic planning and tactical planning are parts of a unitary combined planning process, or they can be structured using a nested plans approach in which strategic planning is undertaken at longer intervals and tactical planning is undertaken at shorter intervals. It is easy to see that the approach selected will considerably influence the nature of the between-cycle activities that are a crucial part of the continuing regional planning routine.

Figure 20.1 is a schematic representation of the general framework for regional development planning. It first shows the steps involved in the alternative approaches for launching the planning process, and then, in turn, shows the general steps in strategic planning and tactical planning. Once the first planning cycle is completed, the routine returns either to strategic and tactical planning on separate schedules or to strategic planning as the first part of a combined strategic and tactical planning cycle.

Actually, the steps involved in launching the planning process with either approach extend all the way through the first planning cycle. In the case of projects to strategies, the launching steps link up with what later becomes the routine planning process just before the evaluating projects step. In the case of the strategies to projects approach, the launching steps link up much earlier with what later become the steps of the general planning routine. But while some steps have the same names in both the launching cycle and in subsequent cycles, their characters are somewhat different in the two cases.

From projects to strategies begins with assembling information on projects recently implemented and soon to be implemented. It then moves on to generating new project proposals. This is done by soliciting the ideas of politicians (who may in turn consult their constituencies), village and town committees, local groups, nongovernmental organizations operating in the region, central government agencies, and the planning staff. Generating new project proposals does not involve project identification procedures like those discussed in Chapter 15, but represents a rapid canvassing of existing development project agendas.

Next, the project proposals are grouped into a programmatic framework as described in Chapter 19, laying the groundwork for eventual refinement in a strategic context. As mentioned in Chapter 19, if it is possible to undertake any regional analysis in the first planning cycle, this is the point at which it would be done; and the way in which it is done would best be a function of the programmatic groupings.

Project proposal evaluation in the first cycle launched with this approach is likely to be a difficult process. Many project proposals will probably be on the

Figure 20.1
A General Framework for Regional Development Planning

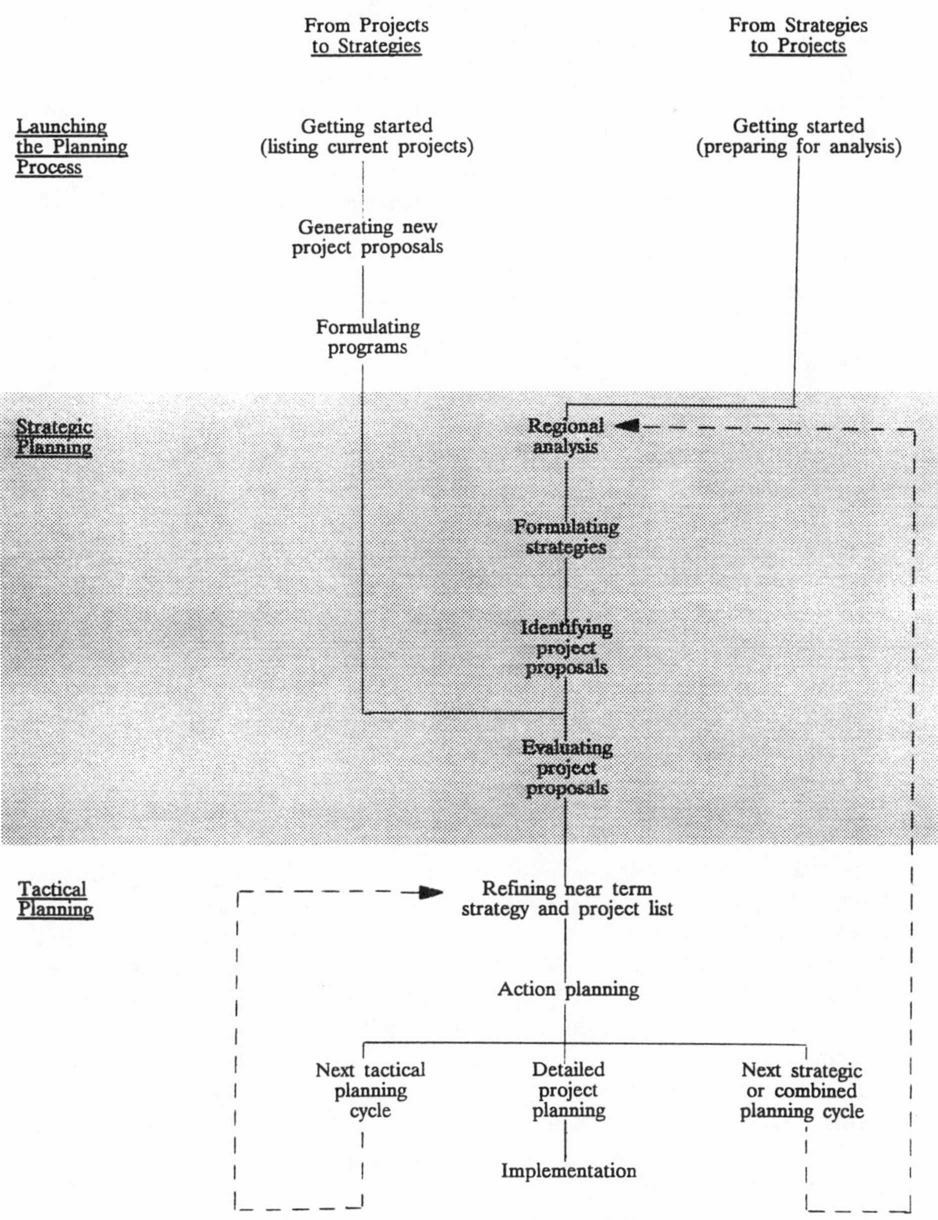

table and, especially if there has been no regional analysis, no consensus will have been established on strategic parameters. In this step and the next, techniques described in the last section of Chapter 15 and in chapters 16 and 17 can go a long way toward eliminating many proposals for the time being in an atmosphere of objectivity. These techniques also encourage evolution of a rudimentary strategic framework and help establish what is necessary for proposals to receive favorable initial evaluation in future planning cycles.

Under the strategies to projects approach, getting started essentially involves preparing for regional analysis. This can entail several elements. As with projects to strategies, information needs to be assembled on projects recently implemented and soon to be implemented. This information can be incorporated into a written overall description of the regional economy, prepared quickly and without field research as described in Chapter 1. The overall description can serve as a basis for formulating preliminary development goals, objectives, and strategies, if possible like those described in Chapter 18. These provide the foundation for determining sets of important aggregate and intraregional analysis questions such as those listed in chapters 1 and 2, and a set of preliminary project opportunity indicators such as those listed in Chapter 15. These questions and indicators, in turn, together with an assessment of data sources, are the basis for designing a framework of methods of aggregate and intraregional analysis drawing on the methods presented in parts II and III of this book, and also for considering special studies that may be needed. The lists of dominant analytical questions addressed by different methods of regional analysis in chapters 1 and 2 can serve in the process of designing the framework of analysis.

All this may not be possible in the course of launching the first regional development planning cycle. If not, the next step, regional analysis, will also reflect the practical limitations of the specific situation. But whatever amount of regional analysis is possible, the methods of regional analysis employed, how they are adapted, and the relationship between aggregate and intraregional analysis are best initially linked to a preliminary strategic framework, including goals and objectives, formulated as part of "getting started."

Aggregate and intraregional analysis, even if minimal, will produce new hard information on the operation and performance of the regional economy. The better understanding of their region as a complex of sectoral and spatial interdependencies that this provides to planning participants offers a basis for rethinking strategic priorities. Thus, in the launching cycle, the formulating strategies step involves a refinement of the preliminary strategic framework in light of the findings of regional analysis.

Here, strategy formulation is a far less casual affair than it may have been during "getting started," when the exercise was not based on formal analysis and its primary purpose was to provide guidance for formal analysis. Now, not only are there analytical findings to be interpreted and considered, but the strategic framework is to be the context for project proposal identification and evaluation. Even though strategies may be—indeed, are likely to be—further altered and refined during upcoming planning steps, their reformulation at this point should be seen as for the first time setting overall parameters for the regional development plan.

"Identifying project proposals" employs techniques such as those presented in Chapter 15. In principle, projects identified should derive from regional analysis and relate directly to the strategic framework. But especially in the first planning cycle, there are likely to be projects previously on the table that must be considered, and in any case owing to the newness of the planning experience, the analysis-to-strategies-to-projects progression is likely to have a good many rough edges. That is one reason it is important to utilize the "evaluating project proposals" step to evaluate projects not just as free-standing interventions in the regional economy, but also as components of development strategies. Doing so not only results in better project evaluation, but also helps refine the strategic development framework.

Evaluating project proposals is where the alternative ways of launching the planning process meet up among the steps of the routine planning process. Whether project proposal identification came about through the steps of one approach or the other to launching the first planning cycle, in principle the tools used for evaluating proposals could be the same, namely, tools such as those presented in the last section of Chapter 15 and in Chapters 16 and 17.

In practice, however, evaluating project proposals is likely to have a different character if the planning process was launched using the projects to strategies approach than if the strategies to projects approach was used. In the former case, this step may represent the first time in the planning process that debate over significant issues has been undertaken, and there may still be no real agreed-on strategic framework to help order the debate. Moreover, this step may represent the first time any significant idea or proposal that has been put forward is rejected. In the latter case, at this point there will be a body of regional analysis and a strategic context as background for project evaluation, and there will also be more experience with ordered decision making and the give-and-take of consensus building. In both cases, evaluating project proposals is likely to be an especially delicate matter in the first planning cycle. It is a step that needs to be designed with great care to achieve good technical results without undermining a broad commitment to the planning process.

In the first planning cycle, evaluating project proposals and refining a near-term strategy and project list are really one step. The equivalent of many iterations may be required before a limited set of priority projects proposed for near-term implementation is agreed upon. The phrase *near-term strategy* here means something different from the strategic framework for regional development. The reference in this case is to the practical strategic considerations related to obtaining support for specific project proposals in the near term.

For example, some project proposals may be included in the current project list because, though less than top priority on development grounds, they are nevertheless important, and it is known that funding will be available for them in the near term. In other words, the near-term strategy and project list takes account of the fact that a lower-priority project with a high probability of implementation may be preferable to a high-priority project with a low probability of implementation. This is not to say that projects in the list of those proposed for near-term implementation need not reflect strategic priorities in development terms; it is only to say that they may reflect practical implementation considerations as well.

Action planning encompasses two principal activities. The first is developing a schedule of tasks and responsibilities for carrying out detailed project planning and implementation for projects in the near-term list. The second is developing a schedule of tasks and responsibilities for the next strategic and tactical planning cycles or combined planning cycle. Developing a schedule of tasks and responsibilities for the next formal cycle of planning really involves considering the activities to be undertaken between cycles or steps within cycles to develop planning information and in other ways prepare for the next round or rounds.

For example, if a projects to strategies approach was used to launch the planning process, the sorts of steps described under "getting started" with a strategies to projects approach should be planned for the interim between formal cycles. This would yield a framework of methods of aggregate and intraregional analysis to be employed in preparation for the next planning cycle, or two such frameworks distributing analysis activities among the interims between strategic and tactical planning cycles in the case of a nested plans approach. In either case, the objective is to schedule activities that begin to change the hurried, somewhat improvisational, rudimentary, and partial character of the planning process in its launching cycle to a more orderly, information-based, continuously supported, and systematic ongoing routine.

THE REGIONAL DEVELOPMENT PLANNING ROUTINE

We return now to "regional analysis" in Figure 20.1, not as the second step in launching a regional planning process using the strategies to projects approach, but as the first step in a periodic formal planning cycle that is part of a continuing regional planning routine. It may be the first step in a combined strategic and tactical planning cycle or, if a nested plans approach is taken, in a strategic planning cycle alone. In either case, the nature of this step would be rather different from what it was when the planning process was launched. For, once a planning routine is in place, most aggregate and intraregional analysis would be conducted between formal cycles, and this step would involve not so much conducting analysis as considering and debating interpretations of the results of the analyses conducted in the interim.

Moreover, "regional analysis," as part of a routine planning process, would in principle include considering all the types of information produced by "data collection and analysis" mentioned in Chapter 18. In addition to the products of special studies and methods of regional analysis like those presented in parts

II and III of this book, for example, this would encompass information on the performance of development projects previously undertaken in the region, including those implemented as a result of the last planning cycle, and on the performance of the planning process itself.

If a combined strategic and tactical planning approach is used, the amount of information developed since the previous cycle will be less than if a nested plans approach is used. In the case of a nested plans approach, not only will more time elapse between strategic planning cycles, but current information and some strategic information will be cumulating as a result of work done in connection with the more frequent tactical planning cycles.

Between formal cycles, strategy reformulation will also be continuing. In fact, during formal cycles planning staff can present participants in the planning process with analytical findings and their implications, in the eyes of the staff, for a revised framework of regional development strategies. Thus, once a routine planning process is in place, planning participants can focus with greater deliberation on hard information and on debating its strategic implications as a framework for identifying and evaluating projects, and less on the procedural aspects of analysis and strategy formulation. The work done between cycles is meant to facilitate a concentration on substance rather than procedure during formal planning cycles.

Indeed, new project proposals will continue to be developed, and old but good ones previously insufficiently developed will be strengthened between planning cycles. While the opportunity to introduce new project proposals during formal planning cycles is never foreclosed, between cycles the planning staff continues to pursue project identification activities. In addition to following up on project proposal ideas arising from regional analysis work, the staff would maintain active communication with sectoral agencies, village and town committees, local officials, nongovernmental organizations, local groups, and other potential sources of project ideas as part of its work between planning cycles.

This between-cycle work of the staff and special committees that may be established needs to be pursued with great care. Its purpose must be clearly demonstrated not to preempt the participatory process of formal planning cycles, but to facilitate it by presenting information and ideas for consideration, debate, consensus, and decision making. If this is done properly, both the "identifying project proposals" and "evaluating project proposals" steps will be far more productive as a matter of routine than was possible in the initial planning cycle.

If a combined strategic and tactical planning approach is employed, project proposals will have to be identified and evaluated fully toward refining a near-term project list. If a nested plans approach is employed, it will be necessary to resolve the questions of how far to carry project evaluation in the context of strategic planning, and what is to be the relationship between project proposals identified during strategic planning and those that emerge in connection with tactical planning cycles.

Even between tactical planning cycles under a nested plans approach, some regional analysis will be undertaken and project performance will be monitored. Also, information on the changing regional, national, and international economic and policy environment will be incorporated into the first step of the tactical planning cycle, "refining near-term strategy and project list." As a result, part of the "refinement" in this step may involve examining project proposals that were not generated during the less frequent and therefore less current strategic planning cycle.

Action planning in the context of a routine regional planning process is similar to the way the step was described earlier. But as cycle succeeds cycle, the tasks to be planned become clearer as each round builds on the experience and cumulating information of previous rounds. For example, experience will demonstrate that certain methods of regional analysis are impractical or produce information of limited planning value for the situation at hand; that some are useful only in connection with strategic planning while others are more useful in support of tactical planning; that certain methods of aggregate and intraregional analysis are important complements; and that some can be easily updated while others involve a major effort each time. This knowledge makes the job of scheduling regional analysis tasks a much easier one.

Most important, planning procedures, and the relationship between the planning staff and its continuing work on the one hand, and participants in the periodic planning cycles on the other, increasingly achieve routine status. This also eases the job of scheduling tasks and responsibilities for the next planning cycle or cycles. But it also facilitates coordination of regional planning activities with the other decision-making procedures of local authorities, because political leaders and personnel of administrative departments participate in the planning process and may even be members of the regional planning staff.

This in turn builds confidence in the regional development planning process as one that serves the interests of the region's population effectively without usurping the responsibilities or circumscribing the prerogatives of administrative officials and political leadership. It builds confidence in the regional planning process as a vehicle for broader participation in regional development decision making.

Bibliography

PART I: THE ECONOMIC AND DEVELOPMENT CONTEXT

Abler, Ronald, et al. 1971. *Spatial Organization: The Geographer's View of the World*. Englewood Cliffs, NJ: Prentice-Hall.

Barbosa, Tulio. 1981. "The Farm-Nonfarm Interface, with Special Reference to Rural Brazil," in G. Johnson and A. Maunder (eds.), *Rural Change: The Challenge for Agricultural Economists*. Totowa, NJ: Allanheld, Osmun, Inc.

Bar-El, Raphael, et al., eds. 1987. *Patterns of Change in Developing Rural Regions*. Boulder, CO: Westview Press.

Bell, Clive, et al. 1982. *Project Evaluation in Regional Perspective: A Study of an Irrigation Project in Northwest Malaysia*. Baltimore: Johns Hopkins University Press.

Bendavid-Val, Avrom. 1989. "Rural-Urban Linkages: Farming and Farm Households in Regional and Town Economies." *Review of Urban and Regional Development Studies*, Vol. 1, No. 2, pp. 89–97.

———. 1990. *Rural Area Development Planning: A Review and Synthesis of Approaches*. Rome: Food and Agriculture Organization of the United Nations.

De Janvry, Alain. 1983. "Growth and Equity: A Strategy for Reconciliation," in K. Nobe and R. Sampath (eds.), *Issues in Third World Development*. Boulder, CO: Westview Press.

Dickinson, Robert E. 1964. *City and Region: A Geographical Interpretation*. New York: Humanities Press.

Evans, Hugh, and Peter Ngau. forthcoming. "Rural-Urban Relations, Household Income Diversification and Agricultural Productivity."

Freeman, Donald B., and G. B. Norcliffe. 1985. *Rural Enterprise in Kenya: Development and Spatial Organization of the Non-Farm Sector*. Research Paper No. 214. Chicago, IL: University of Chicago, Department of Geography.

Friedmann, John. 1966. *Regional Development Policy: A Case Study of Venezuela*. Cambridge, MA: MIT Press.

Friedmann, John, and William Alonso. 1975. *Regional Policy: Readings in Theory and Applications*. Cambridge, MA: MIT Press.

Friedmann, John, and Clyde Weaver. 1979. *Territory and Function*. Berkeley: University of California Press.

Gibb, Arthur, Jr. 1984. "Tertiary Urbanization: The Agricultural Market Centre as a Consumption Related Phenomenon." *Regional Development Dialogue*, 5, No. 1.

Gilbert, A., ed. 1976. *Development Planning and Spatial Structure*. London: John Wiley and Sons.

Haggblade, Steven, et al. 1989. "Farm-Nonfarm Linkages in Rural Sub-Saharan Africa." *World Development*, 17, No. 8., pp. 1173–1201.

Haggblade, Steven, and Peter Hazell. 1989. "Agricultural Technology and Farm-Nonfarm Growth Linkages." *Agricultural Economics*, No. 3, pp. 345–364.

Hardoy, Jorge E., and David Satterthwaite, eds. 1986. *Small and Intermediate Urban Centres: Their Role in National and Regional Development in the Third World*. London: Hodder and Stoughton in association with the International Institute for Environment and Development.

Hazell, Peter, and Ailsa Roell. 1983. *Rural Growth Linkages: Household Expenditure Patterns in Malaysia and Nigeria*. Research Report No. 41. Washington, DC: International Food Policy Research Institute.

Hoover, Edgar M. 1948. *The Location of Economic Activity*. New York: McGraw-Hill.

———. 1971. *An Introduction to Regional Economics*. New York: Alfred A. Knopf.

Isard, Walter. 1956. *Location and Space Economy*. New York: MIT Press and John Wiley and Sons.

———. 1975. *Introduction to Regional Science*. Englewood Cliffs, NJ: Prentice-Hall.

ISSAS (G. Lathrop, J. P. Meindertsma, and H. G. T. van Raay). 1986. *The Theory and Practice of Regional Rural Development and Planning: A Review of the Literature*. The Hague: Food and Agriculture Organization of the United Nations.

Johnson, E. A. J. 1970. *The Organization of Space in Developing Countries*. Cambridge, MA: Harvard University Press.

Johnston, Bruce F., and Peter Kilby. 1975. *Agriculture and Structural Transformation: Economic Strategies in Late-Developing Countries*. London: Oxford University Press.

Karaska, Gerald, et al. 1985. *Rural-Urban Dynamics in Ecuador: Agricultural Marketing in the Ambato Region*. SARSA research report for USAID and the Government of Ecuador. Worcester, MA: Clark University.

Kenya, Republic of. 1986. *Economic Management for Renewed Growth*. Sessional Paper No. 1. Nairobi.

Kuklinski, A., ed. 1975. *Regional Development and Planning: International Perspectives*. The Hague: Mouton.

Liedholm, Carl, and Donald Mead. 1987. *Small-Scale Industries in Developing Countries: Empirical Evidence and Policy Implications*. East Lansing, MI: Michigan State University.

Losch, August. 1954. *The Economics of Location* (trans. from the 2nd rev. ed. by W. H. Woglom). New Haven, CT: Yale University Press.

Maro, S., and Wifred Milay. 1979. *Small Urban Centers in Rural Development in Africa* (ed. Southall Aidan). University of Wisconsin: African Studies Program.

Mathur, Om Prakash, ed. 1984. *The Role of Small Cities in Regional Development*. Japan: United Nations Centre for Regional Development.

Mellor, John W. 1976. *The New Economics of Growth: A Strategy for India and the Developing World*. Ithaca, NY: Cornell University Press.

———. 1986. ''Agriculture on the Road to Industrialization,'' in J. Lewis and V. Kallab (eds.), *Development Strategies Reconsidered*. Washington, DC: Overseas Development Council.

Richardson, Harry W. 1969. *Elements of Regional Economics*. Harmondsworth, U.K.: Penguin Books.

———. 1973. *Regional Growth Theory*. London: Macmillan Press.

———. 1979. *Regional and Urban Economics*. London: Penguin Books.

Rondinelli, Dennis A. 1985. *Applied Methods of Regional Analysis: The Spatial Dimensions of Development Policy*. Boulder, CO: Westview Press.

———. 1987. *Agriculture, Employment and Enterprise: Rural-Urban Dynamics in AID Development Strategy*. Washington, DC: U.S. Agency for International Development.

SARSA (A. Bendavid-Val, J. Littlefield, and G. McDowell). 1990. *Market Towns in Uganda's Recovery and Development*. SARSA research report for USAID and the Government of Uganda. Blacksburg, VA: Virginia Polytechnic Institute and State University.

SARSA (A. Bendavid-Val, J. Downing, and G. Karaska). 1988c. ''Rural-Urban Dynamics Synthesis Report.'' SARSA research report for USAID. Worcester, MA: Clark University.

Sharpley, Jennifer. 1981. ''Resource Transfers between the Agricultural and Non-Agricultural Sectors: 1964–1977,'' in T. Killick (ed.), *Papers on the Kenyan Economy: Performance, Problems and Policies*. Portsmouth, NH: Heinemann Educational Books, Inc.

Siebert, Horst. 1969. *Regional Economic Growth: Theory and Policy*. Scranton, PA: International Textbook.

Smith, Carol Ann, ed. 1976. *Regional Analysis*, Vols. 1 and 2. New York: Academic Press.

Soto, Hernando de. 1989. *The Other Path: The Invisible Revolution in the Third World*. New York: Harper and Row.

Wanmali, Sudhir. 1988. *Market Towns and Service Linkage in Sub-saharan Africa: A Case Study of Chipata, Zambia; Salima, Malawi; and Chipinge, Zimbabwe*. Washington, DC: International Food Policy Research Institute.

Weitz, Raanan. 1971. *From Peasant to Farmer: A Revolutionary Strategy for Development*. New York: Columbia University Press.

———. 1979. *Integrated Rural Development: The Rehovot Approach*. Rehovot Israel: Settlement Study Center.

PART II: METHODS OF AGGREGATE REGIONAL ANALYSIS

Armstrong, Regina Belz. 1980. *Regional Accounts: Structure and Performance of the New York Region's Economy in the Seventies*. Bloomington: Indiana University Press.

Chenery, Hollis B., and Paul G. Clark. 1959. *Interindustry Economics*. New York: John Wiley and Sons.

Hammer, Thomas. 1969. *The Estimation of Economic Base Multipliers*. RSRI Discussion Paper Series, No. 22. Philadelphia: Regional Science Research Institute.

Hirsch, Werner Z., ed. 1964. *Elements of Regional Accounts*. Conference on Regional Accounts, 1962. Papers presented at the conference, sponsored by the Committee on Regional Accounts. Baltimore: Johns Hopkins University Press.

Isard, Walter. 1960. *Methods of Regional Analysis: An Introduction to Regional Science*. New York: MIT Press and John Wiley and Sons.

Leven, Charles L., et al. 1970. *An Analytical Framework for Regional Development Policy*. Cambridge, MA: MIT Press.

Miernyk, William H. 1970. *Simulating Regional Economic Development*. Lexington, MA: Heath-Lexington Books.

Nijkamp, Peter, ed. 1988. *Handbook of Regional Economics*. Amsterdam: North Holland Publishing Company.

Nijkamp, Peter, et al. 1985. *Measuring the Unmeasurable*. Dordrecht: Martinus Nijhosf, Publishers.

Raay, H. G. T. van, et al., eds. 1989. *Tanzania Planners' Handbook: A Guide for Regional and Rural Development Planning*. The Hague: Institute for Rural Development and Planning and Institute of Social Studies Advisory Service.

Rhoda, Richard. 1982. *Urban and Regional Analysis for Development Planning*. Boulder, CO: Westview Press.

Richardson, Harry W. 1972. *Input-Output and Regional Economics*. London: Weidenfield and Nicolson.

Stone, Richard. 1961. *Input-Output and National Accounts*. Paris: Organization for Economic Cooperation and Development.

Tiebout, Charles M. 1962. *The Community Economic Base Study*. Supplementary Paper No. 16. New York: Committee for Economic Development.

United Nations Environment Programme and United Nations Centre for Human Settlements. 1987. *Environmental Guidelines for Settlements Planning and Management*, Vols. 1, 2, and 3. Nairobi: UNEP and UNCHS.

PART III: METHODS OF INTRAREGIONAL ANALYSIS

Burrough, P. A. 1986. *Principles of Geographical Information Systems for Land Resources Assessments*. Oxford: Clarendon Press.

Miernyk, William H. 1965. *The Elements of Input-Output Analysis*. New York: Random House.

Raay, H.G.T. van, et al., eds. 1989. *Tanzania Planners' Handbook: A Guide for Regional and Rural Development Planning*. The Hague: Institute for Rural Development and Planning and Institute of Social Studies Advisory Service.

Rhoda, Richard. 1982. *Urban and Regional Analysis for Development Planning*. Boulder, CO: Westview Press.

Rondinelli, Dennis A. 1985. *Applied Methods of Regional Analysis: The Spatial Dimensions of Development Policy*. Boulder, CO: Westview Press.

SARSA (A. Bendavid-Val, M. Cullen, H. Evans, and P. Little). 1988a. *Rural-Urban Exchange in the Kismayo Region of Somalia*. SARSA research report for USAID and the Government of Somalia. Worcester, MA: Clark University.

SARSA (A. Bendavid-Val, H. Evans, B. Lewis, M. Murray, and P. Ngau). 1988b. *Rural-Urban Exchange in Kutus Town and Its Hinterland*. SARSA research report for USAID and the Government of Kenya. Worcester, MA: Clark University.

SARSA (A. Bendavid-Val, J. Downing, and G. Karaska). 1988c. "Rural-Urban Dynamics Synthesis Report." SARSA research report for USAID. Worcester, MA: Clark University.

Star, Jeffrey, and John Estes. 1990. *Geographic Information Systems: An Introduction*. Englewood Cliffs, NJ: Prentice-Hall.

Tiebout, Charles M. 1962. *The Community Economic Base Study*. Supplementary Paper No. 16. New York: Committee for Economic Development.

United Nations Environment Programme and United Nations Centre for Human Settlements. 1987. *Environmental Guidelines for Settlements Planning and Management*, Vols. 1, 2, and 3. Nairobi: UNEP and UNCHS.

PART IV: METHODS OF PROJECT IDENTIFICATION AND EVALUATION

Bendavid-Val, Avrom. 1980. *Local Economic Development Planning: From Goals to Projects*. Planning Association Series, No. 353. Chicago: American Planning Association.

Delp, Peter, et al. 1977. *Systems Tools for Project Planning*. Bloomington: Indiana University, International Development Institute/PASITAM.

Food and Agriculture Organization of the United Nations. 1986. *Guide for Training in the Formulation of Agricultural and Rural Investment Projects*. Rome: FAO.

Gittinger, J. Price. 1975. *Economic Analysis of Agricultural Projects*. Baltimore: Johns Hopkins University Press.

Hansen, J. 1978. *Guide to Practical Project Appraisal: Social Cost-Benefit Analysis in Developing Countries*. Vienna: United Nations Institute for Development Organizations.

Irvin, George. 1978. *Modern Cost-Benefit Methods*. London: Macmillan.

Little, M. D., and J. A. Mirrlees. 1974. *Project Appraisal and Planning for Developing Countries*. New York: Basic Books.

MacArthur, J. D., et al. 1976. *Project Appraisal in Practice*. London: Heinemann Educational Books.

SARSA (A. Bendavid-Val, J. Downing, and G. Karaska). 1988c. "Rural-Urban Dynamics Synthesis Report." SARSA research report for USAID. Worcester, MA: Clark University.

Sasonne, Peter J., and William A. Schaffer. 1978. *Cost-Benefit Analysis: A Handbook*. New York: Academic Press.

Squire, Lynn, and Herman G. van der Tak. 1975. *Economic Analysis of Projects*. Baltimore: Johns Hopkins University Press.

UNIDO. 1972. *Guidelines for Project Evaluation*. New York: United Nations.

———. 1978. *Guide to Practical Project Appraisal: Social Benefit-Cost Analysis in the Developing Countries*. New York: United Nations.

United Nations Environment Programme and United Nations Centre for Human Settlements. 1987. *Environmental Guidelines for Settlements Planning and Management*, Vols. 1, 2, and 3. Nairobi: UNEP and UNCHS.

PART V: APPROACHES TO REGIONAL DEVELOPMENT PLANNING

Alden, Jeremy, and Robert Morgan. 1974. *Regional Planning: A Comprehensive View*. United Kingdom: Leonard Hill Books.

Arizona Office of Economic Planning and Development. 1977. *Planning Handbook for Communities*. Phoenix.

Arkansas, University of, Department of Community and Governmental Affairs. 1981. *Citizen Participation: Overview and Selected Techniques*. Fayetteville.

Association of Voluntary Agencies for Rural Development. 1980. *Block Level Planning*. New Dehli: Vikas.

Auerbach, Devora, et al. 1980. *Regional Plans of Developing Countries: An Annotated Bibliography*. Giessen, W. Germany: Centre for Regional Development Research and Settlement Study Centre.

Belshaw, D. G. R. 1979. ''Regional Planning in Tanzania: The Choice of Methodology for Iringa Region,'' in I. Livingstone, ed., *Issues in Development Studies: Essays in Honor of Athole Mackintosh*. Farnborough U.K.: Dover Press.

Bendavid-Val, Avrom. 1980. *Local Economic Development Planning: From Goals to Projects*. Planning Advisory Service Publication No. 353. Chicago: American Planning Association.

———. 1987. *More with Less: Managing Energy and Resource Efficient Cities*. Washington, DC: Agency for International Development.

———. 1990. *Rural Area Development Planning: A Review and Synthesis of Approaches*. Rome: Food and Agriculture Organization of the United Nations.

Bendavid-Val, Avrom, and Peter P. Waller, eds. 1975. *Action-Oriented Approaches to Regional Development Planning*. New York: Praeger.

Dias, Hiran D., and B. W. E. Wickramanayake. 1983. *Manual for Training in Rural Development Planning*. Bangkok: Human Settlements Division, Asian Institute of Technology.

Faludi, A. 1973. *Planning Theory*. Oxford: Pergamon Press.

Friedmann, John. 1973. *Retracking America: A Theory of Transactive Planning*. New York: Anchor Press.

Gillie, F.B. 1967. *Basic Thinking in Regional Planning*. The Hague: Mouton.

Gillinwater, David, and Douglas Hart, eds. 1978. *The Regional Planning Process*. Westmead, U.K.: Saxon House.

Government of Zimbabwe. 1986. *District Development Plan Handbook*. Harare, Zimbabwe: Ministry of Local Government.

Hilhorst, J. G. M. 1971. *Regional Planning: A Systems Approach*. Rotterdam: Rotterdam University Press.

ISSAS (G. Lathrop, J. P. Meindertsma, and H. G. T. van Raay). 1986. *The Theory and Practice of Rural Development Planning: A Review of the Literature*. The Hague: Food and Agriculture Organization of the United Nations.

Kelly, Rita Mae. 1976. *Community Participation in Directing Economic Development*. Cambridge, MA: Center for Community Economic Development.

Krieger, Martin H. 1981. *Advice and Planning*. Philadelphia: Temple University Press.

Kuklinski, A., ed. 1975. *Regional Development and Planning: International Perspectives*. The Hague: Mouton.

Maetz, Materne, and Maria G. Quieti. 1987. *Training for Decentralized Planning: Lessons from Experience*, Vols. 1 and 2. Rome: Food and Agriculture Organization of the United Nations.

O'Regan, Fred M., et al. 1980. *Public Participation in Regional Development Planning: A Strategy for Popular Involvement*. Washington, DC: The Development Group for Alternative Policies.

Oregon Department of Economic Development. 1977. *Shaping Your Community's Economic Future*. Eugene.

Organization of American States, Department of Regional Development, Secretariat for Economic and Social Affairs. 1984. *Integrated Regional Development Planning: Guidelines and Case Studies from OAS Experience*. Washington, DC: OAS.

Raay, H. G. T. van, et al. (eds.). 1989. *Tanzania Planners' Handbook: A Guide for Regional and Rural Development Planning*. The Hague: Institute for Rural Development and Planning and Institute of Social Studies Advisory Service.

Republic of Kenya. 1987. *Local Authority Development Programme*, Vols. 1–8. Nairobi: Ministry of Local Government.

Richardson, Harry W. 1969. *Elements of Regional Economics*. Harmondsworth, U.K.: Penguin Books.

Rondinelli, Dennis A. 1975. *Urban and Regional Development: Policy and Administration*. Ithaca, N.Y.: Cornell University Press.

———. 1985. *Applied Methods of Regional Analysis: The Spatial Dimensions of Development Policy*. Boulder, CO: Westview Press.

United Nations Environment Programme and United Nations Centre for Human Settlements. 1987. *Environmental Guidelines for Settlements Planning and Management*, Vols. 1, 2, and 3. Nairobi: UNEP and UNCHS.

Weitz, Raanan. 1979. *Integrated Rural Development: the Rehovot Approach*. Rehovot, Israel: Settlement Study Center.

Index

ABOUT THE AUTHOR

AVROM BENDAVID-VAL works as Research Associate with Virginia Polytechnic Institute and State University's Center for Development Policy and as a consultant to governments and development assistance organizations. Since 1966 he has been active as a planner, analyst, researcher, government official, consultant, author, and teacher in the fields of regional development, urban development, and natural resource management, and has been associated with over 75 projects in these fields in both Western countries and the developing world. His other books and monographs include *Action-Oriented Approaches to Regional Development Planning*, *Starting Your Own Energy Business*, *Patterns of Change in Developing Rural Regions*, *More with Less: Managing Energy and Resource Efficient Cities*, *Mobilizing Savings and Rural Finance: The A.I.D. Experience*, *Local Economic Development Planning: From Goals to Projects*, and three earlier editions of this book. Mr. Bendavid-Val brings to his work an intense concern with strengthening indigenous capacity to plan and manage development activity, which is amply reflected in this volume.